This book is dedicated to friends and family … in these challenging times, they are more important than ever.

The 2021 Cheltenham Festival Stallion Guide is printed by
Penrose Group
01784 461464
Ian.how@dcwpenrose.co.uk

Front Cover:
Champ ridden by Barry Geraghty (White Cap) wins the RSA Insurance Novices' Chase from Minella Indo (Striped Cap) and Allaho (Blue Cap)
Cheltenham Festival - 11th March 2020
Photograph by Grossick Racing Photography (racingpost.com/photos)

THE 2021 CHELTENHAM FESTIVAL STALLION GUIDE

Welcome to the seventh edition of the

Cheltenham Festival Stallion Guide

Introduction from the Author – James Iddiols

The coronavirus pandemic. It has been and continues to be a complete pain in the backside. It has killed enough already, and in its aftermath, the actions taken to tackle the problem will leave a devastating impact on society. I'm fed up with hearing about it. I'm fed up talking about it. And I'm not going to write any more about it. Let's pray that the world can either get rid of this awful virus or learn to live with it. And soon. I'm impatient for the roaring twenties to kick in.

When providing their opinions on who will be victorious at the festival, most pundits ignore a horse's genetics. In making a selection, they pay scant attention to the DNA inherited from their sire and whether the genes will help or hinder their fancy as it applies itself to Cheltenham's stiff course and undulations before raising its game further to stay on up that famous hill finish. The Cheltenham Festival Stallion Guide, now in its seventh year, thinks differently and provides compelling evidence that a horse's breeding is a critical factor when it comes to picking winners at the Cheltenham Festival. A commentary is provided on the prevailing stallions whose progeny are consistently successful at festivals as well as advising on those sires to avoid. The Guide consists of insightful betting recommendations based upon forensic research into the results and trends of some 32 stallions' progeny who have raced at previous festivals, punctuated with thought-provoking observations on several of the races.

History has shown us that the offspring of some stallions perform creditably at the festival time and time again, whereas others consistently struggle. Stallions that have entries that consistently perform at the Cheltenham Festival include **Beat Hollow**, **Kalanisi**, **Milan**, **Network**, **Oscar**, **Poliglote**, **Saddler Maker**, **Saint Des Saints** and **Shantou**. Sires that you may wish to avoid are **Al Namix**, **Kapgarde**, **Kayf Tara** and **Martaline**.

The Guide's central theme is how the offspring of predominant stallions perform at Cheltenham Festivals, but the book delivers so much more, including the low-down on some of the festival's leading contenders, emotional memories of previous meetings, and recommendations on betting strategies.

The 2020 Cheltenham Festival welcomed soft ground for the 3rd year in succession, with all bar the three chases on the Friday (that took place on good to soft), taking place on ground officially described as 'soft'. To summarise, of the 84 races that have taken place at the last three festivals, 62 have taken place on 'Soft'; 17 on 'Good to Soft'; and 5 on Heavy, clearly portraying the difference in conditions at the past three Cheltenham Festivals. Preceding the 2018 Cheltenham Festival, inclusive of all 17 festivals between 2000 and 2017, there had been 420 races of which just 24 (5.7%) had been run on going officially described as soft. Although the offspring of some stallions may perform better on soft or firmer ground, when it comes to the festival, the impact appears to be quite marginal. My analysis of the festival results shows that if a high-quality racehorse has been trained to its peak condition and is better than its rivals, then there is a strong possibility that the horse will always take the beating whatever the ground conditions.

I suffered a little from "seconditis" at the 2020 Cheltenham Festival. Many of my tips advised in this Guide and other wagers that were placed at the meeting seemed to just miss out in the closing stages, none more so than when ***Champ*** appeared from nowhere to win the *RSA Insurance Novices' Chase* from ***Minella Indo***. I decided to put ***Champ*** on this year's cover as a reminder of my success rate in picking horses that finished 2nd. Other selections that found one (or perhaps) two in front of them at the line included ***The Storyteller, Kildisart, Kilfilum Cross, Plan Of Attack, Saint D'oroux, Elfile, Saint Calvados*** and ***Shantou Flyer***.

The 2021 Cheltenham Festival Stallion Guide features four "new entries", generally younger stallions whose offspring have started to provide some early positive or negative festival trends. The sires making their debut appearance in this year's Guide are **Doyen, Getaway, Mahler and Shirocco.** I have also dropped two stallions from the Guide, either because the sire is not producing the quality of progeny rated high enough to get a run at the festival or simply due to the fact that the stallion's offspring are now too old to race. The two who have appeared in previous Stallion Guides but are not featured in 2021 are ***Midnight Legend*** and ***Robin Des Champs***.

The layout has changed a little from previous Guides which I hope readers see as an improvement. Previously, I had an index table at the back of the Guide of the featured stallions' stock with Official Ratings of 135+. This same information is now provided within each chapter after the sire's analysis. The tables for each stallion show the British Horseracing Association (BHA) and Irish Horseracing Regulatory Board (I.H.R.B) Official Ratings for National Hunt horses with a rating of 135 or greater on 9th February 2021. In addition, I have separated out, and have now placed after the stallion's commentary, my views and recommendations on some of the potential entries for the 2021 Cheltenham Festival. I believe and hope that these changes will make it easier for readers to navigate through the strengths and weaknesses of a stallion's progeny and my rationale for supporting or avoiding selected entries for this year's festival meeting. Any feedback on the new layout will be very much welcomed.

477 horses took part at the 2020 Cheltenham Festival, of which 237 runners (50%) were sired by stallions featured in this year's Guide and whose offspring recorded 51 of the 92 win and place positions (55%). For the record, a total of 643 stallions have been responsible for the 4,796 entries to have run at the festival in the past decade, and of those, 115 (18%) have sired ten or more festival runners.

I have a sense that the 2021 Cheltenham Festival has several short-priced 'dead-certs' where many will consider it unthinkable that any will lose. As so often at Cheltenham, some of these favourites will win and we will be in awe of our new festival heroes. For other nailed on certainties and for some inexplicable reason, perhaps even genetics, they will be beaten, and we will be scratching our heads looking for explanations. All this is part and parcel of watching the greatest show on earth.

Enjoy the 2021 Cheltenham Festival and thank you for purchasing this year's Cheltenham Festival Stallion Guide. If you have any views or comments, please feel free to contact me on Twitter @festivalsires.

Finally, I would like to offer a genuine and heartfelt thank you to my wife, Katherine, for her unwavering support and patience in allowing me the space and time required to write this Guide.

James Iddiols @festivalsires

Highlights from the 2020 Cheltenham Festival Stallion Guide

Quotes from the 2020 Cheltenham Festival Stallion Guide	What happened at the 2020 Cheltenham Festival?
"On paper, there are several talented racehorses by **Stowaway** that will be competing this March, and I'm certain that at least two or three of them will make their presence felt."	***Monkfish*** (5/1) finished 1st and ***Fury Road*** (5/1) finished 3rd in the *Albert Bartlett Novices' Hurdle* . ***Put The Kettle On*** (16/1) won the *Arkle* . ***Us and Them*** (10/1) finished 3rd in the *Grand Annual*
"I fully expect results to be in line with previous trends whereby horses by **Poliglote** will secure a win or place for one in every three festival runs."	From **Poliglote**'s six festival entries, ***Sire Du Berlais*** (10/1) won the 2020 *Pertemps Network Final Handicap Hurdle* . ***Politologue*** (6/1) won the *Queen Mother Champion Chase*
"If you are one of those punters that doesn't fancy odds-on favourites, and so will give ***Paisley Park*** a miss, I can advise that there may well be 2-3 other horses by **Oscar** lining up in the *Stayers'* such as ***Lisnager Oscar*** , ***Kilbricken Storm*** and ***Not Many Left*** ."	***Lisnager Oscar*** (50/1) won the *Stayers' Hurdle*
"As of early January, ***Saint D'oroux*** is a big outsider for either the *Triumph* or *Fred Winter* , but then again, three horses by **Saint Des Saints** have already achieved big-priced placings in both races already."	***Saint D'oroux*** (14/1) secured 3rd place in the *Boodles (Fred Winter) Juvenile Handicap Hurdle*
"Providing ***Delta Work*** and ***Easywork*** (both by **Network**) are sent off at odds of 16/1 or shorter, then they are guaranteed to finish in the first six places and have a more than 50% chance of rewarding each-way supporters."	***Easywork*** (12/1) finished 2nd in the *Ballymore Novices' Hurdle* . ***Delta Work*** (5/1) finished 5th in the *Cheltenham Gold Cup*
"Horses by **Great Pretender** that are big priced outsiders (22/1 to 200/1) have performed better than anticipated at the festival."	***Cracking Smart*** by **Great Pretender** secured a 4th place dividend in the *Coral Cup* @ 33/1
"As for ***A Plus Tard*** and ***Fakir D'oudairies*** , I can see at least one of them, if not both, finishing in the top three but for either of them to provide **Kapgarde** supporters with a second festival victory may just be out of reach. For this festival anyway."	***A Plus Tard*** (7/4 favourite) finished 3rd in the *Ryanair Chase* . ***Fakir D'oudairies*** (3/1) finished 2nd in the *Arkle*
"Kayf Tara's stock has failed to achieve a top three finish in the *Albert Bartlett* from six attempts. ***Thyme Hill*** 's record is clean, neat and tidy. 3 wins out of 3 in three high quality Graded Hurdle events. Be that as it may, on Friday 13th March 2020, I shall be opposing ***Thyme Hill*** ."	4/1 favourite ***Thyme Hill*** by **Kayf Tara** finished in 4th place in the *Albert Bartlett Novices' Hurdle*
"My guess is that **Martaline** will once again be well represented at this year's festival with probably 8-12 entries and I'm not especially keen on any of them."	Nine horse by **Martaline** took part at the 2020 Cheltenham Festival. The highest finishing position was recorded by ***Thatsy*** (8/1) who finished 7th in the *County Handicap Hurdle*

Cheltenham Festival 2021 – Race Schedule *(as of 9th February 2021)*

Tuesday 16th March 2021		*Hurdles*			*Chases*				*Bumper*
		2m	*2½m*	*3m*	*2m*	*2½m*	*3m*	*4m*	*2m*
1.30pm	*The Sky Bet Supreme Novices' Hurdle Race*	✓							
2.10pm	*The Sporting Life Arkle Challenge Trophy Steeple Chase*				✓				
2.50pm	*The Ultima Handicap Steeple Chase*						✓		
3.30pm	*The Unibet Champion Hurdle Challenge Trophy*	✓							
4.10pm	*The Close Brothers Mares' Hurdle Race*		✓						
4.50pm	*The Boodles Juvenile Handicap Hurdle Race*	✓							
5.30pm	*The National Hunt (Amateur Riders' Novices' Steeple Chase) Challenge Cup*							✓	

Wednesday 17th March 2021		*Hurdles*			*Chases*				*Bumper*
		2m	*2½m*	*3m*	*2m*	*2½m*	*3m*	*4m*	*2m*
1.30pm	*The Ballymore Novices' Hurdle Race*		✓						
2.10pm	*The Brown Advisory Novices' Steeple Chase*						✓		
2.50pm	*The Coral Cup Hurdle (A Handicap Hurdle Race)*		✓						
3.30pm	*The Betway Queen Mother Champion Steeple Chase*				✓				
4.10pm	*The Glenfarclas Cross Country Steeple Chase*							✓	
4.50pm	*The Johnny Henderson Grand Annual Handicap Chase*				✓				
5.30pm	*The Weatherbys Champion Bumper (A Standard Open NH Flat Race)*								✓

Thursday 18th March 2021		*Hurdles*			*Chases*				*Bumper*
		2m	*2½m*	*3m*	*2m*	*2½m*	*3m*	*4m*	*2m*
1.30pm	*The Marsh Novices' Chase*					✓			
2.10pm	*The Pertemps Network Final (A Handicap Hurdle Race)*			✓					
2.50pm	*The Ryanair Steeple Chase*					✓			
3.30pm	*The Paddy Power Stayers' Hurdle*			✓					
4.10pm	*The Paddy Power Plate (A Handicap Steeple Chase)*					✓			
4.50pm	*The Festival Mares Novices' Hurdle*	✓							
5.30pm	*The Fulke Walwyn Kim Muir Challenge Cup Handicap Steeple Chase*						✓		

Friday 19th March 2021		*Hurdles*			*Chases*				*Bumper*
		2m	*2½m*	*3m*	*2m*	*2½m*	*3m*	*4m*	*2m*
1.30pm	*The JCB Triumph Hurdle*	✓							
2.10pm	*The County Handicap Hurdle Race*	✓							
2.50pm	*The Albert Bartlett Novices' Hurdle Race*			✓					
3.30pm	*The WellChild Cheltenham Gold Cup Steeple Chase*						✓		
4.10pm	*The St. James's Place Festival Challenge Cup Open Hunters' Steeple Chase*						✓		
4.50pm	*The Mrs Paddy Power Mares' Steeple Chase*					✓			
5.30pm	*The Martin Pipe Conditional Jockeys' Handicap Hurdle*		✓						

Right hand columns show race categories (by race format and nearest distance to a half mile)

Contents

Introduction 1
Highlights from the 2020 Cheltenham Festival Stallion Guide 3
Cheltenham Festival 2021 – Race Schedule 4

Stallions

Al Namix 6
Arcadio 8
Authorized 14
Beat Hollow 19
Beneficial 27
Court Cave 33
Doyen 38
Dubai Destination 41
Flemensfirth 45
Getaway 52
Gold Well 56
Great Pretender 60
Jeremy 65
Kalanisi 70
Kapgarde 75
Kayf Tara 80
King's Theatre 84
Mahler 90
Martaline 94
Milan 97
Network 101
Oscar 105
Poliglote 110
Presenting 113
Saddler Maker 118
Saint Des Saints 121
Shantou 126
Shirocco – 132
Stowaway 135
Voix Du Nord 141
Westerner 146
Yeats 150

Al Namix (FR)

Quote from the 2020 Cheltenham Festival Stallion Guide - "Facts are facts. Ignore entries by **Al Namix** at the 2020 Cheltenham Festival."

Al Namix (23-y-o)							
Race Format	*Miles*	*Won*	*Placed*	*Unplaced*	*Total*	*Win %*	*Place %*
Hurdles	About 2m	0	2	12	14	0%	14%
	About 2m 4f	0	0	6	6	0%	0%
	About 3m	0	1	4	5	0%	20%
Chases	About 2m	0	0	3	3	0%	0%
	About 2m 4f	0	0	2	2	0%	0%
	About 3m	0	0	3	3	0%	0%
	About 4m	0	0	2	2	0%	0%
Bumper	About 2m	0	0	0	0	-	-
Total	2011-2020	**0**	**3**	**32**	**35**	**0%**	**9%**

In July 2020, it was announced at *Haras de Mirande* that the stud career of **Al Namix** had come to an end. The stallion was retired as a result of declining fertility. As of today, the top three national hunt racehorses to be sired by **Al Namix**, based on Best Official Ratings (OR) are ***Grandouet*** (OR 166), ***Saphir Du Rheu*** (165) and ***Petit Mouchoir*** (164).

Eighteen horses by **Al Namix** have had 35 opportunities to win a race at the Cheltenham Festival. None of them have achieved it, not even the top three of **Al Namix**'s stock that are mentioned above. The trio, however, are responsible for delivering the rather dismal showing of just three placings, these being from ***Grandout*** (13/2) 3rd in the *2011 JCB Triumph Hurdle;* ***Saphir Du Rheu*** (5/1 Favourite) 2nd in the 2015 *Ladbrokes World Hurdle;* and ***Petit Mouchoir*** (6/1) 3rd in the 2017 *Stan James Champion Hurdle Challenge Trophy.* In 11 of the 35 Cheltenham Festival starts, horses by **Al Namix** have lined up at single figure odds which probably points to the some of the progeny performing quite well in the festival build-up, only to disappoint at the festival.

Only two of the **Al Namix**'s progeny made the trip to the 2021 Cheltenham Festival. ***Petit Mouchoir*** was making what could be termed his 'annual visit' as his entry in last year's *Champion Hurdle* was his fifth festival appearance. The second runner of last year's two entries was ***Al Dancer***, who was to take his chance in the festival's second event, the *Racing Post Arkle Challenge Trophy Novices' Chase.* It was the grey's second trip to the festival, having made his debut as one of the 9/2 joint favourites in the 2020 *Sky Bet Supreme Novices' Hurdle.* Having enjoyed four unbeaten starts over hurdles, many punters (well, those that ignore breeding as a factor) considered this to be a great opportunity for ***Al Dancer***. I wasn't surprised when ***Al Dancer*** delivered a hugely disappointing performance to finish in 10th place. The result was in line with how the progeny had performed at previous festivals.

Al Dancer took his place in a field of 11 runners in the 2021 *Racing Post Arkle Challenge Trophy Novices' Chase.* Trained by *Nigel Twiston-Davies,* ***Al Dancer*** had won one of his four novice chases, and the biggest field he had experienced before last year's *Arkle* was six runners. The 16/1 chance never seemed particularly comfortable in the race and ***Al Dancer*** was beaten by more than 20 lengths when finishing 5th of six finishers.

Less than 90 minutes later, ***Petit Mouchoir***, at a price of 25/1, would also take 5th place when taking on sixteen rivals in the *Unibet Champion Hurdle Challenge Trophy*. To be fair, it was a fair performance by ***Petit Mouchoir*** who pretty much led the field all the way nearing the final hurdle, before the more fancied contenders asserted their class as they cleared the final obstacle before running on to eat up the ground of the famous Cheltenham uphill finish. As previously highlighted, it was the second time that ***Petit Mouchoir*** had competed in the *Champion Hurdle*, having secured a 3rd place finish in the 2017 renewal.

Four races down of the twenty-eight events of last year's Cheltenham Festival and it was all over as far as **Al Namix** was concerned. And the two defeats by ***Al Dancer*** and ***Petit Mouchoir*** can be added to the 30 defeats that have gone before. Backing **Al Namix**'s festival representatives is financially ruinous. If one had placed a £10.00 each-way stake on all 35 festival appearances by **Al Namix**'s offspring, the outcome would be a loss of £625.00.

My advice hasn't changed. Ignore horses by **Al Namix** at the 2021 Cheltenham Festival.

Al Namix (FR) – Progeny with Official Rating of 135+

Horses by this sire with an Official Rating of 135 or greater on 9th February 2021. Horses registered with the Irish Horseracing Regulatory Board (I.H.R.B) are shown in *italics*.

				Official Ratings as of 9th February 2021		
Sire	***Horse***	***Age***	***Sex***	***Hurdles***	***Chase***	***Trainer***
Al Namix	Al Dancer	8	g		153	Nigel Twiston-Davies
Al Namix	Cervaro Mix	7	g	137		Oliver Sherwood
Al Namix	Cut The Mustard	9	f		140	Paul Nicholls
Al Namix	Dear Sire	9	g	138		Donald McCain
Al Namix	Elixir De Nutz	7	g		144	Colin Tizzard
Al Namix	*Petit Mouchoir*	*10*	*g*	*155*		*Gordon Elliott*
Al Namix	Pinson Du Rheu	10	g	125	135	Alexandra Dunn
Al Namix	Raf Tavel	5	g	141		Ben Pauling

Commentary on selected potential entries for 2021 Festival

Al Dancer – Paddy Power Plate 2m5f (4:10 Thursday 18th March)

My commentary on **Al Namix** suggests that horses by this stallion should be ignored at the Cheltenham Festival. From 35 outings, the offspring have managed just three places. The highest rated chaser by **Al Namix** is ***Al Dancer***, and the 8yo had a couple of outings at Cheltenham at the end of last year. He was the 5/1 favourite for both races but failed to reward favourite backers in either the *Paddy Power Gold Cup Handicap Chase* for which he finished 3rd or the *Caspian Caviar Gold Cup Handicap Chase* for which he finished 9th. At the time of writing, ***Al Dancer*** can be backed at 25/1 for the newly named *Paddy Power Plate*. Don't waste your money.

Footnote:

For further insight to the *Paddy Power Plate*, read the commentary on ***Mister Whitaker*** by **Court Cave**.

Arcadio (GER)

Quote from the 2020 Cheltenham Festival Stallion Guide - "Even though my findings are based upon a small number of festival appearances, the early signs suggest that, specifically at the Cheltenham Festival, **Arcadio**'s offspring perform well over longer distance events and perform dismally in races at two miles where they simply struggle to get involved."

Arcadio (19-y-o)							
Race Format	*Miles*	*Won*	*Placed*	*Unplaced*	*Total*	*Win %*	*Place %*
Hurdles	About 2m	0	0	7	7	0%	0%
	About 2m 4f	0	2	0	2	0%	100%
	About 3m	0	0	1	1	0%	0%
Chases	About 2m	0	0	3	3	0%	0%
	About 2m 4f	1	0	2	3	33%	33%
	About 3m	0	1	3	4	0%	25%
	About 4m	0	0	0	0	-	-
Bumper	About 2m	0	0	2	2	0%	0%
Total	**2011-2020**	**1**	**3**	**18**	**22**	**5%**	**18%**

In looking back at the entry of **Arcadio** in the 2020 Cheltenham Festival Stallion Guide, albeit there isn't an abundance of data to make such judgements, it is noticeable how I was very positive about **Arcadio**'s progeny in the longer distance races and yet very negative about the offspring's chances in races over two miles. I quote, *"There are just eight more festival races to consider, all of which have been contested over 2½ miles or more. In these contests, again with the caveat of limited data being available, I am quite positive about the performances of* ***Arcadio****'s offspring."* And in races over the minimum distance, I said, *"Based on the evidence to date, not only would I recommend keeping clear of horses by* ***Arcadio*** *in 2m hurdle races at the 2020 Cheltenham Festival, but I would also extend that to all two-mile race disciplines."*

Bearing the above two statements in mind, four horses by **Arcadio** took part at last year's Cheltenham Festival, with two entries racing in events covering two miles, and the other two runners competing in longer distance chases. ***Simply The Betts***, trained by *Harry Whittington*, was a warm favourite in the 2020 *Brown Advisory & Merriebelle Stable Plate Handicap Chase*, mainly due to emerging from a 340-day break in stupendous form, winning three of his four races over fences. His race performances and novice handicap wins had resulted in him rising in the weights from an Official Rating of 125 in November 2019 to racing off a mark of 149 when he lined up for the 2m4½f *Stable Plate*. ***Simply The Betts***, the 100/30 favourite, raced prominently in the race and took over the lead two fences from home. His challenger, *Happy Diva*, headed ***Simply The Betts*** as they jumped the last, but jockey *Gavin Sheehan* rallied his mount to regain the lead up the Cheltenham hill, and, in staying on strongly, ***Simply The Betts*** emerged to win by 1¼ lengths, to give *Harry Whittington* his first festival winner. It was also the first festival winner from the stock of **Arcadio**.

The victory of ***Simply The Betts*** was a nice 'tick in the box' for my confident views as regards supporting **Arcadio**'s offspring in longer distance festival contests. Having one's views reinforced by a 100/30 favourite is one thing, but I was less convinced about how a nine-year-old 40/1 chance would fare in the *Fulke Walwyn Kim Muir Challenge Cup Amateur Riders' Handicap Chase*. The **Arcadio** sired ***Flying Angel*** was making his 4th festival appearance when lining up for the *Kim Muir*. He had finished runner-up on his debut in the 2016 *Martin Pipe Conditional Jockeys' Handicap Hurdle* and followed up by finishing last of six finishers in a field of 8 in the 2017 *JLT Novices' Chase*. Having missed the 2018 Cheltenham Festival, he returned in 2019 to compete in the *Ultima Handicap Chase* where he just missed out on a place when finishing fifth at a price of 25/1. In the *Kim Muir* of 2020, ***Flying Angel*** was never in the race and finished 9th.

So, in the longer distance national hunt races, one great run from a **Arcadio** sired favourite and one poor run from an outsider. As for the two races at two miles, there was one promising run from a 16/1 chance and one poor run from a 33/1 outsider. Let's start with the promising run from ***Third Time Lucki***, who finished in 4th place in the *Weatherbys Champion Bumper*. Trained by *Dan Skelton*, ***Third Time Lucki*** delivered a very good performance in the *Bumper*, not quite having the pace of the Irish trained trio in front of him but staying on well at the finish and just missing out on a place dividend by a neck. Horses by **Arcadio** have competed in two-mile events on twelve occasions at Cheltenham Festivals, and ***Third Time Lucki***'s 4th place in this race has undoubtedly been the best performance of the dozen so far. The Racing Post commented that the horse seems more about stamina than speed, so it will be interesting where he turns up at the 2021 Cheltenham Festival.

The other festival appearance at two miles by **Arcadio**'s progeny, took place in the *Randox Health County Handicap Hurdle*, where ***Zanza*** (33/1) was never in contention and struggled at the rear of the field to finish in 21st position. The run was very much in keeping with the other five appearances in which **Arcadio** has had a representative in this race. Starting with the earliest in 2015, the finishing positions of **Arcadio**'s offspring in the *County Hurdle* read as 9th, 14th, 13th, 13th, 20th and 21st. These six finishing positions present a somewhat compelling case for avoiding **Arcadio**'s entries in the *County Hurdle*. On the other six occasions in which horses by **Arcadio** have competed in festival races that cover two miles, there have been three poor performances in two-mile chases, a 22nd place finish to go with ***Third Time Lucki***'s 4th place in the *Weatherbys Champion Bumper* and a 10th place finish by ***Simply The Betts*** (40/1) in the 2018 *Sky Bet Supreme Novices' Hurdle*.

With the exception of ***Third Time Lucki***, none of these outings are telling me to support **Arcadio**'s progeny in the festival's two-mile races. That said, I am quite intrigued that four of the horses by **Arcadio** that made no impression on their festival debut in a two-mile hurdle event, returned to Prestbury Park to deliver a far better performance on their second visit. ***The Game Changer*** (8/1) who finished in 9th place in the 2015 *County Hurdle*, delivered an improved performance to finish 4th at 14/1 in the following year's *Arkle*, albeit nowhere near to securing a place position. ***Mad Jack Mytton*** (28/1) who finished 14th in the 2016 *County Hurdle* returned twelve months later in the *Brown Advisory & Merriebelle Stable Plate*. Racing at the same price of 28/1 as in the *County Hurdle*, ***Mad Jack Mytton*** had just emerged out of the mid-division pack to dispute 4th place when he fell at the 2nd last fence. Without that fall, he may well have secured a placing. ***Crievehill***, at 33/1 in the 2017 *County Hurdle*, appeared two years later in the 2019 *Kim Muir* and bagged a 4th place dividend rewarding each way backers with odds of 40/1. And finally, we have ***Simply The Betts***, 10th at a price of 40/1 in the 2018 *Supreme Hurdle*, who returned on his next visit two years later to claim victory as the 100/30 favourite in the 2020 *Stable Plate*. Based on these follow-up runs to mediocre two-mile hurdle festival debut runs, punters may wish to have a second glance should ***Zanza*** (2020 *County Hurdle* debut) or ***Thistle Do Nicely*** (2019 *County Hurdle* debut) turn up at Cheltenham this March.

Arcadio's festival statistics table tells us that the offspring that have competed in the festival's two-mile races are naught from twelve, whereas there is a very different picture when considering the other ten festival outings at distances of 2½ miles and 3 miles that when combined together, indicate one win, three places and six unplaced efforts. Of the ten appearances by **Arcadio**'s progeny in these longer distance races, there has been seven excellent performances and three poor ones. One of these feeble performances occurred when ***Walk To Freedom*** was pulled up in the 2019 *Pertemps Network Final Handicap*, the only occasion that a horse by **Arcadio** has competed in a festival hurdle contest covering three miles. And ***Flying Angel*** is the culprit for the other two mediocre runs in longer distance outings, when finishing 6th in the 2017 *JLT Novices' Chase* and 9th in the 2020 *Kim Muir*, either side of a strong performance when finishing 5th in the 2019 *Ultima Handicap Chase*. Two years prior to ***Flying Angel***'s 5th placing in the *Ultima*, another horse by **Arcadio**, ***Go Conquer*** (20/1) filled the exact same position when racing in the 2017 renewal. Four of the other five outings resulted in a pay-out on each-way bets as follows: ***Simply The Betts*** (100/30) winner of the 2020 *Stable Plate*; ***Flying Angel*** (8/1) 2nd in the 2016 *Martin Pipe*; ***Bright Forecast*** (25/1) 3rd in the *Ballymore*; and ***Crievehill*** (40/1) 4th in the *Kim Muir*.

As was referenced earlier, the only **Arcadio** sired horse to fall in 22 festival outings is ***Mad Jack Mytton***. I carried out some research on the real *John "Mad Jack" Mytton* and it is highly appropriate that the one festival faller from **Arcadio**'s stock is his namesake. *Mad Jack Mytton* was a British eccentric and I encourage all readers to google his name to really understand why he was known as "*Mad Jack*". He once tried to cure his hiccups by setting his shirt on fire and was instantly enveloped in flames. As a servant beat out the flames, *Mytton* was heard to say, "The hiccup is gone, by God!"

Thirteen horses by **Arcadio** have raced at the Cheltenham Festival on 22 occasions, and four of those 13 horses have rewarded each-way bets, all of them in races covering a distance of 2½ miles or more. Had one placed a £10.00 each-way bet on all 22 festival appearances, the outcome would be a loss of £178.38. However, had one only supported the 10 of **Arcadio**'s offspring that had competed in the mid to long distance festival races, the loss would instead turn into a £61.63 profit.

Despite ***Third Time Lucki***'s excellent performance in recording a 4th place finish in last year's *Weatherbys Champion Bumper*, I still recommend avoiding horses by **Arcadio** that are entered in festival races covering a distance of around two miles. My advice to punters is to take note of **Arcadio**'s offspring that are taking part in races covering a distance of 2½ miles or greater and perhaps be even more interested if any of those entries are returning to a Cheltenham Festival having delivered what could be considered an unsatisfactory performance in a two-mile hurdle contest on their festival debut. To that end, punters should have a quick check to see whether there are any 2020 Cheltenham Festival entries by the name of ***Thistle Do Nicely*** and/or ***Zanza***.

Arcadio (GER) – Progeny with Official Rating of 135+

Horses by this sire with an Official Rating of 135 or greater on 9th February 2021. Horses registered with the Irish Horseracing Regulatory Board (I.H.R.B) are shown in *italics*.

				Official Ratings as of 9th February 2021		
Sire	***Horse***	***Age***	***Sex***	***Hurdles***	***Chase***	***Trainer***
Arcadio	Bear Ghylls	6	g	140		Nicky Martin
Arcadio	Crievehill	9	g		140	Nigel Twiston-Davies
Arcadio	Flying Angel	10	g		139	Nigel Twiston-Davies
Arcadio	*Hardline*	*9*	*g*		*157*	*Gordon Elliott*
Arcadio	Simply The Betts	8	g		157	Harry Whittington
Arcadio	Third Time Lucki	6	g	144		Dan Skelton
Arcadio	Up The Straight	7	g	135	135	Richard Rowe
Arcadio	Zanza	7	g		145	Philip Hobbs

Commentary on selected potential entries for 2021 Festival

Third Time Lucki – Sky Bet Supreme Novices' Hurdle 2m½f (1:30 Tuesday 16th March)

Despite a fine performance in last year's *Weatherbys Champion Bumper*, I don't believe ***Third Time Lucki*** will trouble the judge in this year's renewal of the *Sky Bet Supreme Novices' Hurdle.* I am not keen on **Arcadio**'s festival contenders in 2m distance events and ***Third Time Lucki*** also falls short on several of the achievements required to win the festival's opener. There is no doubt that ***Third Time Lucki*** is a talented horse and I believe he will deliver a very respectable performance in the *Supreme.* Available at around 25/1, I can see him finishing just outside the top six.

Footnote:

For further insight to the *Sky Bet Supreme Novices' Hurdle*, read the commentary on ***Appreciate It*** by **Jeremy**.

Bear Ghylls – Ballymore Novices' Hurdle 2m5f (1:30 Wednesday 17th March)

At the time of writing, ***Bear Ghylls*** is priced at around 20/1 for the *Ballymore Novices' Hurdle* and it would be a Cheltenham Fairytale for trainer *Nicky Martin* if this talented six-year-old could cause an upset and win Wednesday's opening race. ***Bear Ghylls*** is so far unbeaten in four racecourse outings of one national hunt flat race at *Warwick* followed by three wins over hurdles, the last of which was a class 3 handicap at *Exeter*. It is a huge step up in class from a class 3 to a Grade 1 event at Cheltenham and almost certainly too ambitious. That said, it will be interesting to see how ***Bear Ghylls*** performs against the best of national hunt's 2½m novice hurdlers which should help connections determine where the horse is engaged for the 2021-22 season. There is the option, perhaps, of ***Bear Ghylls*** going for one of the handicaps instead, such as the *Martin Pipe Conditional Jockeys Handicap Hurdle* but the trends of that contest aren't pointing me towards ***Bear Ghylls*** as the winner.

Footnote:

For further insight to the *Ballymore Novices' Hurdle*, read the commentary on ***Galliard Du Mesnil*** by **Saint Des Saints**.

Zanza – Johnny Henderson Grand Annual Handicap Chase 2m½f (4:50 Wednesday 17th March)

There is a lot I like about ***Zanza***'s chances in the *Grand Annual*. I certainly think that at a price of 25/1, he offers better value than the early February favourite for the race, *Sky Pirate* who is available at around 7/1. *Sky Pirate* and ***Zanza*** raced against each other in the 2m½f *Spreadex Handicap Chase* at Cheltenham on 12th December 2020. *Sky Pirate* (4/1) won easily off an Official Rating (OR) of 134. ***Zanza*** (OR 145), at 11/2, was close up and going easily when falling three out. As the Racing Post analysis advised on ***Zanza***, *"It's hard to say he'd have won given how easy Sky Pirate did it, but he'd likely have given him something to think about"*. ***Zanza*** has not raced since, whereas *Sky Pirate* was raised 11lb and then followed up with another 2m chase victory at *Warwick* and raised another 7lb, so now has an OR of 152. Connections advise that they have finally found the right distance race for *Sky Pirate*, which is a strongly run 2m chase, and they know far more than I will ever know. That said, the horse has had 12 chase starts, the first five at 3m+, then another five at distances between 2m3f and 2m5f, before these two recent 2m chase successes. In the previous 10 outings, *Sky Pirate* had finished runner-up on five occasions.

I'm intrigued. If ***Zanza*** was about to finish close to the winner in that Cheltenham race when carrying 11lb more, should he really be 3-4 times the price of *Sky Pirate* in the *Grand Annual*, when he will be carrying 7lb less? Looking at the list of credentials that have regularly popped up for the winner of the *Grand Annual*, there are a number of positives, but also a very significant negative as advised below:

1) 9 of the past 10 winners of the Grand Annual were rated between 139 and 147. ***(Zanza has an Official Rating of 145)***
2) Only two winners this century had raced more than 12 times over fences. Nine of those winners had competed in 3-7 chases. ***(Zanza has had 4 chase outings)***
3) In the past 11 renewals, only three horses had won a race during the season. All three were novices. ***(Zanza is a novice but has won a handicap chase at Newbury)***
4) 13 of the past 16 winners had run at the festival previously. ***(Zanza finished down the field in the 2020 County Handicap Hurdle)***
5) 5 of the past 7 winners had been off the course for more than 90 days. ***(If Zanza goes straight to the Grand Annual from that fall at Newbury, he will have been off the course for 95 days)***
6) Here is the big negative which isn't good for either Sky Pirate or Zanza - In the past 16 renewals, horses that had won a handicap chase during the season are 0-126. ***(Both horses have won a handicap chase during the season)***

Based on some of these pointers above, ***Zanza*** may possibly sneak into a place in the *Grand Annual*, but on balance, I will resist the temptation to place a bet. There are three other factors that I find off-putting, probably the biggest one being the festival record of **Arcadio**'s offspring in races at two miles which stands at 0-12. ***Zanza*** is trained by *Philip Hobbs* who, in recent years, other than the success that he has had with *Defi Du Seuil*, has found it difficult to find festival winners. Even when he was picking up festival winners over many years, he has never yet saddled the winner of the *Grand Annual*. We need to go down memory lane to find the trainer's two festival winners within the 2m chase category. They are *Flagship Uberalles* in the 2002 *Queen Mother Champion Chase* and *Captain Chris* in the 2011 *Irish Independent Arkle Challenge Trophy Chase*. My final concern about ***Zanza***'s chances is his lack of experience in the hustle and bustle of a big field 2m chase which is highly competitive. The *Grand Annual* can be a bit bruising, with jockeys jostling for position throughout whilst still being able to negotiate tough fences at speed. This is the reason, I believe, why 8 of the past 15 winners had run in the *Grand Annual* previously. ***Zanza*** hasn't yet had that experience and none of her four chase runs to date have involved more than 9 runners.

Simply The Betts – Paddy Power Plate 2m5f (4:10 Thursday 18th March)

The top weight in last year's *Stable Plate* was on an Official Rating (OR) of 157, so when ***Simply The Betts***, off a mark of 149, won this event at the 2020 Cheltenham Festival, he was 8lb off the top weight. *The Storyteller* was also successful in this race when being 8lb off top weight. He won off a mark of 147, the top weight having an OR of 155. Over the past ten years, in order to win the *Stable Plate*, it would appear that being provided with a weight quite a bit below top weight has been proven to be crucial in the past decade. *The Storyteller* and ***Simply The Betts*** were 8lb away from the top weight but the other eight winners had a weight gap to the top weight ranging from 13lbs to 21lbs. I mention all of this technical detail because as a result of his success in this race last year, ***Simply The Betts*** now possesses an OR of 157 which is pretty much bang on when it comes to the typical OR of the top weight in this race. In the past 8 years, the OR of the top weight has been between 155 and 158. All of which means that if ***Simply The Betts*** does take up the chance to compete in this race again, he will find it rather tougher than he did last year. To win, he is going to have to defy all the trends that have been present over the past 10 years, which is why he is a 25/1 chance.

Simply The Betts also holds an entry in the *Betway Queen Mother Champion Chase* (40/1); the *Ryanair* (25/1); and the *Wellchild Cheltenham Gold* Cup (50/1). He won't win these either. If we combine the last ten years of these races and look at the Official Ratings of the thirty winners, only two horses have been on Official Ratings below 160. *Special Tiara* won the *Champion Chase* in 2017 off an Official Rating of 159, and the lowest OR of the 30 comes from *Lord Windermere* who won the 2014 *Gold Cup* off 152.

In humans, we often say, "*He or she is at that awkward age*". In racing, we say, "*He or she is at that awkward weight*". Whatever event he turns up in, I will be very surprised if ***Simply The Betts*** manages to trouble the judge.

Footnote:

For further insight to the *Paddy Power Plate*, read the commentary on ***Mister Whitaker*** by **Court Cave**.

Authorized (IRE)

Quote from the 2020 Cheltenham Festival Stallion Guide - "I suggest that punters keep their eyes on the racing cards throughout February to see if any potential festival entries by **Authorized**, and that includes ***Tiger Roll***, are taking in another prep race before the festival start on 10th March. In my view, in will be the progeny's racing performances during February that will determine the offspring's success or otherwise at the 2020 Cheltenham Festival."

Authorized (17-y-o)							
Race Format	*Miles*	*Won*	*Placed*	*Unplaced*	*Total*	*Win %*	*Place %*
Hurdles	About 2m	1	4	15	20	5%	25%
	About 2m 4f	0	1	2	3	0%	33%
	About 3m	1	0	2	3	33%	33%
Chases	About 2m	0	0	0	0	-	-
	About 2m 4f	0	0	1	1	0%	0%
	About 3m	0	0	0	0	-	-
	About 4m	3	1	0	4	75%	100%
Bumper	About 2m	0	0	1	1	0%	0%
Total	2011-2020	**5**	**6**	**21**	**32**	**16%**	**34%**

The festival statistics table for **Authorized** is impressive, showing a win strike rate of 16% and a win & place strike rate of 34%. I like to look at those strike rates another way. For every six occasions in which a horse by **Authorized** lines up in a festival race, one runner will win, and another will record a place dividend. It follows, therefore, that providing the majority of starting prices of those 5 wins and 6 place dividends are bigger than 5/1, then one is likely to be in profit betting on all of **Authorized** festival contenders blind to level stakes. And indeed, this is true. If one had placed a £10.00 each-way wager on all 32 outings by **Authorized**'s offspring, the outcome would be a £218.20 profit.

Before you start searching for all of **Authorized**'s entries for the forthcoming 2021 Cheltenham Festival, perhaps I should provide some insight to some of the data hidden in the bare figures. Nineteen horses by **Authorized** have raced at Cheltenham Festivals on 32 occasions, but only five of those 19 festival participants have contributed to the five wins and six places advised in **Authorized**'s festival statistics table. More importantly, 50% of the place dividends and all five wins are down to just two of the offspring, these being the illustrious ***Tiger Roll*** and the highly talented, but now sadly departed, ***Nichols Canyon***. Take these two out of calculations, and the £218.20 profit turns into a £286.25 loss. All of which says nothing more than to dig deeper into the data and be selective and smart with our selections. More of that later, but when it comes to **Authorized**, I believe we should start with the star performer. ***Tiger Roll***.

At last year's Cheltenham Festival, ***Tiger Roll*** was making his sixth appearance. This little bay gelding is quite popular with the annual festival lovers as in his previous five visits to the course, ***Tiger Roll*** had secured victory on four occasions. He's been pretty good at *Aintree* too, where every year the course holds a Grade 3 handicap chase named *The Grand National*. The horses that compete in this annual event have to jump huge fences and travel over 4¼ miles, which is why the race lasts about nine minutes to complete. Having to jump so many big fences over such a long distance means that the race is quite a spectacle, so much so that an estimated 500 million people in over 140 countries watch the event on television. It is a very difficult race to win and winning the race twice is almost impossible. Only three horses have managed this feat in the past 100 years and because this is so rare, the horses that achieve it become global stars. And who are they? *Reynoldstown*, *Red Rum* and ... ***Tiger Roll***.

Tiger Roll is a rather versatile racehorse, a bit like an Olympic athlete who could not only win, say, the 400 metres, but also the javelin, long-jump and beach volleyball. On top of his two *Grand National* victories, ***Tiger Roll***'s roll of honour at Cheltenham include the 2014 *JCB Triumph Hurdle* over two miles; the 2017 *JT McNamara National Hunt Challenge Cup Amateur Riders' Novices' Chase* over four miles; and in 2018 and 2019, two victories over Cheltenham's cross-country course to win the *Glenfarclas Cross-Country Chase*. His only defeat at Cheltenham came in the 2015 *Ladbrokes World Hurdle* where he finished 13th.

His second defeat occurred at last year's festival, where he finished runner-up to *Easysland* (3/1) in the 2020 running of the *Glenfarclas Chase*. *Easysland* hails from *David Cottin*'s yard in France and in January 2020, this talented horse, having won five cross-country chases on the bounce, was purchased by *J P McManus*. Aged six, *Easysland* is the youngest horse ever to win the *Glenfarclas Chase*, all previous winners had been aged between 8 and 12. ***Tiger Roll***, at 10 years old, was the 8/11 odds on favourite for the race, and although he performed nowhere near the level of his victory in the previous year's renewal, he still ran well in the soft going which certainly wouldn't have been to his liking when tiring after the last fence. Interestingly, the winning time was more than 40 seconds slower than the 2019 renewal of the *Glenfarclas* and eight seconds slower than the winning time of the 2019 *Grand National*!

The highest rated of **Authorized**'s progeny is, as one would expect, ***Tiger Roll***, whose best Official Rating (OR) is 171. Next in line is ***Nichols Canyon*** (best OR 164). Trained by *Willie Mullins*, ***Nichols Canyon*** secured 3rd place finishes on his first two festival appearances, the first in the 2015 *Neptune Investment Management Novices' Hurdle*, and on the second occasion when a 15/2 chance in the 2016 *Stan James Champion Hurdle Challenge Trophy*. The third Cheltenham Festival contest for ***Nichols Canyon*** turned out to be his best performance as he came from off the pace to win the 2017 *Sun Bets Stayers' Hurdle* at 10/1. Tragically, later in that year, on 28th December, ***Nichols Canyon*** suffered a fatal fall in what was his 20th race over hurdles whilst racing in the *Squared Financial Christmas Hurdle* at *Leopardstown*. It was the third time in seven runs at *Leopardstown* where he had parted company with his jockey. In his other seventeen races, ***Nichols Canyon*** had never finished outside the front three.

They say that Friday 13th is unlucky. Well, it certainly was for the **Authorized** bred ***Goshen***, who along with ***Zamdy Man***, is rated the 3rd best of **Authorized**'s progeny with a best Official Rating of 156. At precisely 54 seconds past 1:33pm on Friday 13th March 2020, I was about to put down **Authorized** as the sire of the *JCB Triumph Hurdle* winner, when disaster struck. ***Goshen*** was in command, about 10 lengths ahead of his nearest pursuer, when a clumsy jump at the last resulted in jockey *Jamie Moore* being unseated. According to trainer *Gary Moore*, it was a freak incident as ***Goshen***'s back foot got caught on the overhang of his shoe on his front foot. One can't help but feel sympathy for connections when hit with such misfortune. And things haven't gone right for ***Goshen*** ever since, as he finished last in a Grade 2 hurdle at Cheltenham in December which followed two defeats in a couple of handicaps on the flat. I hope connections can find out what's wrong with him.

In last year's Cheltenham Festival Stallion Guide, I highlighted that the majority of **Authorized**'s festival contenders make their first trip to Prestbury Park as four-year-olds and make their debut appearance in one of the festival's two juvenile hurdle events, these being the *Triumph Hurdle* (where ***Tiger Roll*** and ***Goshen*** made their debuts) or the *Boodles Juvenile Handicap Hurdle (Registered as the Fred Winter)*. Indeed, of the 19 horses by **Authorized** that have made their way to Prestbury Park for the Cheltenham Festival, 13 of them competed as four-year-olds in either the *Fred Winter* or *Triumph*

Hurdle contests. In six appearances by the offspring in the *Triumph Hurdle*, with the obvious exceptions of both ***Goshen*** and ***Tiger Roll***, the four remaining appearances have been uninspiring. None of the four runners have been back to the festival since. In the Grade 3 *Fred Winter*, the first five four-year-olds by **Authorized** to enter the race were all beaten, with all performances being no great shakes, with the exception perhaps of ***Totalize***, who just missed out on a placing when finishing in 5th place in the 2013 race. The past two runs by **Authorized**'s youthful stock, however, have been encouraging, with ***Ciel De Neige*** claiming a 3rd place finish in 2019 and ***Night Edition*** taking the runner-up spot last season.

Like many contenders for the *Boodles Juvenile Handicap Hurdle*, ***Night Edition*** started his racing career in France, contesting three races on the flat in the first half of 2019, before coming to Britain, changing ownership and trainer, in December 2019. Now trained by *David Pipe*, it wasn't long before ***Night Edition*** made his British debut, in a Class 4 juvenile race for three-year-olds at *Taunton* on 30th December. It was a pleasing introduction to hurdling, rather than anything special, as ***Night Edition*** finished in 4th place at a price of 9/1. Up in class, ***Night Edition*** appeared next at Cheltenham, running well at a big price to finish 2nd in Cheltenham's Grade 2 *Finesse Hurdle*, a recognised trial for the *Triumph Hurdle*. Less than two months later following a maiden hurdle success at *Ludlow*, ***Night Edition*** was at Cheltenham again for the *Boodles Juvenile Handicap Hurdle* (*Fred Winter*). Having been held up in the early stages, ***Night Edition*** (16/1) made headway three out, putting in a strong run approaching the last but had no more to give at the finish and so settled for the runner-up spot, beaten a length by the 15/2 winner, *Aramax*.

Only four horses by **Authorized** made it to the 2020 Cheltenham Festival – ***Tiger Roll***, ***Goshen***, ***Night Edition*** and ***Ciel De Neige***. The last named, having finished 3rd in the 2019 renewal of the *Fred Winter*, lined up in the 2020 *Randox Health County Handicap Hurdle*. The two horses at the front of the betting market were both five-year-old geldings owned by *J P McManus* and trained by *Willie Mullins*, the two being 11/2 favourite *Saint Roi* and 6/1 second favourite ***Ciel De Neige***. The latter had previously performed well in the Grade 3 *Betfair Hurdle* at *Newbury* in February, where backed into favouritism at 13/2, he just missed out on losing his maiden tag, beaten into the runner-up spot by 33/1 outsider *Pic D'Orhy*. In the *County Hurdle*, *Barry Geraghty* had the choice of either *Saint Roi* or ***Ciel De Neige***, and opted for *Saint Roi*. It was clearly the right choice as his mount quickened impressively to win the race whilst ***Ciel De Neige*** was hugely disappointing, dropping away tamely to finish in 15th place some 20 lengths behind his stablemate.

Earlier on in this chapter, I hinted that we need to be selective and smart with our **Authorized** sired selections, (which does not mean, of course, that we shouldn't be smart and selective all the time), but I consider there to be a couple of simple rules when it comes to looking at festival entries by **Authorized**. With this stallion's offspring, the place to start is with the juveniles. As advised earlier, 13 of the 19 horses by **Authorized** that have competed at Cheltenham Festivals made their festival debuts as four-year-olds, of which ***Tiger Roll*** is the only winner, although ***Goshen*** would almost certainly have won last year's *Triumph Hurdle* had it not been for that last hurdle fall. In the *Fred Winter Handicap Hurdle*, two more horses by **Authorized** have secured place dividends. If one assumes, ***Goshen*** would have won, then of those 13 four-year-old's, close to one third of them will reward backers with a win or place. The issue facing punters is that for these two races, several contenders don't make themselves known to the public until February (and certainly after this Guide and others have gone to print). ***Ciel De Neige*** is a case in point. He had raced three times in *France* for trainer *Guy Cherel*, finishing just outside the places on all three occasions, before being sent over to *Willie Mullins*' yard on 31st January 2019 and just six weeks before his appearance in the *Fred Winter*. My first piece of advice to punters is to keep their eyes peeled on two-mile hurdle races throughout February to check if any potential 4yo festival entries by **Authorized** are showing potential, especially those that started their careers in France.

There is a saying, *"If at first you don't succeed, try and try again."* Wise advice in many situations, but when it comes to **Authorized**'s festival representatives, more apt advice would be, *"If you are by **Authorized**, raced at the Cheltenham Festival without securing at least a placing on your debut, give up"*. And this provides my second recommendation to punters. Of the five horses by **Authorized** that have won or placed at the Cheltenham Festival, all five of them finished in the first three positions on their debut, and of those five, only ***Nichols Canyon*** and ***Tiger Roll*** went onto further festival success. To be fair, the majority of festival entries by **Authorized** that are unable to record a top three finish on their debuts do give up and never again appear at the Cheltenham Festival. Of the 19 that have made the trip to Prestbury Park in March, eleven of the offspring made just one appearance having failed to trouble the judge on their festival debuts. Two of **Authorized**'s stock, however, didn't follow this rule and returned to compete at the festival another day. ***Boite*** finished in 19th place in the 2017 *County Hurdle* and then returned in 2018 to finish in 20th position in the *Pertemps Network Final*. And ***Zamdy Man*** returned twice more following his debut defeat in the 2013 *Fred Winter Handicap Hurdle*. Trained by *Venetia Williams*, ***Zamdy Man*** returned to the festival in 2016 to compete in the *County Hurdle* where he finished 18th and then tried his luck over jumps at the following year's festival meeting when he was the last of those that completed the course, registering a 10th place finish in the *Close Brothers Novices' Handicap Chase*. When it comes to the progeny of ***Authorized***, my rule will be to ignore any entries that are returning to compete at a festival, having not secured at least a place position on their debut run.

Taking into account my two pieces of advice as highlighted above, where does that leave us as we look at **Authorized**'s entries for the 2021 Cheltenham Festival. If we start with the rule about ignoring those unplaced on their debut run, then what shall we decide about ***Goshen***? My view is that in betting decisions, use common sense rather than sticking rigidly to some trend or set of statistics, and so I would list ***Goshen*** as a 'qualifier' for being placed on his debut. That said, there are other factors to consider with ***Goshen*** at present, as he clearly isn't himself based on his outings since that unfortunate fall in the *Triumph Hurdle*. As for the other three horses that appeared at the 2020 Cheltenham Festival, ***Tiger Roll***, ***Ciel De Neige*** and ***Night Edition***, you can't rule any of them out as they all secured a top three finish on their festival debut.

And finally, we need to scan through the potential runners for the *Boodles Juvenile Handicap Hurdle* and the *JCB Triumph Hurdle* and look at the form and chances of any entries sired by **Authorized**. At the past two Cheltenham Festivals, three four-year-old horses by **Authorized** have made their mark; ***Ciel De Neige***, ***Night Edition*** and the unfortunate ***Goshen***. We will wait to see if any **Authorized** bred candidates emerge during February to make it three years in a row for this stallion's juveniles to deliver a top three finish.

Authorized (IRE) – Progeny with Official Rating of 135+

Horses by this sire with an Official Rating of 135 or greater on 9th February 2021. Horses registered with the Irish Horseracing Regulatory Board (I.H.R.B) are shown in *italics*.

				Official Ratings as of 9th February 2021		
Sire	***Horse***	***Age***	***Sex***	***Hurdles***	***Chase***	***Trainer***
Authorized	*Ciel De Neige*	*6*	*g*	*137*		*W.P. Mullins*
Authorized	*Foveros*	*6*	*g*	*136*		*W.P. Mullins*
Authorized	Goshen	5	g	156		Gary Moore
Authorized	Joke Dancer	8	g	132	140	Sue Smith
Authorized	Lucky One	6	g	143		Paul Nicholls
Authorized	*Maze Runner*	*6*	*g*	*135*		*W.P. Mullins*
Authorized	Mister Coffey	6	g	138		Nicky Henderson
Authorized	Pipesmoker	6	g	137		Nicky Henderson
Authorized	Sternrubin	10	g	137		Fergal O'Brien

Commentary on selected potential entries for 2021 Festival

Tiger Roll – Glenfarclas Cross-Country Chase 3m6f (4:10 Wednesday 17th March)

Tiger Roll is aged 11 now and the last horse aged older than 11 to win the cross-country chase was *A New Story* in 2010. He has been onto a racecourse on four occasions without winning since his second *Grand National* triumph in 2019 and however easy he made those two *Grand National* victories appear, this fabulous horse is getting older, not younger, so he is not going to be improving. It will be fantastic if he turns up and wins the *Glenfarclas* for a 3rd time, but if that is going to happen, then it will mean that 2-3 of his rivals will need to have an off day. I won't be backing him that's for sure, but I will be cheering him on. As all of us should be. What a truly amazing horse he is.

Beat Hollow (GB)

Quote from the 2020 Cheltenham Festival Stallion Guide - "So long as three turn up, it will be the biggest turn-out at a festival by this stallion's progeny since 2014. My recommendation to punters is to support any horse by **Beat Hollow** that lines up in a festival race that is outside the two-mile events."

Beat Hollow (24-y-o)								
Race Format	*Miles*	*Won*	*Placed*	*Unplaced*	*Total*	*Win %*	*Place %*
Hurdles	About 2m	2	0	11	13	15%	15%
	About 2m 4f	0	2	1	3	0%	67%
	About 3m	1	0	0	1	100%	100%
Chases	About 2m	0	0	0	0	-	-
	About 2m 4f	0	1	1	2	0%	50%
	About 3m	0	1	0	1	0%	100%
	About 4m	0	0	0	0	-	-
Bumper	About 2m	0	0	1	1	0%	0%
Total	**2011-2020**	**3**	**4**	**14**	**21**	**14%**	**33%**

I followed my own advice as per the quote above. At the 2020 Cheltenham Festival, I backed the horse by **Beat Hollow** that was competing in a chase covering a distance of three miles, and I ignored the two horses entered in two of the festival's two-mile hurdle contests. In these selections, I was probably in a group of thousands of punters, as the horse I supported was fancied to win and lined up at a price of 3/1, whereas the two hurdlers by **Beat Hollow** were outsiders, one priced at 33/1 and the other at 150/1.

Today, in professional football, we have a Video Assistant Referee or VAR, and as a result, when a football supporter sees his team score a goal, he is more cautious about celebrating that goal until he is sure that VAR isn't going to rule it out. The feeling that goes through a football fan today must be similar to those occasional situations in horse-racing, when having placed a big bet on a horse and you see it win, you hear the dreaded bell that announces a steward's enquiry. Or similarly, when your selection is involved in a photo-finish. Or sometimes, when your selection is out in front, yards from the finishing line, when suddenly completely out of the blue, another horse appears from nowhere, and in similar fashion to Usain Bolt sprints past your 'almost walking' selection, and your winnings which you had just started counting, are suddenly snatched away from you.

At 14:17 on Wednesday 11th March, I was very tempted to set myself some homework to write 100 times the sentence, "*I must not count my chickens until they've hatched.*" I had backed ***Minella Indo*** to win the *RSA Insurance Novices' Chase* and despite an awkward jump at the last that stopped his momentum a little, my selection kept on going up the Cheltenham Hill and looked certain to win having seen off the challenge of favourite *Allaho*. Apparently, ***Minella Indo*** was matched at 1.06 on the betting exchanges when suddenly *Barry Geraghty* appeared from nowhere on *Champ*, who I thought had been beaten off ages ago. But he motored up the Cheltenham Hill whilst my selection faltered and won going away to beat ***Minella Indo*** by 1 length. A few lucky punters had backed *Champ* in running on the exchanges at over 400. "What the hell happened there?", I exclaimed to my fellow punters.

As for the two hurdlers by **Beat Hollow**. ***Hollow Sound*** (150/1) finished 10th in the *Sky Bet Supreme Novices' Hurdle* and ***Not So Sleepy*** (33/1) was pulled up in the *Unibet Champion Hurdle Challenge*

Trophy. And that was it for **Beat Hollow**'s progeny at the 2020 Cheltenham Festival. All done and dusted by 2.20pm on the second day of the meeting. The last time that there had been as many as three horses by **Beat Hollow** entered at a Cheltenham Festival was back in 2014. This stallion doesn't have too many runners at Cheltenham festivals, but when the racing conditions are right, I would advise punters to sit up and take notice.

Eleven horses by **Beat Hollow** have raced on 22 occasions at Cheltenham Festivals, of which all bar one has taken place within the past decade. The sole outing that isn't showing in the festival table was when an unconsidered 100/1 chance named ***Sleepy Hollow***, lined up in the 2010 *Neptune Investment Management Novices' Hurdle*. Trained by *Hughie Morrison*, ***Sleepy Hollow*** ran by far his best race over hurdles, leading from the front but coming under pressure when he ducked out through the wing at the second last hurdle.

The 3 wins and 4 places showing in **Beat Hollow**'s festival statistics table have been recorded by four of the stallion's offspring, the quartet being responsible for 13 of the progeny's 22 festival appearances. The *Donald McCain* trained ***Cinders And Ashes*** lined up in four festival contests and achieved a 10/1 festival success, when winning the opening event of the 2012 Cheltenham Festival, the *William Hill Supreme Novices' Hurdle*, twelve months after he finished 5th in the 2011 *Weatherbys Champion Bumper*. ***Cinders And Ashes*** competed in ten more races following his *Supreme* victory, but never managed to win again, his last racecourse appearance taking place in May 2015. Two of those 10 races were back at Prestbury Park for the Cheltenham Festival meeting, but his performances were as different as chalk and cheese to his win in the *Supreme*, ***Cinders And Ashes*** being pulled up in both the 2013 *Champion Hurdle* and the 2014 *County Handicap Hurdle*.

Racing at the festival even more than ***Cinders And Ashes*** was ***Wicklow Brave***, who made a festival appearance on five occasions, the first of which was when taking 6th place in the 2014 *Sky Bet Supreme Novices' Hurdle*. His one festival victory came in the 2015 *Vincent O'Brien County Handicap Hurdle* which he followed with two consecutive 7th place finishes in the *Champion Hurdles* of 2017 and 2018. ***Wicklow Brave***'s last festival appearance was in the 2019 *Coral Cup Handicap Hurdle* when, priced at 28/1, and aged ten, he secured a runner-up spot when just caught at the finish by the year younger *William Henry*. He was beaten by a short head. For those not familiar with ***Wicklow Brave***, he was a highly talented versatile maverick who won races on the flat, in bumpers, over hurdles and fences. Based with *Willie Mullins* at *Closutton*, ***Wicklow Brave*** won 17 of his 59 races, winning over £900,000 in prize money during his career, his top successes being the Group 1 *Palmerston House Estate Irish St. Leger* in September 2016 at *The Curragh*, followed less than eight months later with victory at *Punchestown* in the *BETDAQ Champion Hurdle*. Sadly, in the autumn of 2019, when on the verge of adding yet another win to his record at *Far Hills, New Jersey*, in the *American Grand National*, he fell at the last fence, which sadly resulted in a fractured shoulder. It was a tragic end to a brilliant racehorse.

The other two horses by **Beat Hollow** that have rewarded punters with each-way bets are ***Battle Group*** and ***Minella Indo***. ***Battle Group***, hailing from *David Pipe*'s yard in Devon, travelled to Prestbury Park in March on two occasions and made something of an art in finishing in 4th place at 33/1 in festival handicap races. He ran well to claim the 4th place dividend in the 2011 *Coral Cup* at a price of 33/1 and then returned twelve months later to compete in the *Pulteney Land Investments Novices' Handicap Chase*. Déjà vu. ***Battle Group*** finished 4th at 33/1, rewarding each way backers for the second year in succession. ***Minella Indo***'s runner-up finish in last year's *RSA Insurance Novices' Chase* has already been painfully mentioned, but in the preceding year, the horse caused something of a surprise when under a confident ride by the excellent *Rachael Blackmore*, **Minella Indo** won the Grade 1 *Albert Bartlett Novices' Hurdle* at the hugely rewarding odds of 50/1.

Fourteen festival races contested by **Beat Hollow**'s offspring have been at the minimum distance of two miles, consisting of thirteen hurdle events and one run in the *Bumper*. ***Wicklow Brave*** and ***Cinders And Ashes*** account for eight of these 14 runs delivering one win apiece. Those wins aside, the next highest positions achieved are the 5th place in the *Bumper* by ***Cinders and Ashes*** and the 6th place secured by ***Wicklow Brave*** in the 2014 *Supreme Novices' Hurdle*. The remaining six 2m hurdle runs from five other horses by **Beat Hollow** were fruitless, with finishing positions of 7th, 10th, 14th, 18th, 23rd and pulled up. My view is that **Beat Hollow**'s offspring show a trend in two-mile hurdle races of being 'also-rans', unable to trouble the judge or to finish in the top-six places. That said, the trend has been interrupted on a couple of occasions by ***Wicklow Brave*** and ***Cinders And Ashes***. ***Wicklow Brave*** is the highest rated of **Beat Hollow**'s progeny with a best Official Rating of 166 and I would consider him an exception. Racing at the festival on five occasions with four results in two-mile hurdle events of 1st, 6th, 7th and 7th, are out of sync compared with the trend showing from the other **Beat Hollow** bred hurdlers who ran within this race category. ***Cinders And Ashes***' best Official Rating is 15lb lower than ***Wicklow Brave*** and I'm more inclined to suggest that the former's victory was more of a one-off. When he won the 2012 *Supreme Hurdle*, he was in form no doubt, having won his previous three hurdle events, but his Official Rating on the day was 142, and the eight *Supreme* winners since have been rated higher, six of them officially rated at 150+. Both ***Wicklow Brave*** and ***Cinders And Ashes*** won their festival events at attractive starting prices, so financially, had one placed a £10.00 each way wager on all 14 of **Beat Hollow**'s representatives who had participated in these two-mile festival races, the outcome would be a tidy profit of £192.50. Despite this profit, I am uneasy to support this stallion's runners in two-mile events when the profit has been generated by the odd sporadic big-priced win buried amongst several 'also-ran' performances. When it comes to backing **Beat Hollow**'s festival representatives, the races that cover a distance of two miles are not the contests to which I'm attracted. But I am very interested in this stallion's few entries that race over further.

Let's take a look at those eight festival runs where horses by **Beat Hollow** have travelled further than 2m4f. Six different horses by **Beat Hollow** make up the eight runs and I have listed the races below (Wins and placings are in bold):

Year	Festival Race	Name of horse	Position	Odds
2020	**RSA Insurance Novices' Chase (3m½f)**	**Minella Indo**	**2nd**	**3/1**
2019	**Albert Bartlett Novices' Hurdle (3m)**	**Minella Indo**	**1st**	**50/1**
2019	**Coral Cup Handicap Hurdle (2m5f)**	**Wicklow Brave**	**2nd**	**28/1**
2015	Brown Advisory & Merriebelle Stable Plate (2m5f)	Hollow Penny	5th	33/1
2013	Coral Cup Handicap Hurdle (2m5f)	Hollow Tree	11th	33/1
2012	**Pulteney Land Investments Novices' Handicap Chase (2m4½f)**	**Battle Group**	**4th**	**33/1**
2011	**Coral Cup Handicap Hurdle (2m5f)**	**Battle Group**	**4th**	**33/1**
2010	Neptune Investment Management Novices' Hurdle (2m5f)	Sleepy Hollow	RO	100/1

There are several elements within these results that I find highly attractive: (1) only two runners have failed to finish in the first five places which includes one win and four places; (2) the starting prices. These results are more akin to runners priced at single figures, not outsiders priced at 28/1 or more; (3) the results and figures are not dominated by just one or two horses, but rather spread across six of **Beat Hollow**'s offspring, of which four have recorded finishing positions in the front five places; (4) Financially, one would have done rather well backing all 8 runners blind to level stakes. To a £10.00 each-way stake, profits would amount to £741.00.

Clearly, there needs to be some caution when looking at the above results, especially as it is based on just eight festival outings. One could point out, for example, that a big slice of that huge profit figure is down to ***Minella Indo***'s 50/1 win, but even if you take ***Minella Indo***'s results out of the financial calculations, there is still a profit of £145.00 to be gained. And it is worth noting that ***Hollow Penny*** was very close to adding to the profit tally when missing out on a place by under a length in the 2015 *Stable Plate*. Whatever the starting prices on offer, I would be very pleased with a list of results showing that out of eight festival outings from a stallion's offspring, six of the runners achieved top five finishes, from four different horses. And if one adds into the mix, that of those six top five finishes, five of them returned starting prices of 28/1 or bigger – well that's eye-popping.

Not many horses by **Beat Hollow** will be at the Cheltenham Festival, but for those that do make the trip, take a very close look at those entries that are engaged in races of 2m4f or further. If I find one, I treat it like gold-dust and very often back it.

Beat Hollow (GB) – Progeny with Official Rating of 135+

Horses by this sire with an Official Rating of 135 or greater on 9th February 2021. Horses registered with the Irish Horseracing Regulatory Board (I.H.R.B) are shown in *italics*.

					Official Ratings as of 9th February 2021	
Sire	**Horse**	**Age**	**Sex**	**Hurdles**	**Chase**	**Trainer**
Beat Hollow	Benson	6	g	137		Dr Richard Newland
Beat Hollow	*Flanking Maneuver*	*6*	*g*	*137*		*Noel Meade*
Beat Hollow	*Minella Indo*	*8*	*g*		*164*	*Henry de Bromhead*
Beat Hollow	*Mt Leinster*	*7*	*g*	*142*		*W.P. Mullins*
Beat Hollow	Not So Sleepy	9	g	149		Hughie Morrison
Beat Hollow	*Roseys Hollow*	*7*	*f*	*136*		*Jonathan Sweeney*

Commentary on selected potential entries for 2021 Festival

Benson – Coral Cup 2m5f (2:50 Wednesday 17th March)

I watched ***Benson*** win the *Betfair Exchange December Handicap Hurdle* at *Sandown* on 5th December where despite making a bad blunder two hurdles from home, he recovered and put in a strong run up *Sandown*'s finishing hill to win going away. I was very impressed and immediately thought he may be suited for a run in the *Coral Cup*. Two weeks after that *Sandown* run, he finished in 4th place in the Grade 3 *Betfair Exchange Trophy* at *Ascot*. He looked to be going nowhere as they turned into *Ascot*'s straight where he was ridden along and last but one of the seventeen runners. Then, out of nowhere he flew up the straight to take 4th place and finished 10 lengths clear of the 6th horse. The furthest ***Benson*** has ever run is 2m½f, and frankly, I can't wait to see him tackle an extra ½ mile at Cheltenham.

As it states in my summary of **Beat Hollow**, the stallion has very few runners at the Cheltenham Festival, but if one is found that is engaged in a race of 2m4f or more, then they are well worth a bet. Of the 8 horses by **Beat Hollow** that have raced in festival races of 2½m or more, six have finished in the first 5 places.

At the time of writing, ***Benson*** is available at around 16/1 for the *Coral Cup*. I've already backed him. Not only am I a huge fan of horses by **Beat Hollow** that tackle festival races at 2½m but ***Benson*** does possess some of the traits that are required for a *Coral Cup* winner. See below:

1) Only 3 winners this century had contested more than 9 hurdle races. **(Benson has had 6 hurdle runs)**

2) 7 of the past 10 winners had raced in Graded Company within the past 18 months. 5 of those 7 had competed in 2 or more graded races. ***(2 of Benson's 6 Hurdle races have been in Graded races, both within the past 18 months)***
3) 11 of the last 19 winners had never run as far as 2m5f. **(All of Benson's races to date have been at 2m)**
4) 7 of the past 10 winners had a win strike rate over hurdles of between 33% and 50% **(Benson's win strike rate stands at 50%)**
5) The last nine Coral Cup winners had all raced at least once in a bumper. **(Benson competed in 4 bumpers, winning one)**

Benson's current Official Rating is 137 which I hope will be just high enough to get him a run in the *Coral Cup*. The bottom weight has been 136 or below in 7 of the past 10 years, so fingers crossed. And it could potentially be a winning mark, as 3 of the past 10 winners have been within 2lb of the bottom weight. If ***Benson*** does line up in the *Coral Cup*, he will be the 4th horse by **Beat Hollow** to do so and hopefully he will go one better than the great ***Wicklow Brave*** who finished in 2nd place in this event two years ago.

Finally, ***Benson***'s trainer is *Dr Richard Newland*, who over the past five years, possesses a healthy win strike rate over hurdles of 22%. He has only ever had one Cheltenham Festival winner which happened way back in 2007 with *Burntoakboy*. The race that the trainer won with *Burntoakboy* was the *Coral Cup*.

Footnote:

As well as the *Coral Cup*, ***Benson*** is showing in the betting markets for both the *County Handicap Hurdle* and the *Martin Pipe Conditional Jockeys Handicap Hurdle*, which are both scheduled for the last day of the festival. I'm guessing that these are an option should his handicap mark not be quite high enough to have a run in the *Coral Cup*. Should this happen, I won't be backing ***Benson*** in either contest. The *County Handicap Hurdle* at two miles isn't far enough and the trends are against him in the *Martin Pipe* even if the distance isn't.

Roseys Hollow – Festival Mares' Novices' Hurdle 2m1f (4:50 Thursday 18th March)

After the first three renewals of this race were won by three short-priced favourites, the event now appears to be much more open. At the time of writing, there are around half-a-dozen horses vying for favouritism around the 6/1 mark and ***Roseys Hollow*** is one of them. Trained by *Jonathan Sweeney*, ***Roseys Hollow*** (17/2) showed clear improvement to win the *Race Displays Solerina Mares Novice Hurdle* at *Fairyhouse* on 8th February. This race is a good pointer to the Cheltenham contest, having been won by *Limini* and *Laurina* who both went onto to win the *Festival Mares' Novices' Hurdle*. That said, last year's winner of the *Solerina* was *Minella Melody*, who was unbeaten over hurdles before arriving at the 2020 Cheltenham Festival, where she started as the 11/4 favourite. She flopped in the *Mares' Hurdle*, finishing down the field in 18th.

There were two big differences about *Minella Melody* compared to the previous four winners of the *Mares' Novices' Hurdle*. For starters, *Minella Melody* had not started her career in France, like the previous four (now 5) *Mares' Novices'* winners. And the trainer (not that I have anything negative to say about him) was *Henry De Bromhead*. For this event specifically (sorry Henry), it is probably better to have your horse trained by *Willie Mullins*, purely because he has trained all five winners of this race to date. These two attributes of starting life in France and not being trained by *Willie Mullins*, potentially compromised *Minella Melody*'s chances. And both elements apply to ***Roseys Hollow*** too. This is also a race that is over 2m1f, and although **Beat Hollow** has picked up two festival wins at this distance, they have come pretty much out of the blue, hidden amongst 12 forgettable outings. She definitely has a chance, but so do 4-5 others in the race. Not for me.

Not So Sleepy – County Handicap Hurdle 2m1f (2:10 Friday 19th March)

Not So Sleepy is aged nine and trained by *Hughie Morrison*. At last year's Cheltenham Festival, he lined up at 33/1 in the *Unibet Champion Hurdle Challenge Trophy* and was pulled up. He does hold an entry in this year's *Champion Hurdle* too, but I believe it unlikely that connections will enter him for a second tilt to upset the odds. He won't win if he is entered as his Official Rating is 149. In the past decade, the lowest rated *Champion Hurdle* winner was *Buveur D'Air* (157) in 2017.

Connections may try their luck by entering ***Not So Sleepy*** in the *County Hurdle* for which the 9yo can currently be backed at 25/1. But I don't see the horse winning this either. The race is over a distance of 2m1f and **Beat Hollow**'s offspring are much, much better in festival races at 2½ miles plus. ***Not So Sleepy*** is nine years old. No horse aged nine has won this race in the past decade. And ***Not So Sleepy***'s Official Rating of 149 isn't much help either. In the past 10 years, 8 winners were rated below 140. Indeed, six winners held an Official Rating of either 138 or 139. The winners nearer the top of the weights were *Ch'tibello* (146) in 2019 and *Arctic Fire* (158) in 2017.

There are just too many negatives for me surrounding ***Not So Sleepy***.

Minella Escape – Albert Bartlett Novices' Hurdle 3m (2:50 Friday 19th March)

Minella Indo was born on 18th April 2013. Sire is **Beat Hollow**. Dam is *Carigeen Lady*. Dam's sire is *Supreme Leader*. Owner *Barry Maloney* and trained by *Henry De Bromhead*. ***Minella Indo*** won a Point-to-Point on 18th March 2018, finished 3rd in a bumper, 3rd in a maiden hurdle and then was 2nd to *Allaho* in the Grade 3 *Surehaul Mercedez-Benz Novice Hurdle* (3m) at *Clonmel* on 14th February 2019. ***Minella Indo*** next appeared in the Grade 1 *Albert Bartlett Novices Hurdle* at Cheltenham on 15th March 2019 and won the race by 2 lengths at a price of 50/1.

Minella Escape was born on 14th April 2015. Sire is **Beat Hollow**. Dam is *Be My Leader*. Dam's sire is *Supreme Leader*. Owner *Alan Halsall* and trained by *Henry De Bromhead*. ***Minella Escape*** was 4th in a Point-to-Point on 8th December 2019, before winning in his second Point-to-Point outing on 2nd February 2020. This season, ***Minella Escape*** fell at the last in a maiden hurdle at *Punchestown*, finished 2nd in a Maiden Hurdle at *Navan*, and on 1st January 2021, won a maiden hurdle at *Tramore*. ***Minella Escape*** is entered in a Grade 3 race named the *Surehaul Mercedez-Benz Novice Hurdle* (3m) at *Clonmel* on 18th February 2021 after this Guide has gone to print. The horse is then scheduled to race at the 2021 Cheltenham Festival in the Grade 1 *Albert Bartlett Novices Hurdle* at Cheltenham on 19th March 2021, for which he is currently priced at 33/1.

You may have guessed. I've backed him.

Minella Indo – Magners Cheltenham Gold Cup 3m2½f (3:30 Friday 19th March)

Following a comfortable victory at *Navan* on 22nd November 2020 in the Grade 2 *BetVictor Make Your Best Bet*, ***Minella Indo*** was seen by many commentators as the main threat to *Al Boum Photo* achieving a third successive *Gold Cup* win. Two performances since in Grade 1 chases at *Leopardstown*, however, has blotted the horse's copybook. Following those defeats, a fall in December's *Savills Chase* and a 4th place in the *Paddy Power Irish Gold Cup* on 7th February, ***Minella Indo*** has been pushed out to 14/1 in the *Gold Cup* betting market.

The *Gold Cup* is the blue riband race of the National Hunt season and as a result, and quite rightly, is a very difficult race to win. Horses are up against top quality opposition, all of whom have been trained to peak on the day of this race. Have no doubt, any weakness from a *Gold Cup* hopeful will be exposed. The preparation races before the *Gold Cup* need to go right, everything within the week of the race needs to work out right, and the race itself needs to go just right. In this race, I avoid horses that have made their debut in a previous renewal of the *Gold Cup* yet haven't been victorious. Horses that have been prepared to perfection for their first attempt of triumph only to fail, are going to find it really difficult to reach those same heights of preparation again and improve. The *Gold Cup* is a tough race and takes a lot out of a horse. *Native River* is the only horse this century to have been beaten on his *Gold Cup* debut and come back to win when trying again. When punters talk about a horse benefitting from the experience of putting in a great run (but without winning) in a previous *Gold Cup*, ignore them. The opposite is true. The horses behind the winner often finish tired and the mental and physical scars of battle will usually haunt them in any follow-up bid. (*Native River* proving to be the exception).
Minella Indo does have the advantage that if he runs in this year's *Gold Cup*, it will be his first attempt, and quite frankly, his one and only chance of winning it. There is no doubt, however, that I am hugely concerned that he was unable to win at least one of his two Grade 1 *Leopardstown* prep races. And that alone, is enough for me to believe that he won't win this year's *Cheltenham Gold Cup*. I do, however, believe that ***Minella Indo*** will bounce back from those performances at *Leopardstown* as I'm convinced the horse prefers better ground which could be the case 19 days into March. We shall see, but I can see ***Minella Indo*** finishing in the frame and picking up a place to finish 2nd or 3rd.

As for the two Grade 1 prep races at *Leopardstown*, they haven't pointed to the winner as much as the Cheltenham Festival's Grade 1 novice chase from the previous festival, all of which is a positive sign for the 1-2-3 of the 2020 renewal, *Champ*, ***Minella Indo*** and *Allaho*. In the past decade, four winners of the *Cheltenham Gold Cup* had run in the previous season's *RSA Insurance Novices' Chase*. Two had won the *RSA*, one had finished in 3rd place and another had fallen which was none other than *Al Boum Photo*! Two *Gold Cup* winners apiece, over the past 10 years, have emerged from the two aforementioned *Leopardstown* races. *Synchronised* (2012 *Gold Cup* winner) won the *Savills Chase* before his success, whilst *Lord Windermere* (2014 *Gold Cup* winner) finished down the field in 7th. *Lord Windermere* didn't fare much better in the *Irish Gold Cup* where he finished in 6th, whereas in 2017, *Sizing John* did the *Irish* and *Gold Cup* double.

Some factors that are a positive for ***Minella Indo***'s chances in the *Gold Cup* are as follows:

1) Only 2 Gold Cup winners in the past 21 years had raced more than 12 times over fences and 5 of the past 10 winners had had between 7-9 chase starts. ***(Minella Indo had had 7 chase starts)***
2) The last 21 winners were sent chasing immediately after their novice campaign over hurdles ***(as was Minella Indo)***
3) 9 of the past 10 winners had a win strike rate of 43% or greater. ***(Minella Indo sits on 43% with an identical record to when Al Boum Photo won the 2019 Gold Cup of 3 wins from 7 chase starts)***
4) 16 winners this century had won (9) or been placed (7) at a previous Cheltenham Festival. ***(Minella Indo has a festival record of 1 win and 1 runner-up)***
5) 20 of the last 21 winners of the Gold Cup have been aged 7, 8 or 9. ***(Minella Indo is aged 8)***

Other trends are a negative for ***Minella Indo***:

1) 14 of the past 21 winners had won a graded novice hurdle over 2m-2m4f. ***(Minella Indo's two Grade 1 hurdle wins covered a distance of three miles)***
2) Only 1 of the past 13 winners had raced more than 3 times during the season. ***(Minella Indo has had four outings)***
3) 16 Gold Cup winners this century had won last time out. ***(Minella Indo finished 4th)***
4) 18 of the past 20 winners started at single-figure odds, of which 9 were favourite. ***(I guess Minella Indo will end up borderline at around 10/1 mark)***
5) The last 21 winners had already won a Grade 1 race over fences. ***(This is a huge statistic for Minella Indo to overcome, despite how close he was to victory in last year's RSA Insurance Novices' Chase)***

Beneficial (GB)

Quote from the 2020 Cheltenham Festival Stallion Guide - "Staking £10.00 each way blind on all horses by **Beneficial** that have competed at Cheltenham Festivals from 2004 through to 2019 highlights that on the 28 occasions when the going was Soft, a profit of £112.50 would have been the outcome. In comparison, when the going was anything other than Soft, on 103 appearances by the offspring, the result would have been a loss of £1,118.50."

Beneficial (Died as a 23-y-o in 2013)							
Race Format	*Miles*	*Won*	*Placed*	*Unplaced*	*Total*	*Win %*	*Place %*
Hurdles	About 2m	0	1	9	10	0%	10%
	About 2m 4f	1	3	15	19	5%	21%
	About 3m	1	0	7	8	13%	13%
Chases	About 2m	0	4	15	19	0%	21%
	About 2m 4f	1	2	13	16	6%	19%
	About 3m	2	5	22	29	7%	24%
	About 4m	0	0	6	6	0%	0%
Bumper	About 2m	0	0	3	3	0%	0%
Total	**2011-2020**	**5**	**15**	**90**	**110**	**5%**	**18%**

In last year's Cheltenham Festival Stallion Guide, I advised that if the word 'Good' is mentioned anywhere within the official description of the going, then the wise move would be to give **Beneficial**'s progeny the swerve. The rationale for this conclusion is based upon the statistics from previous Cheltenham Festivals as highlighted in the quote at the top of this page. As the 2020 Cheltenham Festival welcomed soft ground for the 3rd year in succession, then like me, punters may have been looking out for the **Beneficial** sired entries that may have provided the opportunity for profit. As it was, only eight of **Beneficial**'s offspring made it to last year's meeting and four of those were big outsiders, two priced up at 33/1 and another duo at 50/1.

I invested in the two shortest priced of **Beneficial**'s offspring at the 2020 Cheltenham Festival, these being ***Ben Dundee*** (10/1) in the *Brown Advisory & Merriebelle Stable Plate Handicap Chase* and ***Kilfilum Cross*** (8/1) in the *Fulke Walwyn Kim Muir Challenge Cup Amateur Riders' Handicap Chase.* I was fortunate enough to pick a bookie who was offering five places in the *Stable Plate Handicap Chase*, so made a small profit on my ***Ben Dundee*** each way wager. Trained by *Gordon Elliott*, ***Ben Dundee*** had a rather challenging journey throughout the 2m4½f journey, on occasions meeting trouble in the pack of 23 runners before being hampered by a faller two fences from home. One could easily argue that he would have secured an 'official' place position had he enjoyed a clearer passage.

Just over an hour later on the 3rd day of last year's meeting, ***Kilfilum Cross*** lined up for his second appearance in the *Kim Muir Handicap Chase*. On his first visit to the Cheltenham Festival, in 2019, the grey ran well at a price of 7/1 to claim the runner-up spot behind winner, *Any Second Now.* Ridden once again by *Mr Alex Edwards*, I was hoping that ***Kilfilum Cross*** would go one better in the 2020 *Kim Muir* renewal, but it wasn't to be, as once again, the *Henry Oliver* trained gelding found one too good, on this occasion, *Milan Native*, who prevailed over my selection by 1¾ lengths.

Beneficial has been represented at Cheltenham Festivals on 139 occasions, of which 110 runs have taken place within the past decade. Within those 139 runs, there have been just six Cheltenham Festival winners secured by five of **Beneficial**'s progeny, with ***Salsify***, having won the *Foxhunter Chase*

Challenge Cup in 2012 and 2013, being the only one of the offspring to record two festival successes. For punters, the numbers are crystal clear. **Beneficial**'s offspring have a Cheltenham Festival win strike rate of just over 4%, equivalent to a festival victory for one in every 23 occasions that the sire has a festival runner. The total number of festival placings that have been registered by **Beneficial**'s stock is 18 which measures a win & place strike rate of 17%. With statistics like these, it is incredibly difficult to make profits. Placing a £10.00 each way bet on all 139 festival appearances from **Beneficial**'s progeny calculates into a mammoth loss of £1,136.00.

It has been a long time since a horse by **Beneficial** secured a Cheltenham Festival victory. The last time it happened was In 2014 when the *Jonjo O'Neill* trained ***More Of That*** beat off the challenge of the mare, *Annie Power*, to win the 2014 *Ladbrokes World Hurdle*. As we approach the 2021 Cheltenham Festival, it is beginning to look as if ***More Of That*** may well be the last of **Beneficial**'s festival winners. My rationale is that the offspring have not only failed to take advantage of the soft ground that has been so prevalent at the past three festival meetings, but also because **Beneficial**'s stock is now aged eight or greater, meaning that there are far fewer opportunities in which horses by **Beneficial** can be entered.

Readers of earlier editions of the Cheltenham Festival Stallion Guide will be aware that when it comes to **Beneficial**, I typically advise punters to forget about backing any of the stallion's progeny unless there is torrential rain making the going soft or heavy. In short, the festival results recorded by **Beneficial**'s offspring have historically been better in soft ground conditions. At the 2020 Cheltenham Festival, we saw soft ground for the 3rd year in succession, with all bar the three chases on the Friday (that took place on good to soft), taking place on ground officially described as 'soft'. As a result, of the 84 races that have taken place at the last three festivals, 62 have taken place on 'Soft'; 17 on 'Good to Soft'; and 5 on Heavy. Horses by **Beneficial** have been represented on 23 occasions at these predominantly soft ground festivals registering 4 place positions from 19 outings on going officially described as 'Soft' and 1 placing from 4 runners on going officially described as 'Good to Soft'. Based on previous festival results recorded in soft ground conditions preceding the 2018 Cheltenham Festival, one can only conclude that results over the past three festivals have fallen short of what one might have expected. If one had placed a £10.00 each way bet on all 19 horses by **Beneficial** that had competed at the last three festival meetings, when conditions were soft, the outcome would be a loss of £161.50.

In recent years, preceding the most recent three festivals, it has been somewhat of a rarity to witness a festival event taking place on soft ground. Indeed, this century up to and including the 2017 Cheltenham Festival, there were just 24 festival races contested on going described as 'soft'. Within those 24 races, fifteen horses by **Beneficial** lined up in nine of them, registering two victories and four place positions. A £10.00 each way bet on these 15 runners would have resulted in a profit of £184.00 which compares far more favourably than the £161.50 loss suffered at the past three festivals. Combined together then, and despite the underwhelming results at the past three festivals, when horses by **Beneficial** have competed on festival ground that is officially described as 'Soft', supporting all of them blind to level stakes would have resulted in a small profit. This is due to an improved win & place strike rate of 29%, more than double the 13% win & place strike rate result from **Beneficial**'s representatives that have competed in festival events on ground that is described as 'Good to Soft' through to 'Good to Firm'.

I mentioned earlier that **Beneficial**'s festival entries are now aged eight or more as a result of the stallion's death in 2013, which will mean that there are fewer opportunities for this sire's stock to record a first Cheltenham Festival victory since 2014. The majority of older national hunt horses race over fences rather than hurdles, and also are more likely to tackle longer distances too. This century, of the 28 Cheltenham Festival races, there are 11 contests in which horses aged eight or greater have recorded more victories than their younger competitors. So, if I was forced to propose a race in which **Beneficial**'s offspring may have a chance of victory, (chances of which would improve if the going becomes soft), which race would it be? In an analysis of the 11 festival races in question, I immediately discounted the *Wellchild Cheltenham Gold Cup*, the *Ryanair Chase*, and the *Betway Queen Mother Champion Chase*. Typically, only the top-class horses, with Official Ratings of 160 or more win these Grade 1 chases. Over the past decade in these three events, only two victories have been recorded by horses that possessed an Official Rating below 160, these being *Special Tiara* (159), winner of the 2017 *Queen Mother Chase* and the 2014 *Cheltenham Gold Cup* victor, *Lord Windermere* (152). **Beneficial**'s current crop has nothing classy enough to win any of these three events.

Taking the two long distance chases, horses by **Beneficial** have competed without success on 9 occasions in the *National Hunt Chase* and twice in the *Glenfarclas Cross Country Chase*. The best performance by the progeny in these marathon events was recorded by ***Becauseicouldntsee*** who finished runner-up as a seven-year-old in the 2010 *National Hunt Chase Challenge Cup*. At the other end of the scale in distance, is the highly competitive two-mile chase, the *Johnny Henderson Grand Annual Handicap Chase*, which at the 2021 Cheltenham Festival, will take place on the 2nd day of the meeting rather than the event's traditional Friday slot. Horses by **Beneficial** have competed in this race on 16 occasions, and three of them have been placed, all finishing runner-up. ***Tanks For That*** (2012), ***Kid Cassidy*** (2013) and ***Eastlake*** (2015) all found one too good. Experience often counts for horses to be successful in this contest, and it is interesting to note that all three of these horses secured their 2nd placings a year after their debut in the race. ***Kid Cassidy*** and ***Eastlake*** were also helped by the heavens opening and torrential rain causing the going for their races to be run on soft.

In the 2m4½f Grade 3 *Paddy Power Plate Handicap Chase*, horses aged 8 or more have won 12 of the 20 renewals this century. **Beneficial** has been represented on five occasions, twice last year by the previously mentioned ***Ben Dundee*** who finished 5th and ***Livelovelaugh*** who was placed 8th. Both horses had the benefit of soft ground, unlike the three previous contenders, all of whom finished outside of the first ten places.

Of the six Cheltenham Festival victories recorded by **Beneficial**'s stock, four of them have been achieved at three miles, a distance within which there are four races (aside from the *Gold Cup*), where older horses have been more successful than runners aged below eight. The races concerned are the *Ultima Handicap Chase*, the *Fulke Walwyn Kim Muir Handicap Chase*, the *St. James's Place Festival Challenge Hunters Chase* and one hurdle event, the *Pertemps Network Final*. Taking the hurdle event first, it is rather surprising to learn that in 139 festival outings by **Beneficial**'s progeny, only twice has the stallion been represented in the *Pertemps Network Final*. The very first of **Beneficial**'s offspring to appear in a Cheltenham Festival race was named ***G V A Ireland*** and the 14/1 chance almost won the 2004 *Pertemps Final*, beaten in the closing stages by the strong run of 50/1 outsider, *Creon*. More than a decade later, in the 2015 renewal, a 66/1 outsider trained by *Sophie Leech* finished last of 23 runners. The name of the horse, ***Peckhamecho***, makes me smile as it reminds me of an episode of that brilliant comedy, 'Only Fools and Horses', when Del Boy and Rodney were selling tap water as 'Peckham Spring Water'!

All of which leaves us with three races in the 3m chase category and the influence of three of **Beneficial**'s more successful offspring, these being ***Salsify***, ***Kilfilum Cross*** and ***Becauseicouldntsee***. As highlighted towards the beginning of this chapter, ***Salsify*** is the only horse by **Beneficial** to have won twice at the Cheltenham Festival, both victories coming in the *Festival Hunters Chase*. His first victory came in the 2012 renewal when he beat *Chapoturgeon* by a length at a price of 7/1, with *Oscar Delta* (28/1) coming home in 3rd place. The following year's renewal will always be remembered for when *Oscar Delta*, with victory firmly in his grasp, famously jinked left and unseated jockey *Jane Mangan* just 150 yards from the finish. The beneficiary of *Jane Mangan*'s misfortune was ***Salsify***, who claimed his second victory in the race, this time as the 2/1 favourite. **Beneficial** has been represented in the *Festival Hunters Chase* on 7 occasions, and adding to **Salsify**'s two victories in the race, is the runner-up position that was registered by a 50/1 outsider, ***Following Dreams***, in 2015. I should point out that the 2nd placing achieved by ***Following Dreams*** and ***Salsify***'s 2013 victory were both achieved on soft ground following downpours and less than two hours before the previously highlighted successes of ***Kid Cassidy*** and ***Eastlake*** in the 2013 and 2015 *Grand Annual Chase* events. Soft going keeps popping up, doesn't it?

As referenced earlier, ***Becauseicouldntsee*** is the only one of **Beneficial**'s progeny to have registered a placing in the 4m chase category, but the chestnut also finished runner-up two years later in the 2012 *Fulke Walwyn Kim Muir Handicap Chase*, an event where horses by **Beneficial** have appeared on seventeen occasions. ***Becauseicouldntsee*** competed at the Cheltenham Festival for a 3rd and final time in 2013, where he was once again entered for the *Kim Muir*. This time, he just missed out on the places when finishing fifth. The only other horse by **Beneficial** to secure a place in this event for amateur riders is the prior mentioned ***Kilfilum Cross***, who has been the runner-up in the past two renewals. ***Becauseicouldntsee*** and ***Kilfilum Cross*** are the only two of **Beneficial**'s offspring to achieve any sort of success in the *Kim Muir*, with none of the other 13 runners by this sire registering a top six placing.

The final race of the eleven in which older horses have fared better is in the *Ultima Handicap Chase*, where **Beneficial** bred horses have lined up in the race on just three occasions delivering three forgettable performances. Indeed, although all 11 races have now been commented upon, whereby horses older than seven have recorded a higher win-rate than their younger rivals, not one event stands out as being 'the one' for **Beneficial** supporters. The evidence suggests that the stars need to be aligned and all of the pieces falling neatly into place for this stallion to have one of his remaining stock secure a 7th Cheltenham Festival success. In my view, to even consider a second glance at a **Beneficial** sired entry at the 2021 Cheltenham Festival, the going needs to be officially 'Soft' or even worse. If that happens, then the focus should be upon a race distance of three miles (like 4 of the sire's 6 winners) together with a horse that has shown at least some semblance of form in previous races. If 'Good' is mentioned anywhere within the going description, then we can halt our improbable deliberations and simply move on.

Beneficial (GB) – Progeny with Official Rating of 135+

Horses by this sire with an Official Rating of 135 or greater on 9th February 2021. Horses registered with the Irish Horseracing Regulatory Board (I.H.R.B) are shown in *italics*.

				Official Ratings as of 9th February 2021		
Sire	***Horse***	***Age***	***Sex***	***Hurdles***	***Chase***	***Trainer***
Beneficial	*Abbey Magic*	*10*	*f*		*140*	*Henry de Bromhead*
Beneficial	Benatar	9	g		138	Gary Moore
Beneficial	Bennys King	10	g		157	Dan Skelton
Beneficial	*Benruben*	*8*	*g*		*137*	*Henry de Bromhead*
Beneficial	*Chatham Street Lad*	*9*	*g*		*151*	*Michael Winters*
Beneficial	Cloth Cap	9	g		148	Jonjo O'Neill
Beneficial	Crixus's Escape	8	g		135	Gillian Boanas
Beneficial	Kilfilum Cross	10	g		135	Henry Oliver
Beneficial	*Livelovelaugh*	*11*	*g*		*137*	*W.P. Mullins*
Beneficial	Locker Room Talk	8	g	132	142	Stuart Coltherd
Beneficial	Mellow Ben	8	g		135	Chris Gordon
Beneficial	Pistol Whipped	7	g		139	Nicky Henderson
Beneficial	Red River	8	g		135	Kim Bailey
Beneficial	*Snugsborough Benny*	*11*	*g*	*120*	*147*	*Liam P Cusack*
Beneficial	*Snugsborough Hall*	*10*	*g*	*116*	*142*	*Liam P Cusack*
Beneficial	Thomas Darby	8	g	155		Olly Murphy
Beneficial	*Treacysenniscorthy*	*9*	*g*	*139*	*136*	*Robert Widger*
Beneficial	Wishing And Hoping	11	g		137	Mrs Melanie Rowley
Beneficial	Worthy Farm	8	g		135	Paul Nicholls

Commentary on selected potential entries for 2021 Festival

Chatham Street Lad - Paddy Power Plate 2m5f (4:10 Thursday 18th March)

Michael Winters, the trainer of ***Chatham Street Lad*** is a real character. After the **Beneficial** sired horse under his tutelage had secured the *Caspian Caviar Gold Cup Handicap Chase* on 12th December last year at a price of 16/1, you had to admire the joy and excitement within him as he was interviewed by ITV Racing. After the interview, he threw himself to the ground to roll around in the Cheltenham mud. Brilliant! The going was soft that day and so would have suited ***Chatham Street Lad*** as his sire's offspring definitely prefer the softer going. The trainer will be hopeful that the going is exactly like that or even heavy if he sends his horse over to the 2021 Cheltenham Festival.

Connections appear to have entered him in every possible contest. The *Arkle*, The *Champion Chase*, The *Marsh*, The *Ryanair*, The *Brown Advisory Novices' Chase*, The *Paddy Power Plate* as well as Britain's Got Talent! My first message to connections of ***Chatham Street Lad*** is not to enter their pride and joy into any of the Grade 1 contests. If we take the three novice races of the *Arkle*, *Marsh* and now *Brown Advisory* (instead of *RSA*) and total up the number of renewals this century, we have 50 races, (there being only 10 renewals of the *Marsh*). ***Chatham Street Lad*** is nine years old and no horse aged nine or older has won any of those 50 races. Now, let's take the *Champion Chase* and the *Ryanair*. The lowest rated horse to win either of these two contests in the past 10 years is *Special Tiara* who won the *Champion Chase* in 2017 off an Official Rating of 159. ***Chatham Street Lad*** possesses an Irish Official Rating of 151.

It is fun and a dream to consider these Grade 1 events, but I suggest connections look elsewhere, and so we come to the *Paddy Power Plate*, where ***Chatham Street Lad*** (at the time of writing) can be backed at 20/1. He does have a chance in this event, but I still doubt that he will win. In the past ten years, every winner of this event carried 8lb or more less than the top weight, and in the past 8 years, the OR of the top weight has been between 155 and 158. ***Chatham Street Lad*** is currently at 151 and as if often the case, the British Handicapper usually adds a few pounds to the Irish runners as he assesses and compares British and Irish form. 151 is high enough based on historic trends, let alone a few pounds more.

The final reason why I think ***Chatham Street Lad*** won't win is because horses by **Beneficial** haven't won a festival race since 2014 and yet conditions at the past three festivals have played to their advantage. If there is a deluge of rain, I may think again. And it would be great to see *Mr Winters* rolling around in the mud again!

Footnote:

For further insight to the *Paddy Power Plate*, read the commentary on ***Mister Whitaker*** by **Court Cave**.

Court Cave (IRE)

Quote from the 2020 Cheltenham Festival Stallion Guide - "Combining the results of the six chases with the three hurdle runs at this race distance (2½m), produces a very impressive set of statistics; 3 wins, 2 places and 4 other runners that were placed from 5th to 7th. Backing all **Court Cave**'s 2½m festival runners blind to level stakes delivers a profit of £296.25 to a £10.00 each-way stake."

Court Cave (20-y-o)							
Race Format	*Miles*	*Won*	*Placed*	*Unplaced*	*Total*	*Win %*	*Place %*
Hurdles	About 2m	0	0	4	4	0%	0%
	About 2m 4f	2	1	0	3	67%	100%
	About 3m	0	0	2	2	0%	0%
Chases	About 2m	0	0	1	1	0%	0%
	About 2m 4f	1	2	5	8	13%	38%
	About 3m	0	1	4	5	0%	20%
	About 4m	0	0	0	0	-	-
Bumper	About 2m	0	0	1	1	0%	0%
Total	2011-2020	**3**	**4**	**17**	**24**	**13%**	**29%**

Fifteen horses have been responsible for the 24 festival runs of **Court Cave**'s stock, of which all bar five have competed at the Festival just once. ***Champagne Court, City Island and Court Minstrel*** have participated twice, ***Mister Whitaker*** on three occasions, whilst ***Champion Court*** raced at the festival for five consecutive seasons from 2011 through to 2015. ***Champion Court*** was quite consistent, although looking at the overall picture of his half-decade of runs, he was a little bit away from being top class. His best performances occurred when he was at his youngest, finishing just outside the places to take 4th in the 2011 *Albert Bartlett Novices' Hurdle* before securing his one festival placing when finishing runner-up to *Sir Des Champs*, in the 2012 *Jewson Novices' Chase*.

At last year's festival, four horses made the trip to Prestbury Park, with three of those named above making a return visit following success at a previous meeting. ***Champagne Court***, ***City Island*** and ***Mister Whitaker*** all made an appearance at the 2019 Cheltenham Festival with mixed results. ***Mister Whitaker*** was pulled up when disappointing in the 2019 *Ultima Handicap Chase*; ***Champagne Court*** (14/1) secured a 4th place dividend in the 2019 *Martin Pipe Conditional Jockeys' Handicap Hurdle; and* ***City Island*** became the third of **Court Cave**'s progeny to record a Cheltenham Festival victory when winning the 2019 *Ballymore Novices' Hurdle* at a price of 8/1. It was the second time that a horse by **Court Cave** had won the *Ballymore*, ***Willoughby Court*** taking the prize in 2017 to become the very first of **Court Cave**'s offspring to win a festival event. The horse by **Court Cave** that claimed the second of the progeny's festival successes was ***Mister Whitaker*** who won on his festival debut in the 2018 *Close Brothers Novices' Handicap Chase*.

At the 2020 meeting, on ***Mister Whitaker***'s third visit to the Cheltenham Festival, trainer *Mick Channon* had entered the horse in the *Brown Advisory & Merriebelle Stable Plate Handicap Chase*. Personally, as the *Stable Plate* covers a distance of 2m4½f, I think he made the right decision. In ten previous appearances in chases at a distance of between 2m4f and 2m5½f, ***Mister Whitaker*** had won five, been placed twice, and had never finished outside the first five positions. In his two runs at three miles plus, he had been pulled up on both occasions. With an impressive record in middle distance chases, 22/1 was an attractive starting price as he lined up alongside 22 rivals, and he didn't disappoint those who had done their homework, finishing in 3rd place and less than a couple of lengths off winner, *Simply The Betts*.

The other two festival returnees by **Court Cave** that were ***Champagne Court*** and ***City Island*** didn't fare that well at the 2020 Cheltenham Festival. In the *Northern Trust Company Novices' Handicap Chase*, the race that was won by ***Mister Whitaker*** in 2018, ***Champagne Court*** finished in 8th place some 21 lengths behind the winner, *Imperial Aura*. As for ***City Island***, he was pulled up in the *Paddy Power Stayers' Hurdle* in what was his first run over three miles. In the lead up to the race, he had wind surgery following two rather disappointing outings in a couple of novice chases.

The one horse by **Court Cave** that was making his debut at the 2020 Cheltenham Festival was ***Plan Of Attack***, who was entered in the *Fulke Walwyn Kim Muir Challenge Cup Amateur Riders' Handicap Chase*. He had prepared for this race by finishing in 3rd place in the Grade B *Paddy Power Handicap Chase* at *Leopardstown*. This race has been an excellent guide for finding Irish winners of the *Kim Muir* and his solid performance in that race sparked my enthusiasm to place an ante-post each-way wager on him at a price of 33/1. I was rather chuffed that not only had his trainer *Henry De Bromhead* decided to enter ***Plan Of Attack*** in this event rather than any other festival race, but also the gelding's starting price of 10/1. All of which would be irrelevant if he didn't finish in the first four home, which fortunately, he did. In brief, ***Plan Of Attack*** ran well, making headway towards the business end of the race and staying on well but having no extra to give after the last. He finished in 4th place around half a dozen lengths off the winner, *Milan Native*.

In last year's Guide, I advised readers that **Court Cave**'s progeny had failed to finish a 3m festival race over fences, so some readers may have questioned why I had decided to back ***Plan Of Attack*** in the 3m2f *Kim Muir*. In short, I didn't give too much weight to the statistic. Preceding ***Plan Of Attack***'s placing at last year's meeting, two of the previous four runners by **Court Cave** were big priced outsiders in the *St. James's Place Foxhunter Chase Challenge Cup*. ***Cave Hunter*** (66/1) was struggling and well-beaten in 2016 when unseating his rider two out and in 2019, the 100/1 outsider ***Just Cause*** was pulled up. The 2019 Cheltenham Festival also hosted two more of **Court Cave**'s chasers, although these two runners were supported to do well. ***Speaker Connolly*** (14/1) unseated his jockey in the *Kim Muir* and ***Mister Whitaker*** was pulled up in the *Ultima Handicap Chase* as already highlighted earlier in this chapter.

With **Court Cave**'s progeny having made just 24 festival appearances, the data is rather limited to make bold judgements on where to place bets on this stallion's festival entries, and it is too simple to discount a particular race category on just a handful of runs, and the 3m chase category is such an example. It would, perhaps, be rather different if data showed four horses, all at single digit odds, being pulled up in 3m chases. That could be the beginning of a trend developing. If we look at **Court Cave**'s festival statistics table, there are only three race categories where the offspring have made four or more festival appearances, these being 2m hurdles and chases at 2½ miles and 3 miles. I have already highlighted that I'm not reading too much into the figures related to 3m chases, and I'm pretty much ignoring what the table is saying as regards 2m hurdles too. The four outings are made up of two runs in the *County Hurdle* and two runs in the *Mares' Novices' Hurdle*, where none of the four horses were able to record a finishing position in the first nine finishing positions. That could be the beginning of a trend, until one takes into account the starting prices of 33/1, 66/1 and 100/1 twice. Hence, how **Court Cave**'s offspring perform in the festival's two-mile hurdle events is very much a blank sheet of paper. Indeed, at this time, and based on the limited data of 24 festival outings, I am completely open-minded about how horses by **Court Cave** will perform at Cheltenham in March, with one very notable exception – and that is when the offspring line up in a festival contest and are tasked with racing over a distance of 2½ miles. When I spot this scenario, I sit up and take notice, as the evidence suggests that **Court Cave**'s festival contenders in this category perform well.

Turning to the eight chase outings over 2½ miles, the first point to note is that horses by **Court Cave** have never finished outside of the first eight places, although it should be acknowledged that 4 of these 8 appearances are courtesy of ***Champion Court*** whose finishing positions were 2nd, 5th, 7th and 7th. Three of the other four outings have taken place in Tuesday's *Novices' Handicap Chase* which is to be replaced at the 2021 Festival with the *Mrs Paddy Power Mares' Chase*. ***Shady Operator*** finished 7th in 2018, ***Mister Whitaker*** won the race in 2019 and ***Champagne Court*** finished 8th in the last running of the race last season. The 8th appearance by the progeny in 2½m also took place last year and has already been highlighted – ***Mister Whitaker***'s 3rd place in the *Stable Plate*.

The excellent results achieved by **Court Cave**'s runners in the festival's 2½m hurdles category, provide additional weight to the evidence that **Court Cave**'s stock performs best in festival races at around 2½ miles. In three hurdle outings at this distance, horses by **Court Cave** have won twice and recorded a 4th place dividend from the third run. **Court Cave**'s offspring have a 100% strike-rate, 2 from 2, in the *Ballymore Novices' Hurdle*. In 2019, the *Martin Brassil* trained ***City Island*** (8/1), stayed on well to beat *Champ*, winner of last year's *RSA Insurance Novices' Chase* and in 2017, ***Willoughby Court*** (14/1) was victorious, beating favourite *Neon wolf* by a head. The 4th place dividend was achieved by ***Champagne Court*** (14/1) in the 2019 *Martin Pipe Conditional Jockeys' Handicap Hurdle*. Combining the results of the eight chases with the three hurdle runs at this race distance, produces a very impressive set of statistics; 3 wins, 3 places and 5 other runners that were placed from 5th to 8th. Backing all **Court Cave**'s 2½m festival runners blind to level stakes delivers a profit of £321.25 to a £10.00 each-way stake.

The festival results from **Court Cave**'s progeny really started to take off from the 2017 Cheltenham Festival onwards. Up until that point, out of a total of nine festival outings, this stallion had just one placing on the scoreboard, courtesy of ***Champion Court***'s second place in the 2012 *Jewson Novices' Chase*. But in the fifteen appearances by **Court Cave**'s stock that have taken place at the past four festivals, there has been a big improvement in results, where the offspring have recorded three festival victories and three placings. From a financial perspective, if one had started backing **Court Cave**'s progeny from 2017 onwards, the outcome would be a satisfying profit of £250.25 to a £10.00 each-way stake. Incidentally, if one had supported all 24 festival outings by **Court Cave**'s representatives going back to 2011 with the same stake, a profit of £96.25 would be the result.

In conclusion, albeit there is rather little data to make such rash judgements, I am increasingly becoming quite a fan of **Court Cave**'s festival contenders. Punters should take a serious interest in horses by **Court Cave** that are entered into festival races that cover a distance of around 2½ miles, as the historical evidence based on eleven appearances suggests that the progeny will perform well. All eleven outings have resulted in a top 8 finishing position. As for festival contenders by **Court Cave** that are entered in races at other distances, I wouldn't necessarily discount these runners either, so if a horse by **Court Cave** takes your fancy, I suggest you place your bet. I did exactly that last year when backing ***Plan Of Attack*** in a 3m chase.

Court Cave (IRE) – Progeny with Official Rating of 135+

Horses by this sire with an Official Rating of 135 or greater on 9th February 2021. Horses registered with the Irish Horseracing Regulatory Board (I.H.R.B) are shown in *italics*.

				Official Ratings as of 9th February 2021		
Sire	***Horse***	***Age***	***Sex***	***Hurdles***	***Chase***	***Trainer***
Court Cave	Champagne Court	8	g		135	Jeremy Scott
Court Cave	*City Island*	*8*	*g*	*145*		*Martin Brassil*
Court Cave	Clondaw Caitlin	6	f	135	135	Ruth Jefferson
Court Cave	*Court Maid*	*8*	*f*		*152*	*Thomas Mullins*
Court Cave	Courtandbould	7	g	141		Fergal O'Brien
Court Cave	Hill Sixteen	8	g	130	137	Nigel Twiston-Davies
Court Cave	Jersey Bean	8	g		135	Oliver Sherwood
Court Cave	Mister Whitaker	9	g		152	Mick Channon
Court Cave	*Plan Of Attack*	*8*	*g*		*137*	*Henry de Bromhead*
Court Cave	*The Big Lense*	*8*	*g*		*135*	*Gordon Elliott*

Commentary on selected potential entries for 2021 Festival

Mister Whitaker – Paddy Power Plate 2m5f (4:10 Thursday 18th March)

In the commentary on **Court Cave**, I have advised that in the eight festival chase outings over 2½ miles, horses by **Court Cave** have never finished outside of the first eight places. I also commented that ***Mister Whitaker***, who finished in 3rd place in last year's *Stable Plate*, possesses a pretty good record in chases at around 2½ miles, having never finished outside of the first five places. In three races at three miles, ***Mister Whitaker*** has never finished inside the first five places! So, if ***Mister Whitaker*** does turn up at Cheltenham for a 4th consecutive year this March, what are his chances in the newly named *Paddy Power Plate*? Not good, I'm afraid. I'm hoping that trainer, *Mick Channon*, can get a race into him at *Warwick* after this Guide has gone to print. Even then, I don't think that will alter events too much at the Festival. I believe that the best ***Mister Whitaker*** can achieve in the *Plate* on March 18th is to maintain **Court Cave**'s record of all of his festival representatives in 2½m chases finishing in the top eight finishing positions. Here is a list of reasons as to why ***Mister Whitaker*** is likely to find it a struggle in this year's *Paddy Power Plate*:

1) 7 of the past 10 winners of the Stable Plate have won this on the back of 9 or less chase starts. In the past decade, only Carrickboy (2013 winner) had registered more than 12 chase starts ***(Mister Whitaker has had 14 chase starts)***
2) The past ten winners all carried 8lb or more less than the top weight. In the past 8 years, the OR of the top weight has been between 155 and 158. ***(Mister Whitaker is currently rated at 152 and too close to the likely top weight)***
3) Only two of the past 17 winners had not raced in the current year. ***(At the time of writing, Mister Whitaker's last outing was in October 2020. He may manage to race at Warwick after this Guide has gone to print).***
4) 4 of the past 5 winners finished 1st or 2nd last time out. ***(Mister Whitaker finished in 6th place and if he does manage a late run at Warwick and finishes 1st or 2nd, it could result in his handicap mark being raised)***
5) In the past 11 years, 39 entries for this race had won a Point-to-Point at the start of their careers. Four of them won the Stable Plate. ***(Mister Whitaker did not compete in Point-to-Points)***
6) All seven British trained winners in the past decade had raced at least once at Prestbury Park previously. ***(Good news for Mister Whitaker! He has been to the course eight times)***

Several trends for ***Mister Whitaker*** to overcome. Too many in my view, despite the excellent record of his sire's offspring in festival chases at this distance.

Court Maid – Mrs Paddy Power Mares' Chase 2m4½f (4:50 Friday 19th March)

Court Maid, trained by *Thomas Mullins*, has been performing well over fences and is showing in the betting for both the 3m½f *Brown Advisory Novices' Chase* and the *Mrs Paddy Power Mares' Chase* which is ½ mile shorter. On the basis that **Court Cave**'s progeny has shown a liking for 2½m chases, I hope that connections choose the latter, for which at the time of writing, the 8yo mare can be backed at 25/1. ***Court Maid*** has won three of her five chases to date where the shortest and longest distance wins have both come at *Fairyhouse*, winning a novice chase over 2m5f in mid-October and a 3m5f Handicap Chase on 29th November. The question, therefore, will be whether the 2m4½f of the *Mares' Chase* will be too fast for her.

I'm pleased that connections decided to send her over to Cheltenham so that she could experience the course before the festival. Her last run was at Prestbury Park on 11th December where she was one of seven runners in the *Unibet Handicap Chase* (3m2f). ***Court Maid*** ran a strange race at Cheltenham, going well and in contention off the home turn before appearing to struggle and then suddenly rallying again. At least the experience will help her when she returns next month. I like the fact that she has had two wins at *Fairyhouse* and now has experience of the Cheltenham Course as both tracks take a bit of jumping.

An interesting contender for the *Mares' Chase* and *Thomas Mullins* will hope that ***Court Maid*** can provide him with his 3rd festival win, the previous two victories courtesy of *Alderwood* who won festival races in 2012 and 2013.

Doyen (IRE)

Doyen was not featured in the 2020 Cheltenham Festival Stallion Guide.

Doyen (21-y-o)							
Race Format	*Miles*	**Won**	**Placed**	**Unplaced**	**Total**	**Win %**	**Place %**
Hurdles	About 2m	0	1	2	3	0%	33%
	About 2m 4f	0	0	2	2	0%	0%
	About 3m	0	0	1	1	0%	0%
Chases	About 2m	0	3	3	6	0%	50%
	About 2m 4f	0	1	0	1	0%	100%
	About 3m	0	0	1	1	0%	0%
	About 4m	0	0	0	0	-	-
Bumper	About 2m	0	0	0	0	-	-
Total	**2011-2020**	**0**	**5**	**9**	**14**	**0%**	**36%**

Just eight horses by **Doyen** have raced on 14 occasions at Cheltenham Festivals. There has been at least one entry of **Doyen**'s stock at every festival since 2011 which is when the first of this stallion's offspring appeared at a festival meeting. When I write, *"at least one entry"*, perhaps I should have written, *"usually, just one sole lonely entry"*, because in seven of the last ten years, **Doyen** has been represented at festival meetings by just a single one of his progeny. The exceptions occurred in 2014 (2 entries); 2017 (3 entries); and 2019 (2 entries). With just 14 festival outings from 8 horses by **Doyen** over the past decade of festivals, I can quite understand readers questioning the validity of any analysis when it is based upon just 14 festival outings and secondly, therefore, why is **Doyen** included in the 2021 Cheltenham Festival Stallion Guide?

The simple answer is that I am anticipating far more than a single festival entry from **Doyen**'s stock at the 2021 Cheltenham Festival. In fact, I think there may be as many as 5-6 entries. That number of entries, in itself, wouldn't necessitate an entry in this year's Guide, unless there was some sort of trend showing up in the 14 festival outings that have occurred to date. And I do think I've spotted something.

In **Doyen**'s festival statistics table, there are a couple of key factors that strike me. Firstly, horses by **Doyen** have yet to win at the Cheltenham Festival, but they appear to have come close, having been placed on five occasions. Indeed, for every three appearances in which the offspring have lined up in a festival contest, one of those three runs has resulted in the horse by **Doyen** being placed. And it happens a lot more frequently over the bigger obstacles. Every time a punter has backed a horse by **Doyen** in a festival chase, he has historically been rewarded with a pay-out 50% of the time. And more often than not, it looks like **Doyen**'s offspring specialise in two-mile chases. This needs further investigation.

Of the eight horses by **Doyen** that have been to Cheltenham in March, the place positions recorded have come from the efforts of three of **Doyen**'s progeny, these being ***Kumbeshwar***, ***Dandridge*** and ***The Russian Doyen***. So, with such little data, it could be that the results are skewed purely due to three good horses specialising in two-mile chases, and I think there is an element of that, especially when it comes to ***Dandridge*** who was placed in the two-mile *Grand Annual* in his two outings at the Cheltenham Festival, finishing as the runner-up in 2016 and then securing a 4th place dividend twelve months later. ***Dandridge*** was trained by *Arthur Moore* at the time, and this trainer has an exceptional record with two-mile chasers at the Cheltenham Festival.

Kumbeshwar, trained by *Alan King*, was the first of **Doyen**'s progeny to race at the Cheltenham Festival and was the sole festival entry for 2011 through to 2013. ***Kumbeshwar*** was successful. He finished runner-up in the 2011 *Fred Winter Juvenile Handicap Hurdle* at 33/1, beaten by a neck, and followed up twelve months later by claiming 3rd place, at 16/1, in the 2012 *Johnny Henderson Grand Annual Chase Challenge Cup*. He was entered in the 2013 renewal of the *Grand Annual* but fell at the 4th fence. The one remaining placed effort from **Doyen**'s progeny was achieved in the 2019 *Close Brothers Novices' Handicap Chase* by the ***Russian Doyen*** who claimed a 4th place dividend at a price of 20/1. The race has been the only time in which a horse by **Doyen** has appeared in one of the festival's 2½ mile chases. Interestingly, perhaps, is the fact that horses by **Doyen** have also only ever competed on one occasion in one of the festival's chases covering a distance of three miles. The debut of **Doyen**'s offspring within this race category happened at last year's meeting when ***Battleoverdoyen*** finished 4th, but a very long way behind the front three contenders, in the *RSA Insurance Novices' Chase*.

What I find interesting about the eight outings by **Doyen**'s stock in the festival's chase events is that every time that a chaser by **Doyen** has stayed on his feet to complete the race, the horse has never finished out of the front five places. The one chaser by **Doyen** that I haven't yet mentioned is ***Valdez***, who was 6¾ lengths away from the winner when taking 5th place in the 2014 *Racing Post Arkle Challenge Trophy Chase* and then didn't return to the festival until 2018 when he unseated his rider after just three fences. The festival performances by the offspring over the fences at Cheltenham is in stark contrast to the six performances over hurdles, where other than ***Kumbeshwar***'s fine effort in the previously mentioned *Fred Winter Handicap Hurdle*, the next highest placing is 12th!

All told, it is a rather confusing picture, not helped by the limited data available, and the influence, to some extent, of ***Kumbeshwar*** and ***Dandridge***. That said, punters may consider that **Doyen**'s festival entries may be worth a punt should they be entered in a race over fences. I was thinking that this may be a good strategy too, but having carried out some further analysis, I am now a touch wary. First the good news. If one takes a peek at **Doyen**'s statistics overall, it shows that, as of early February, his stock has appeared in a total of 404 chases and won 59 of them which is a healthy win rate of 15%. This compares with win strike rate of 10% for hurdles and 11% for national hunt flat races. This information supports the results that we have witnessed in the 14 festival outings. Now the not so good news. I decided to look at how many wins had **Doyen**'s offspring enjoyed at Prestbury Park across all meetings. The answer is five. Some may say this is a low number whilst others may view five wins as reasonable. I'm in two-minds, but what does concern me more than the number of wins, is the type of race in which those victories were achieved. And the result is completely opposite as to what I would expect. In short, no horse by **Doyen** has ever won a chase at Cheltenham's racecourse. The five victories consist of ***Keys*** winning a national hunt flat race over 14 furlongs in 2011; ***Doyle Carte*** winning a novice mares hurdle over 17 furlongs in April 2013; ***Golden Doyen*** recording two victories at Cheltenham, first over 16½ furlongs in a Grade 2 hurdle in November 2014, followed by a handicap hurdle win over three miles in October 2016; and finally, ***Streets Of Doyen*** registering a novice hurdle success over three miles in October 2020.

I have often said that the Cheltenham Festival is very different from the other Cheltenham meetings, and some stallions will win at the course regularly but find it far more difficult against top opposition on spring ground, and perhaps that explains why **Doyen**'s offspring appear to be performing better in the festival's chase events than over hurdles and why the results are vice versa when looking at Cheltenham meetings all year round. Either way, the influence of a couple of better-quality horses, the limited data available, and the opposite outcome to what one may have anticipated when researching all performances by **Doyen** at Prestbury Park, all adds up to a rather bewildering picture.

Some punters may wish to back chasers by **Doyen** that are entered for the 2021 Cheltenham Festival based upon the eight festival results attained to date. Others may ignore **Doyen**'s offspring in chases as no horse by this stallion has ever won a chase racing around Prestbury Park. Some may even decide to take a chance on a hurdler, based upon ***Kumbeshwar***'s *Fred Winter* 2nd placing a decade ago combined with the knowledge that **Doyen**'s stock has registered four hurdle course wins.

Me? I'm sitting this one out. And will think again at the 2022 Cheltenham Festival.

Doyen (IRE) – Progeny with Official Rating of 135+

Horses by this sire with an Official Rating of 135 or greater on 9th February 2021. Horses registered with the Irish Horseracing Regulatory Board (I.H.R.B) are shown in *italics*.

					Official Ratings as of 9th February 2021	
Sire	***Horse***	***Age***	***Sex***	***Hurdles***	***Chase***	***Trainer***
Doyen	*Andy Dufresne*	*7*	*g*		*149*	*Gordon Elliott*
Doyen	Baddesley Knight	8	g	131	138	Chris Gordon
Doyen	*Battleoverdoyen*	*8*	*g*		*160*	*Gordon Elliott*
Doyen	*Beacon Edge*	*7*	*g*	*154*		*Noel Meade*
Doyen	Hatcher	8	g		139	Dan Skelton
Doyen	Hurricane Harvey	7	g	141	144	Fergal O'Brien
Doyen	*Pont Aven*	*8*	*g*		*137*	*W.P. Mullins*
Doyen	*Power Of Pause*	*6*	*g*	*136*		*W.P. Mullins*
Doyen	*Streets Of Doyen*	*7*	*g*	*135*		*John C. McConnell*

Dubai Destination (USA)

Quote from the 2020 Cheltenham Festival Stallion Guide - "I would imagine there will be somewhere in the region of 4-6 horses by **Dubai Destination** that will be entered in races at the 2020 Cheltenham Festival, and I think the best that supporters of this stallion can wish for is that two of the progeny perform to their best to register top three places. In my view, the two horses that are best positioned to deliver that goal are ***Kildisart*** and ***Roksana***."

Dubai Destination (22-y-o)							
Race Format	*Miles*	*Won*	*Placed*	*Unplaced*	*Total*	*Win %*	*Place %*
Hurdles	About 2m	0	0	2	2	0%	0%
	About 2m 4f	1	1	6	8	13%	25%
	About 3m	0	0	2	2	0%	0%
Chases	About 2m	0	0	1	1	0%	0%
	About 2m 4f	0	0	2	2	-	-
	About 3m	0	2	2	4	0%	50%
	About 4m	0	0	0	0	-	-
Bumper	About 2m	0	0	1	1	0%	0%
Total	2011-2020	**1**	**3**	**16**	**20**	**5%**	**20%**

Four horses by **Dubai Destination** made it to the 2020 Cheltenham Festival, including ***Kildisart*** and ***Roksana*** as mentioned in the quote at the top of the page. I thought that trainer *Ben Pauling* had prepared ***Kildisart*** really well for his attempt to win the *Ultima Handicap Chase*. He had run ***Kildisart*** in December and January in two races where the ground was heavy which would not have been to ***Kildisart***'s liking who finished 6th in both of them. This was followed by a pleasing 5th place finish in a race at *Kempton* three weeks before the festival on good to soft ground with ***Kildisart*** staying on well towards the end of the race. The three outings had put ***Kildisart*** on an Official Rating mark of 150, only two pounds higher than the mark off which he had won the Grade 3 *Betway Handicap Chase* at *Aintree* in April 2019. In last year's Cheltenham Festival Stallion Guide, when referencing ***Kildisart***'s chances at the 2020 meeting, I had written, *"If the word 'good' is mentioned in the official going at Cheltenham for racing on 10th March, then an each-way bet on **Kildisart** may turn out to be a winning one."* Unfortunately for ***Kildisart***'s connections, the going was 'soft' on 10th March 2020 and in my view, soft ground conditions cost ***Kildisart*** the race. Despite the going, I had backed ***Kildisart*** each-way, so I had my beady eye on him for the whole three miles and one furlong of the *Ultima* and I thought he put in a fantastic performance. All the same, it wasn't quite enough, and the 10/1 chance was just held near the line to lose out to *The Conditional* (15/2) by a neck. A super run all the same.

Two races later, following the *Champion Hurdle*, it was ***Roksana***'s turn in the *Close Brothers Mares' Hurdle*. Twelve months earlier, when the race was named the *OLBG Mares' Hurdle*, ***Roksana*** had been triumphant winning the Grade 1 event at a price of 10/1. In that race, she got lucky as the favourite for the race, *Benie Des Dieux* fell at the last hurdle when three lengths to the good. In ***Roksana***'s bid to retain her crown, I was not surprised to see the **Dubai Destination** bred mare was priced at 12/1. She had not just *Benie Des Dieux* to deal with who was the 4/6 favourite but also the new star mare to appear on the scene, *Honeysuckle* (9/4). No fallers this time as the two at the front of the market fought out the finish with *Honeysuckle* coming out on top. ***Roksana*** finished in 4th place a little too far back to get on terms with the two leaders and 3rd place, *Elfile*.

In last year's Guide, I had suggested that the festival entries by **Dubai Destination** fall into two groups, those who effectively aren't good enough to succeed at what is the number one national hunt meeting of the year, and then a handful, such as ***Kildisart***, ***Roksana*** and ***Next Destination***, who can make their presence felt at the Cheltenham Festival if conditions are in their favour, such as the right race, class, distance, ground, and so on. The latter group, having achieved some success, will keep returning to the festival year after year, whereas the former group come to the realisation that they aren't quite good enough and so generally don't return. The one exception to this rule appears to be ***Knight in Dubai***, whose connections have the mistaken belief that one day, just one day, their horse should or could achieve something at a Cheltenham Festival, so the horse keeps coming back. In last year's Guide, I advised, *"**Knight In Dubai** holds an entry in the Grade 1 **Marsh Novices' Chase**, for which he can be backed at 50/1. Don't waste your money. This Dan Skelton trained 7-year-old is out of his depth at Cheltenham."* ***Knight In Dubai*** duly made the trip to Prestbury Park once again, but was entered in a race where connections thought he may have more of a chance, the 6th race on day one of the Cheltenham Festival, the *Northern Trust Company Novices' Handicap Chase*. Lining up at 20/1, ***Knight In Dubai*** was held up, hampered and then unseated his rider at the 3rd fence. Unlucky? Well in his previous two visits to the festival, he had finished 13th on both occasions.

There is one other horse that keeps returning to Cheltenham year after year who I have a great deal of respect for, the *Colin Tizzard* trained, ***Elegant Escape***. The horse appears to have been around for ages and yet is still only nine years old. Last year, he made his 4th visit to the Cheltenham Festival, to take on the very best 3m chasers in the 2020 *Magners Cheltenham Gold Cup Chase*. He was last of those to finish at a price of 66/1 which wasn't a surprise. Having won the *Welsh Grand National* over 3m5½f in 2018, ***Elegant Escape*** has bags of stamina and likes the ground to be soft or heavy. His biggest success at a Cheltenham Festival was when he finished in 3rd place in the 2018 *RSA Insurance Novices' Chase* where he lacked the pace of the front two of *Presenting Percy* and *Monalee* but stayed on well to claim a place dividend at a price of 9/1. ***Elegant Escape*** is likely to miss the 2021 Cheltenham Festival and go straight to *Aintree* and the *Grand National*. I would agree with that.

Twelve horses by **Dubai Destination** have raced at the Cheltenham Festival on 20 occasions and seven of the progeny visited the festival just once, registering, from best to worst, finishing positions of 9th, 10th, 14th, 15th, 17th, BD and Fell. I have already mentioned ***Knight In Dubai*** as having ideas above his station, and I would class him as being in the same class/category, as the seven of **Dubai Destination**'s offspring who just made the single visit. ***Knight In Dubai***'s finishing positions are 13th (twice) and Unseated Rider (UR). That leaves 10 festival outings by four horses by **Dubai Destination** that have the necessary quality to make some sort of impact at Cheltenham Festivals. The gang of four, unsurprisingly, are in the top 4 positions according to their best Official Rating (OR) of **Dubai Destination**'s stock, these being ***Elegant Escape*** (OR of 162), ***Kildisart*** (156), ***Next Destination*** (153) and ***Roksana*** (153). The ten festival outings by the above quartet have produced the following results, again presented from best to worst: 1st, 2nd, 3rd, 3rd, 4th, 4th, 4th, 6th, 7th and 11th. The last three of these results reflect ***Elegant Escape***'s two *Gold Cup* outings and his 100/1 debut in the 2017 *Albert Bartlett Novices' Hurdle*. With ***Elegant Escape*** likely to go straight to *Aintree*, I believe there to be a strong chance of just three horses by **Dubai Destination** making the trip to Cheltenham this March, and it will be the usual suspects of ***Kildisart***, ***Roksana*** and ***Next Destination***. At previous festivals, none of the trio have finished worse than 4th.

From a financial perspective, had one placed a £10.00 each-way wager on all 20 festival outings made by the offspring of **Dubai Destination**, the outcome would be a loss of £179.00, so the 1-4 placings secured by the higher-rated of the offspring have not been enough to offset the losses from those holding lower ratings. When it comes to this stallion's festival entries, my advice to punters is to look no further than ***Kildisart***, ***Roksana*** and ***Next Destination***, and I am looking forward to seeing the last named should he make it to Prestbury Park this March. His last appearance at a Cheltenham Festival was in 2018 when he finished 3rd to *Samcro* in the *Ballymore Novices' Hurdle*, following a 4th place finish in the *Weatherbys Champion Bumper* twelve months earlier. ***Next Destination*** has had a frustrating series of injury setbacks over the past 2½ years but saw a racecourse for the first time in over 900 days when finishing in 2nd place in a Grade 2 hurdle race at *Wetherby* in October 2020. Owner *Malcolm Denmark* has switched trainers for ***Next Destination*** and his horse is now housed at *Paul Nicholls*' yard in Somerset having left *Closutton* and *Willie Mullins* on 10th October last year, three weeks before that *Wetherby* race. Fingers crossed that *Paul Nicholls* can not only get him back to Cheltenham but also close to the form that he was in before those troublesome injuries took hold.

As we approach the 2021 Cheltenham Festival, I would suggest that we should ignore any entries by **Dubai Destination** other than ***Roksana***, ***Kildisart*** and ***Next Destination***. And for these three horses, if it is one, two or all three of them, I strongly recommend that punters think deeply and act smart on whether or not to place a wager. All three have the potential to win – when the race conditions are in their favour, but all three could easily just miss out on a win or placing when circumstances are against them. By way of example, I had backed ***Roksana*** each-way in the 2019 *OLBG Mares' Hurdle*, as she was amongst a group of four horses priced between 7/1 and 12/1 who I believed would be fighting it out for 2nd and 3rd place, plus there was the bonus perhaps of *Benie Des Dieux* having an off-day, a thought aided by my slight concern that the favourite hadn't run for 318 days. I was confident ***Roksana*** would get placed but obviously got lucky in that *Benie Des Dieux* fell at the last. In the 2020 *Mares' Hurdle*, I didn't support ***Roksana***, as she had two very good horses to beat in not only *Benie Des Dieux* but also *Honeysuckle*, and so what were the chances of the mare grabbing a 3rd place? Not much I thought and I quite fancied *Elfile* to run well, which she did, claiming the 3rd place. My write-up on ***Kildisart*** in the very first paragraph of this chapter also provides an example of thinking through the rationale and reasons why a horse is worth a bet or not. My advice is to take your time looking at the race conditions, ground, distance, your selection's rivals, and so on.

Specifically thinking about the offspring of **Dubai Destination**, there is one further potential betting opportunity in my view, which is to consider the markets for betting in-running. Horses by **Dubai Destination**, more often than not, do appear to be staying on at the end of races – the better horses anyway. So, you may want to think about placing an each-way bet in-running. I can easily see any one of ***Roksana***, ***Kildisart*** and ***Next Destination*** staying on up the Cheltenham Hill, either to win or claim a place. Providing conditions are right of course!

Dubai Destination (USA) – Progeny with Official Rating of 135+

Horses by this sire with an Official Rating of 135 or greater on 9th February 2021. Horses registered with the Irish Horseracing Regulatory Board (I.H.R.B) are shown in *italics*.

				Official Ratings as of 9th February 2021		
Sire	***Horse***	***Age***	***Sex***	***Hurdles***	***Chase***	***Trainer***
Dubai Destination	Coole Cody	10	g		143	Evan Williams
Dubai Destination	Cracking Destiny	8	g		135	Alistair Whillans
Dubai Destination	Kildisart	9	g	148	153	Ben Pauling
Dubai Destination	Next Destination	9	g	153	153	Paul Nicholls
Dubai Destination	Roksana	9	f	153		Dan Skelton
Dubai Destination	Young Bull	7	g		136	Harry Whittington

Commentary on selected potential entries for 2021 Festival

Roksana – Close Brothers Mares' Hurdle 2m4f (4:10 Tuesday 16th March)

I'm a fan of ***Roksana***, having backed her to win this event in 2019. You may remember that she was rather fortunate as *Benie Des Dieux* fell at the last hurdle. I believe ***Roksana*** has improved since then and perhaps with some sentimentality, I can see her running on up the Cheltenham Hill to claim victory for a second time in this year's race. The offspring of **Dubai Destination** do seem to have a tendency to stay on really well at the end of their races. With a certain amount of caution, I am backing ***Roksana*** to win this year's *Close Brothers Mares' Hurdle*.

Footnote:

For further insight to the *Close Brothers Mares' Hurdle*, read the commentary on ***Benie Des Dieux*** by **Great Pretender**.

Flemensfirth (USA)

Quote from the 2020 Cheltenham Festival Stallion Guide - "Will **Flemensfirth**'s progeny achieve a 9th festival winner at the 2020 Cheltenham Festival? I think the answer depends on how many of this stallion's offspring, in total, will line up in the *Albert Bartlett Novices' Hurdle*; the *Coral Cup*; and the four non-amateur novice chases? And will a mare by **Flemensfirth** be entered in the *Weatherbys Champion Bumper?"*

Flemensfirth (29-y-o)							
Race Format	*Miles*	*Won*	*Placed*	*Unplaced*	*Total*	*Win %*	*Place %*
Hurdles	About 2m	0	0	7	7	0%	0%
	About 2m 4f	0	4	21	25	0%	16%
	About 3m	0	0	12	12	0%	0%
Chases	About 2m	0	0	4	4	0%	0%
	About 2m 4f	0	3	12	15	0%	20%
	About 3m	1	3	28	32	3%	13%
	About 4m	0	2	13	15	0%	13%
Bumper	About 2m	1	1	7	9	11%	22%
Total	2011-2020	**2**	**13**	**104**	**119**	**2%**	**13%**

In order to avoid any misunderstanding, I should put into context last year's quote shown at the top of the page. Over the past decade, horses by **Flemensfirth** have found it very difficult to win at the Cheltenham Festival, so having broken down results into various race categories and specific races, I concluded that if one of this stallion's offspring were to register a 2020 festival victory, it was most likely to occur in the races listed. With that in mind, fourteen horses by **Flemensfirth** were entered for the 2020 Cheltenham Festival, of which one held an entry in the *Marsh Novices' Chase*, and one made an appearance in the *Coral Cup*.

The **Flemensfirth** sired ***Tornado Flyer*** lined up at a price of 10/1 in the Grade 1 *Marsh Novices' Chase* and although he was never involved with the leaders, he ran a reasonable race to finish in 5th place. Although trained by *Willie Mullins*, who has saddled 4 of the 10 winners of this race, I advised readers last year that if ***Tornado Flyer*** was to take part, to leave well alone. He was up against it having not run in the previous year's festival (like 8 of the 9 previous winners) and neither had he won a graded novice chase last time out, as had 7 of the previous 9 winners. The winner incidentally didn't meet these criteria either! *Samcro* (4/1), trained by *Gordon Elliott*, won the 10th running of this race, beating *Melon* by a nose. *Samcro* did have a big advantage however, in that his sire is *Germany*, who was also represented by the 3rd home in this race, *Faugheen*. *Germany*'s festival win rate stands at 32% and win and place strike rate at over 50%. *Germany* was a routine entry in my previous Cheltenham Festival Stallion Guides, but I didn't cover him in last year's Guide as his stock is petering out due to his death in 2013 and he has so few festival runners anyway. His progeny, that has been represented just 19 times at Cheltenham Festivals, has been hugely successful, recording six wins and four places. I digress. Going back to **Flemensfirth** and the one entry from the sire that took part in the *Coral Cup*. It would have been a major shock if the 50/1 outsider, ***Ballymoy***, was to provide this stallion with a 9th Cheltenham Festival success in Wednesday's *Coral Cup Handicap Hurdle*. There was to be no surprise as the 7-year-old came home in 17th place.

Of the 14 horses by **Flemensfirth** that made the journey to Cheltenham last year, there was only one that I seriously considered did have some sort of chance of victory, and that was ***Lostintranslation*** who lined up in what was, in my view, a very open *Magners Cheltenham Gold Cup*. I thought any of five could claim victory, my shortlist being *Al Boum Photo, Santini, Kemboy, Delta Work* and the *Colin Tizzard* trained, ***Lostintranslation***. Ten years earlier, in 2010, a **Flemensfirth** bred chaser, hailing from the stable of *Nigel Twiston-Davies*, took the blue riband prize, in the shape of ***Imperial Commander*** (7/1) who spoilt the party for the *Paul Nicholls* trained duo of *Kauto Star* and *Denman*. There were some uncanny similarities between ***Lostintranslation*** and ***Imperial Star*** in their results and preparations before their respective *Gold Cup* appearances, and one wondered whether history would repeat itself. When it came to the big day of last year's *Magners Cheltenham Gold Cup Chase*, although ***Lostintranslation*** travelled well throughout the race, when he needed to pull out that critical little bit extra after the last, it wasn't there and perhaps he didn't quite have the stamina reserves of winner, *Al Boum Photo* and runner-up, *Santini*. It was a thrilling *Gold Cup*. The 3rd place achieved by ***Lostintranslation*** was as good as it got for **Flemensfirth** supporters at last year's meeting, the 10/1 chance being the only one of the 14 **Flemensfirth** bred representatives to provide a reward on each way bets.

Six of **Flemensfirth**'s offspring managed to register finishing places between 4th and 6th last year, so weren't too far from sneaking into a place position. In the festival's newest event, the *Daylesford Mares' Novices' Hurdle (registered as the Dawn Run)*, four **Flemensfirth** sired half-sisters lined up at the start, including ***Minella Melody***, the *Henry De Bromhead* trained 11/4 favourite. Unbeaten in her three hurdle starts, and with the excellent *Rachael Blackmore* in the saddle, punters were hopeful on ***Minella Melody*** making it 4 from 4 over hurdles, despite the burden of a 5lb penalty. But the mare was a huge disappointment, taking a strong hold in the early stages before weakening rapidly towards the end of the race to finish towards the rear of the field in 18th. The other three **Flemensfirth** bred mares all finished in front of the favourite, with the *Willie Mullins* trained duo of ***Yukon Lil*** (20/1) and ***Colreevy*** (4/1) finishing just outside of the place positions, filling 4th and 5th places respectively. It was a good race for *Willie Mullins* as his other pair of runners in the race finished 1st and 2nd, *Concertista* (9/2) taking the prize by 12 lengths from runner-up *Dolcita* (9/1). Last year was the 4th renewal of this event, a contest in which *Willie Mullins* has saddled all four winners.

Almost three hours before ***Minella Melody***'s disappointing run on the Thursday at last year's meeting, another mare by **Flemensfirth**, ***Relegate***, was fancied to win the *Pertemps Network Final Handicap Hurdle*, sent off as one of the 11/2 joint favourites. Two years earlier, in 2018, ***Relegate*** had won the *Weatherbys Champion Bumper* at a price of 25/1. Since then, the mare had moved stables from *Willie Mullins*' yard to *Colm Murphy*'s stables in *County Wexford*. In the *Pertemps Final*, the mare just missed out on a 4th place dividend when filling 5th place and just a short head behind the 4th placed horse, *Third Wind*.

The other three horses by **Flemensfirth** that recorded top 6 finishes at last year's Cheltenham Festival were ***Eskylane*** (5th @ 16/1) in the *Weatherbys Champion Bumper*; ***Fitzhenry*** (6th @ 7/1) in the *Fulke Walwyn Kim Muir Challenge Cup Amateur Riders' Handicap Chase*; and as mentioned earlier, ***Tornado Flyer*** (5th @ 10/1) in the *Marsh Novices' Chase*.

Over the past ten Cheltenham festivals, there has been little to cheer for supporters of **Flemensfirth**'s stock. In the last 119 appearances by the progeny, only two horses have registered a festival win since ***Imperial Commander*** won the 2010 *Cheltenham Gold Cup*, the victories coming from the previously mentioned ***Relegate*** in the 2018 *Weatherbys Champion Bumper* and ***Topofthegame***, who won an exciting renewal of the *RSA Insurance Novices' Chase* in 2019. ***Topofthegame*** was one of the first three in the betting for that race and he came out on top of his two main rivals, *Santini* and *Delta Work*, to prevail by ½ length in a thrilling finish. Trained by *Paul Nicholls*, ***Topofthegame*** was a leading ante-post contender for the 2020 *Cheltenham Gold Cup*, but sadly, the horse suffered a leg injury in late September 2019 that ruled him out for the season. Like many others, I was very much looking forward to seeing this excellent chaser for the 2020-21 National Hunt season, but regrettably, more bad luck for the connections of this nine-year-old, as trainer *Paul Nicholls* announced in November that ***Topofthegame*** would be out for another season. The trainer advised, "The warning lights have been flashing for the last couple of weeks. I was not happy with him last week and we had the vet scan him today and although there is no tear, he just needs more time to recover, so we will leave him for the rest of the season and get him back for next season." I wish horse, trainer and connections the very best of luck.

Festival performances from **Flemensfirth**'s crop in the middle of the past decade were dire. Between 2014 and 2016, only five of **Flemensfirth**'s 35 festival representatives were able to record a finishing position higher than 8th. More recently, there has been a notable improvement. In the past four years, there have been 58 festival appearances from **Flemensfirth**'s offspring, within which 21 have registered a top six placing which equates to slightly better than a top 6 finish for 1 in every 3 runs. With two victories and seven place dividends, the win & place strike rate stands at 15.5%. Not that these statistics are any good for making profits. A £10.00 each way bet on all of the **Flemensfirth** sired competitors over the past four years would have resulted in a loss of £581.75. In the previous three years between 2014 and 2016, where horses by **Flemensfirth** raced on 35 occasions, to the same staking plan, the losses would have amounted to £513.00.

These losses of well over £1,000, if betting £10.00 each-way blind on all 93 of this stallion's offspring over the past 7 years, is in stark contrast to when **Flemensfirth**'s stock first started competing at the festival. In the first seven years in which **Flemensfirth** was represented at the festival, the progeny registered 6 winners and 8 places from just 38 festival appearances, which would have yielded a profit of £712.00 to a £10.00 each-way stake wagered on all 38 runs. These were the glory years for **Flemensfirth** supporters; imagine it – for every bet placed on a **Flemensfirth** runner, there was a 1 in 3 chance of picking up a return. Although there has been an improvement in results over the past few years, I think it is unlikely that festival results for this sire will revert back to the pre-2010 years.

If one is to make money on **Flemensfirth**'s festival entries, the strong recommendation is to be selective and focus on specific races and race categories where historically the offspring have demonstrated stronger performances. And perhaps the starting point is the *Weatherbys Champion Bumper*, a race that has produced 25%, or two of **Flemensfirth**'s eight festival victories. The first two horses by **Flemensfirth** to take their chance at a Cheltenham Festival both competed in the 2004 *Champion Bumper*. The *Jamie Codd* ridden, and *Willie Mullins* trained bay gelding, ***Major Vernon*** (20/1) finished down the field but his half-sister, ***Total Enjoyment*** (7/1) ridden by *Jim Culloty*, travelled smoothly and won readily for trainer *Thomas Cooper*. She was the second mare to win the bumper following *Mucklemeg*'s success a decade earlier in the 1994 running. Thirteen years would pass before a third mare would win the *Bumper*, *Fayonagh* coming from the clouds to sprint past a dozen of her rivals to win in 2017. And a **Flemensfirth** bred mare would provide the 4th victory for the female sex in this event at the 2018 Cheltenham Festival, when *Katie Walsh* rode the 25/1 outsider ***Relegate*** to beat stablemate *Carefully Selected* by a neck. Since the *Champion Bumper* was introduced at the Cheltenham Festival in 1992, 4 of 26 renewals have been won by mares and on the basis that **Flemensfirth** has been responsible for producing two of those victories for the girls, we should be very interested should another **Flemensfirth** bred mare be entered for the 2021 renewal.

Having recorded a victory from the first two of his offspring to appear at the festival, the stallion provided another winner from his only representative to compete at the 2005 meeting, courtesy of the *Venetia Williams* trained, ***Idole First***, who romped home by five lengths to win the *Coral Cup* at a price of 33/1. Having been the very first of the progeny to jump a hurdle at a Cheltenham Festival, ***Idole First*** has been followed by 47 horses who have appeared on 58 occasions, in an attempt to record a second hurdles victory for **Flemensfirth**'s stock at a Cheltenham Festival. All have failed. Against this backdrop, the simple strategy at this year's meeting is to strike a line through the stallion's hurdle entries, but if one really wants to persevere, I suggest that the most likely races in which a second hurdle success may be achieved by the progeny is in the *Albert Bartlett Novices' Hurdle*, the *Stayers' Hurdle*, the *Coral Cup* and the *Martin Pipe Conditional Jockeys' Handicap Hurdle.* My rationale, admittedly based on a rather small sample of data, is that in 59 hurdle outings by **Flemensfirth**'s offspring, the sole victory and 6 of the 8 place positions have occurred in these four races.

Top of the list is the Coral Cup. ***Idole First***'s big priced 33/1 victory has ensured that a sizable profit of £327.50 would have ensued for anyone who had staked £10.00 each-way blind on all eleven of **Flemensfirth**'s *Coral Cup* representatives. Of the other ten of the offspring to have lined up in the *Coral*, three of them have finished runner-up; ***Kicks for Free*** at 11/1 in 2008; ***Meister Eckhart*** at 14/1 in 2013; and ***Topofthegame*** at 9/1 in 2018. A 36% strike rate of finishing in the first two positions in this highly competitive contest is impressive. Other than the *Coral Cup*, the only other handicap hurdle that is run within the 2½m race distance category at the Cheltenham Festival is the *Martin Pipe Conditional Jockeys' Handicap Hurdle*. **Flemensfirth**'s offspring have only appeared on four occasions in this event, so it is with caution that I have suggested that it may be an event where a horse by **Flemensfirth** may be successful. The four races so far provide some green shoots of hope. ***Noble Endeavor*** (14/1) was beaten by a head when he finished runner-up in the 2015 renewal and four years later, in 2019, finishing just outside the places in 5th position was ***Coolanly***, trained by *Fergal O'Brien*.

Going up in distance, within the 3m category, with the exception of ***Relegate*** who finished 5th in last year's renewal, the other eight runs in the *Pertemps Network Final Handicap Hurdle* have been woeful, with all eight being unable to achieve a single digit finishing position. By contrast, in the 3m hurdle event for novices, the *Albert Bartlett Novices' Hurdle*, performances have been much more encouraging. Albeit that horses by **Flemensfirth** are yet to record a victory in the *Albert Bartlett*, they have certainly been knocking at the door. The first **Flemensfirth** bred competitor in this race was ***Black Harry*** (13/2) who fell at the last in 2007 having just been headed by eventual winner, *Wichita Lineman*, the 11/8 favourite. Had ***Black Harry*** stayed on his feet, he would have been a clear second. In the remaining six appearances by **Flemensfirth**'s offspring in this event, four of the runners finished within the first five places, although only one of them has rewarded punters with a pay-out, delivered by ***The Midnight Club*** (14/1) who secured 3rd place in 2009. The remaining five finishing positions and starting prices for **Flemensfirth** competitors in this race have been 4th @ 9/1, 5th @ 22/1, Pulled Up @ 20/1, 4th @ 20/1 and 10th @ 10/1. It is difficult to draw any conclusions on the festival's one other 3m hurdle race, the *Paddy Power Stayers' Hurdle*. The only two horses by **Flemensfirth** to take their chance in this race, lined up in the 2010 renewal which was won by *Big Buck's*, who was winning the second of his four victories in this event. Runner-up to *Big Buck's* in 2010 was the **Flemensfirth** sired and *Paul Webber* trained, ***Time For Rupert*** (16/1). Some 15 lengths behind his half-brother runner-up and crossing the line in 7th was ***Tidal Bay*** (8/1), who had won the *Irish Independent Arkle Challenge Trophy Chase* in 2008. ***Tidal Bay*** is the only horse by **Flemensfirth** to have competed in this two-mile novice chase, so as far as this sire is concerned with respect to the *Arkle*, his stock has a win strike rate of 100%!

In last year's Guide, I advised that when it comes to the bigger obstacles, with the exception of the *National Hunt Challenge Cup Amateur Riders' Novices' Chase*, **Flemensfirth**'s offspring have a far better record in novice chases than in other classifications. So, if we take the 3m6f *National Hunt Novices' Chase* out of the equation, as well as Tuesday's *Novices' Handicap Chase*, which has been replaced with the new *Mares' Chase*, we are left with three novice chase races at the 2021 Cheltenham Festival. As mentioned earlier, no conclusions can be drawn about the *Arkle Challenge Trophy Steeple Chase* (2m½f) as ***Tidal Bay*** has been the one and only **Flemensfirth** bred entry in the race. Therefore, the two novice chases upon which to focus our attention is Wednesday's *RSA Insurance Novices' Chase* (3m½f) and Thursday's *Marsh Novices' Chase* (2m4f).

Combined together, **Flemensfirth**'s offspring have competed in ten renewals of these two novice chases, five in the *RSA Insurance Novices' Chase* and five in the *Marsh Novices' Chase*. Two of the entries were pulled up in their races, both of which occurred at the 2018 Cheltenham Festival. ***Full Irish*** was not unanticipated, considering he was a 100/1 outsider in the *RSA*, but more was expected of ***Invitation Only*** in the *Marsh Novices' Chase*, but the 9/2 chance slipped badly four fences from home and his race was over. The remaining eight contestants of these novice chases all registered a top six finish, although only two horses were rewarded with a top three finish. In the *RSA Insurance Novices' Chase*, in addition to ***Topofthegame*** who won the 2019 renewal, ***Joe Lively*** (7/1) finished in 6th place in 2008; ***Time For Rupert*** (7/4 favourite) finished in 5th place in 2011, his chance of victory gone due to bursting a blood vessel mid-race; and ***O O Seven*** (2017) also registered a 5th placing, tailed off and 48 lengths behind winner, *Might Bite*. In the *Marsh Novices' Chase*, three horses by **Flemensfirth** have finished in 4th, 5th and 6th place. ***Sizing Gold*** finished in 6th place in 2014 and two years later, ***Three Musketeers*** (8/1) was thereabouts and just over five lengths from winner *Black Hercules*, when registering a 4th place finish in 2016. The 5th placing has been highlighted previously, this being the result of ***Tornado Flyer***'s efforts at the 2020 Cheltenham Festival. The best performance in this event took place in 2019, when ***Lostintranslation*** finished 2nd at a price of 4/1 to 3/1 favourite, *Defi Du Seuil*.

It has been a tough decade for **Flemensfirth**'s offspring at Cheltenham Festival meetings, but the recent wins from ***Relegate*** (2018) and ***Topofthegame*** (2019) offer renewed hope that perhaps more festival winners will be forthcoming. With that in mind, I have suggested that the chances of success are perhaps more likely in the *Brown Advisory Novices' Chase*, the *Marsh Novices' Chase*, the *Albert Bartlett Novices' Hurdle*, the two handicap hurdle events within the 2½m distance category and the *Weatherbys Champion Bumper*, especially if there is a **Flemensfirth** bred mare amongst the entries.

As a footnote, I should advise that in August 2020, *The Beeches Stud*, *Coolmore*'s division in *County Waterford*, announced that **Flemensfirth** had been retired from stud duties. **Flemensfirth** has been at the *Beeches Stud* throughout this century and regularly produced crops of more than 200. Even in recent years, his numbers have been in three-figures, so there will be many more young prospects racing at Cheltenham Festivals for many years to come. Let's hope they can bring about a return to the performances and festival winners that **Flemensfirth**'s offspring enjoyed prior to 2010.

Flemensfirth (USA) – Progeny with Official Rating of 135+

Horses by this sire with an Official Rating of 135 or greater on 9th February 2021. Horses registered with the Irish Horseracing Regulatory Board (I.H.R.B) are shown in *italics*.

				Official Ratings as of 9th February 2021		
Sire	***Horse***	***Age***	***Sex***	***Hurdles***	***Chase***	***Trainer***
Flemensfirth	Ashtown Lad	7	g	135		Dan Skelton
Flemensfirth	Ballymoy	8	g	140	137	Nigel Twiston-Davies
Flemensfirth	*Castlegrace Paddy*	*10*	*g*		*153*	*P.A.Fahy*
Flemensfirth	*Colreevy*	*8*	*f*		*148*	*W.P. Mullins*
Flemensfirth	Conrad Hastings	10	g		140	S. C. Robinson
Flemensfirth	Coolanly	9	g	136	138	Fergal O'Brien
Flemensfirth	Craigneiche	7	g	139		Nicky Henderson
Flemensfirth	Demachine	7	g		140	Kerry Lee
Flemensfirth	*Fitzhenry*	*9*	*g*	*122*	*136*	*Paul Nolan*
Flemensfirth	Gala Ball	11	g		146	Philip Hobbs
Flemensfirth	Good Boy Bobby	8	g		142	Nigel Twiston-Davies
Flemensfirth	*Impact Factor*	*9*	*g*		*152*	*Mrs John Harrington*
Flemensfirth	*Jett*	*10*	*g*		*150*	*Mrs John Harrington*
Flemensfirth	Kimberlite Candy	9	g		153	Tom Lacey
Flemensfirth	Lostintranslation	9	g		169	Colin Tizzard
Flemensfirth	*Magic Of Light*	*10*	*f*	*147*	*155*	*Mrs John Harrington*
Flemensfirth	Minella Drama	6	g	142		Donald McCain
Flemensfirth	*Minella Fair*	*10*	*g*		*136*	*Noel Meade*
Flemensfirth	*Minella Melody*	*7*	*f*	*142*		*Henry de Bromhead*
Flemensfirth	Mrs Hyde	8	f	140		Brian Ellison
Flemensfirth	Queenohearts	8	f	136		Stuart Edmunds
Flemensfirth	Rath An Iuir	8	g		137	Rose Dobbin
Flemensfirth	*Royal Kahala*	*6*	*f*	*138*		*Peter Fahey*
Flemensfirth	Secret Reprieve	7	g		144	Evan Williams
Flemensfirth	Shakem Up'Arry	7	g	136		Ben Pauling
Flemensfirth	Sizing Codelco	12	g		137	Colin Tizzard
Flemensfirth	*Ten Ten*	*8*	*g*	*124*	*135*	*J.P.Dempsey*
Flemensfirth	*Three Musketeers*	*11*	*g*		*137*	*Gordon Elliott*
Flemensfirth	*Tornado Flyer*	*8*	*g*		*160*	*W.P. Mullins*
Flemensfirth	Two Taffs	11	g		141	Nigel Twiston-Davies
Flemensfirth	Waiting Patiently	10	g		167	Ruth Jefferson
Flemensfirth	Wandrin Star	10	g		140	Kim Bailey
Flemensfirth	West To The Bridge	8	g	137		Dan Skelton
Flemensfirth	Winningseverything	7	g		135	Harry Fry

Commentary on selected potential entries for 2021 Festival

Colreevy – Mrs Paddy Power Mares' Chase 2m4½f (4:50 Friday 19th March)

Flemensfirth will no doubt be represented by several of his offspring at Cheltenham and perhaps the best chance of claiming a victory may come from ***Colreevy*** who has won her three novice chases quite comfortably. She is jostling for favouritism with stablemate *Elimay*. The race is difficult to predict as other quality horses are entered both here and elsewhere, so I recommend that punters wait until nearer the time before deciding which mare takes your fancy.

Getaway (GER)

Getaway was not featured in the 2020 Cheltenham Festival Stallion Guide.

Getaway (18-y-o)							
Race Format	*Miles*	*Won*	*Placed*	*Unplaced*	*Total*	*Win %*	*Place %*
Hurdles	About 2m	0	0	9	9	0%	0%
	About 2m 4f	0	2	5	7	0%	29%
	About 3m	0	0	1	1	0%	0%
Chases	About 2m	0	0	0	0	-	-
	About 2m 4f	0	0	2	2	0%	0%
	About 3m	0	0	0	0	-	-
	About 4m	0	0	1	1	0%	0%
Bumper	About 2m	0	0	2	2	0%	0%
Total	2011-2020	**0**	**2**	**20**	**22**	**0%**	**9%**

The first two horses by **Getaway** to race at a Cheltenham Festival were both mares and the two of them made their festival debuts in March 2017, to take part in the Grade 2 *Trull House Stud Mares' Novices' Hurdle (Registered as the Dawn Run)*. By all accounts, the two mares produced a satisfactory start for **Getaway**'s first festival runners. Out of the 16 mares to line up, five of them were 100/1 outsiders, one of which was the **Getaway** sired ***Awayinthewest***, who contradicted her 100/1 price, to deliver an eye-catching run, staying on up the Cheltenham run-in to finish just 8½ lengths off the winner to take 6th place. Ahead of her was half-sister, ***Verdana Blue*** (25/1), who took up the lead just before the last hurdle but then edged right under pressure before being outpaced by the winner, *Let's Dance*, who quickened away to draw clear. Unfortunately, in the final 100 yards, the **Getaway** bred mare had no extra to give and lost 2nd and 3rd place to *Barra* and *Dusky Legend* to finish a close 4th. So, **Getaway** just missed out on his stock recording a place position with his first two festival representatives. Over the next three festivals, another dozen horses by **Getaway** would attempt to register a festival placing but all would fail, the drought finally coming to an end in last year's *Ballymore Novices' Hurdle*.

The 2018 festival came and went with two more horses by **Getaway** making the March trip to Prestbury Park but leaving empty-handed. **Getaway**'s 3rd representative at a Cheltenham festival was ***Getabird***, who, in the hands of the powerful connections of owner *Susannah Ricci* and trained by *Willie Mullins*, was sent off as the 7/4 favourite in the festival's opening event, the *Sky Bet Supreme Novices' Hurdle*. In preparation for his run in the *Supreme*, ***Getabird*** had won all four of his Rules Races to date but when it came to the big one, ***Getabird*** flopped, finishing in 11th place. The stallion's other runner at the 2018 meeting was pulled up in the *Albert Bartlett Novices' Hurdle*.

In 2019, seven entries by **Getaway** made their way to the Festival but all seven failed to trouble the judge. The highest placed horse was ***Verdana Blue*** who put in a good effort at a price of 33/1 in the *Unibet Champion Hurdle* to claim 5th place, but she was never anywhere near the leaders, beaten in the end by 24 lengths. Eleven festival runs to date and eleven losses for **Getaway**'s stock. The highest two placings to date belonged to the *Nicky Henderson* trained ***Verdana Blue*** – 4th in the 2017 *Mares' Novices' Hurdle* and 5th in the 2019 *Champion Hurdle*. More horses by **Getaway** made the trip to the 2020 Festival, eleven in total, thereby doubling the number of **Getaway**'s offspring that had raced at the festival previously. And at last, the stallion's progeny would finally succeed in securing a festival place position, and not one, but two! Alleluia!

Two festival placings? Pah! More importantly, with 22 festival appearances on board, there is now enough data on this stallion for **Getaway** to make it into the 2021 Cheltenham Festival Stallion Guide! Now, that really is something worth celebrating!

Nineteen horses by **Getaway** have raced at the Cheltenham Festival on 22 occasions. None of **Getaway**'s offspring have been able to finish in the first two places at a Cheltenham Festival and only two of those 19 horses have rewarded each-way bets, in both cases by securing 3rd place finishes. Although horses by **Getaway** succeeded in picking up those two place positions at last year's meeting from the eleven appearances, that isn't enough to make a sizable dent in financial losses had one been backing **Getaway**'s progeny blind at level stakes. Had one placed a £10.00 each-way bet on all 22 festival appearances from this stallion's offspring, the outcome would be a loss of £377.00. **Getaway** needs his stock to start winning festival races.

The 2020 Cheltenham Festival was better for **Getaway**'s supporters than the performances from the seven appearances at the 2019 meeting, but then again, there were four more of the offspring participating. Looking at the results in detail, horses by **Getaway** delivered three solid outings from five outings in the festival's hurdle events that covered a distance of around 2½ miles, whereas the six performances by **Getaway** sired runners outside of this race category were just as dismal as those that had gone before at the previous two festival meetings.

Four of the five horses by **Getaway** that registered an outing in the 2½m hurdle race category lined up in one race, the *Ballymore Novices' Hurdle*. It would have been a huge performance from the progeny if any of this quartet had managed to trouble the 4/7 favourite and winner of this event, the highly talented *Envoi Allen*. As expected, ***Getaway Fred*** at 100/1, got nowhere near the winner. He was held up, then struggled, then was pulled up. The shortest priced of **Getaway**'s gang of four was the *Philip Hobbs* trained, ***Sporting John***, unbeaten in three starts over hurdles and who was sent off as the race's 5/1 second favourite. His run was too bad to be true and before the field was even halfway, jockey *Barry Geraghty* was hard at work pushing the gelding along. He finished in 7th place more than 30 lengths off the winner. When questioned about the poor performance, trainer *Philip Hobbs* advised that the horse finished distressed. The other two runners by **Getaway** performed much better, although if I had backed either of them, I would have been rather stressed out trying to recall which one of the similar named duo I had backed. Finishing in 3rd place was the *Willie Mullins* trained 9/1 shot (and 4th favourite for this race), ***The Big Getaway***. He wasn't especially fluent during the race but didn't seem short on stamina as he kicked for home between the last two, before being outpaced by runner-up *Easywork* and winner, *Envoi Allen*. He became the first horse by **Getaway** to achieve a festival placing when taking 3rd place, eight lengths away from the winner. Just over six lengths behind ***The Big Getaway*** and finishing in 4th position at a price of 8/1, was the *Colin Tizzard* trained, ***The Big Breakaway***. He looked in some difficulty mid-way through the race when being pushed along, but with the assistance of *Robbie Power* in the saddle, the horse managed to make headway two hurdles from home before being outpaced and coming home in his own time to finish 4th.

The one other run by **Getaway**'s progeny in the 2½m category came from ***Thosedaysaregone***, who lined up at a price of 10/1 in the 2m5f *Coral Cup Handicap Hurdle*. His canny trainer, *Charles Byrnes*, had managed to get the gelding into the bottom end of this competitive handicap, as a result of ***Thosedaysaregone*** winning a valuable Grade B Handicap at *Leopardstown* on his previous outing, which raised the horse's handicap mark by 13lb to an Official Rating of 139. Bottom weight for this running of the *Coral Cup* was 138. In my view, of all 22 outings by **Getaway**'s stock, the performance by ***Thosedaysaregone*** is probably the best so far. In the race, jockey *Kevin Brouder* had the horse settled in midfield, before the partnership made headway three hurdles from home. As they approached the last, the horse switched left and then stayed on to claim 3rd place, less than 5 lengths off the winner, *Dame De Compagnie*.

In conclusion, of the 22 festival appearances that we have seen from **Getaway**'s offspring, there are just a few that I would consider to be a positive sign for this stallion's future festival contenders. ***The Big Getaway***, ***The Big Breakaway*** and ***Thosedaysaregone*** all put in respectable performances, and I would add to this list, the two festival runs by the mare, ***Verdana Blue***. The other 17 outings are forgettable. Amongst those 22 runs, admittedly there have been some big outsiders. Indeed, seven horses by **Getaway** lined up in races priced at 50/1 upwards. That said, a further seven festival runners had starting prices ranging from 7/4 favourite through to 12/1. I don't think there are any real excuses as to why horses by **Getaway** are yet to set the world alight when it comes to the stallion's festival contenders, but in reality, it is still early days.

There is likely to be another large number of horses by **Getaway** that make the trip to the Cheltenham Festival this year and should the higher quality members of his stock not be quite good enough to claim a first festival victory for this sire, then I'm sure that whether it is at this festival or future meetings, a winner will one day materialise simply because of the sheer volume of this stallion's festival entries. It is still very early in **Getaway**'s career as a stallion and the data is minimal. Nevertheless, as of today, I'm not much of a fan **Getaway**'s offspring at Cheltenham Festivals. Unless results pick up very soon, **Getaway** is very much in danger of becoming a stallion where his stock is to be avoided at festivals rather than supported. Let's see what 2021 brings.

Getaway (GER) – Progeny with Official Rating of 135+

Horses by this sire with an Official Rating of 135 or greater on 9th February 2021. Horses registered with the Irish Horseracing Regulatory Board (I.H.R.B) are shown in *italics*.

				Official Ratings as of 9th February 2021		
Sire	***Horse***	***Age***	***Sex***	***Hurdles***	***Chase***	***Trainer***
Getaway	*Assemble*	*7*	*g*		*144*	*Joseph Patrick O'Brien*
Getaway	Barbados Buck's	6	g	139		Paul Nicholls
Getaway	Captain Drake	8	g	140	140	Harry Fry
Getaway	Danny Whizzbang	8	g		140	Paul Nicholls
Getaway	Getaround	6	g	135		Ella Pickard
Getaway	Getaway Totherock	8	f	135	135	Alastair Ralph
Getaway	Getaway Trump	8	g		140	Paul Nicholls
Getaway	I Can't Explain	8	g		136	Kim Bailey
Getaway	Jarveys Plate	8	g	136	136	Fergal O'Brien
Getaway	Killer Clown	7	g		136	Emma Lavelle
Getaway	Lust For Glory	8	f		136	Nicky Henderson
Getaway	Musical Slave	8	g		137	Philip Hobbs
Getaway	Newtide	8	g		141	Kim Bailey
Getaway	One For Rosie	8	g		141	Kim Bailey
Getaway	Return Ticket	8	g		140	Rebecca Menzies
Getaway	Sojourn	8	g		142	Anthony Honeyball
Getaway	Sporting John	6	g		153	Philip Hobbs
Getaway	Talkischeap	9	g		155	Alan King
Getaway	The Big Breakaway	6	g		148	Colin Tizzard
Getaway	The Dellercheckout	8	g		135	Mrs C. J. Robinson
Getaway	Truckin Away	8	g		137	Philip Hobbs
Getaway	Verdana Blue	9	f	151		Nicky Henderson

Gold Well (GB)

Quote from the 2020 Cheltenham Festival Stallion Guide - "In analysing the festival statistics associated with **Gold Well**, one needs to be fully aware of ***Holywell***'s major influence on the figures. From a financial perspective, if one takes ***Holywell*** out of calculations, a level stakes £10.00 each way bet on the remaining 27 festival appearances by **Gold Well**'s stock, results in a loss of £345.00. Punters may be bewildered to learn that, to the same staking plan, a profit of £62.50 is the outcome if ***Holywell***'s results are included."

Gold Well (Died as a 12-y-o in 2013)							
Race Format	*Miles*	*Won*	*Placed*	*Unplaced*	*Total*	*Win %*	*Place %*
Hurdles	About 2m	0	0	3	3	0%	0%
	About 2m 4f	0	1	3	4	0%	25%
	About 3m	1	0	6	7	14%	14%
Chases	About 2m	0	0	0	0	-	-
	About 2m 4f	0	2	4	6	0%	33%
	About 3m	1	2	8	11	9%	27%
	About 4m	0	0	9	9	0%	0%
Bumper	About 2m	0	0	2	2	0%	0%
Total	**2011-2020**	**2**	**5**	**35**	**42**	**5%**	**17%**

When the sadly now departed *Alan Ball* first became the manager of Southampton Football Club, he gathered all the players around him except for *Matthew Le Tissier*. He told the highly talented maverick to stand in the corner. With the players assembled together, *Alan Ball* advised them that they needed to do their jobs professionally, especially working hard to get the ball back from the opposition. When they had the ball, he told them that their next responsibility was to get the ball to *Matt Le Tissier*, because although they were good players, *Le Tissier* was a fantastic player and the team needed to rely on him to get Southampton out of relegation trouble. *Le Tissier* is still nicknamed 'Le God' by Southampton fans. He kept Southampton from being relegated on countless occasions.

Matthew Le Tissier was to Southampton what ***Holywell*** is to **Gold Well**. The quote at the top of the page highlights the impact and influence that ***Holywell*** has on **Gold Well**'s festival statistics. Bizarrely, preceding the 2020 Cheltenham Festival, one would have made a profit backing blind to level stakes all of **Gold Well**'s representatives that had participated in festival races. I say bizarrely because it would have involved just 2 wins, 4 places and 26 losing bets. As anticipated, none of the ten entries by **Gold Well** that made the trip to the 2020 Cheltenham Festival were able to come anywhere near to the achievements of ***Holywell***, and so the £62.50 profit attributable to backing all of **Gold Well**'s festival runners blind to a £10.00 each way stake has now disappeared. As of today, had one supported all 42 festival appearances of **Gold Well**'s offspring to the same staking plan, the outcome would be a loss of £117.50. Without ***Holywell***'s presence, the losses would be £525.00.

Holywell is the only horse by **Gold Well** to have registered a festival victory, something that he achieved twice. In 2013, he won the *Pertemps Final* at a price of 25/1, and followed that up with his second success, at 10/1, in the 2014 *Baylis & Harding Affordable Luxury Handicap Chase*, beating *Ma Filleule* by 1¾ lengths. In 2015, ***Holywell*** took a major step up in class to compete in the *Betfred Cheltenham Gold Cup Chase*, where he finished just outside the place positions with a sound performance to finish fourth. The following season, he was once again entered for the renewal of the race that he won in 2014, now named the *Ultima Handicap Chase*. This time he had to settle for the runner-up spot at odds of 8/1, as *Un Temps Pour Tout* won readily by 7 lengths. In the 2017 running of the *Ultima*, ***Holywell*** was to take on *Un Temps Pour Tout* once again, but their performances could not have been wider apart. *Un Temps Pour Tout* went on to win the contest for a second time, whereas, ***Holywell***, now a 10-year-old, jumped with no fluency whatsoever and was pulled up half-way round.

The 25 horses by **Gold Well** that have made 42 appearances at Cheltenham Festivals are typically unfancied in the betting market before they set off in their respective festival races. And far more often than not, the punters and bookies are right. Within those 42 festival outings by **Gold Well's** stock, on 21 occasions, the offspring have made up the numbers, either failing to complete the race or finishing at the back of the field outside of the first ten home. Of the remaining 21 festival runs by the progeny, they can be divided into two groups, of which the first group consists of 14 occasions in which the **Gold Well** sired runner failed to win or place, but nevertheless delivered a respectable performance, occupying a finishing position somewhere between 4th and 7th. The remaining group consists of 5 horses by **Gold Well** that recorded two wins and five places from seven runs.

One of those place positions was achieved at last year's Cheltenham Festival in the *Northern Trust Company Novices' Handicap Chase*, in which the 4/1 joint favourite for the race, ***Galvin***, finished in second place beaten by 3¼ lengths by the other joint favourite, *Imperial Aura*. It was the first time that a horse by **Gold Well** had finished in the first three places at a Cheltenham Festival since ***Legacy Gold***, a 40/1 outsider, finished in third place in the 2016 *OLBG Hurdle*. ***Galvin*** set a record too at last year's festival, becoming the shortest priced runner out of all 42 of **Gold Well**'s festival representatives. Only on nine occasions at Cheltenham Festivals has a horse by **Gold Well** lined up at single figure odds, and seven of those were at odds of 8/1 or 9/1. ***Galvin*** returned an SP of 4/1 as one of the joint favourites and did a lot better than the one other occasion where **Gold Well** was represented at a festival by a joint favourite. That was ***John's Spirit***, who was pulled up at a price of 11/2 in the *2016 Brown Advisory & Merriebelle Stable Plate.*

Gold Well's festival statistics table shows a win strike rate of 5% and a 17% win & place strike rate. Without ***Holywell***, however, those strike rates change dramatically. The win strike rate of 6% disappears to zero and the 17% win and place strike rate comes down to just 11%, all of which means that if one is interested in a festival entry by **Gold Well**, there needs to be a recognition that historically, the offspring have delivered a place position for once in every nine festival outings. Confidence is drained further when one is reminded that the only horse by **Gold Well** ever to win at a Cheltenham Festival is ***Holywell***. And then there are the financial implications. Without ***Holywell***, staking a £10.00 each-way bet on all 42 of **Gold Well**'s festival representatives calculates to a loss of £525.00.

At the 2021 Cheltenham Festival, perhaps one of **Gold Well**'s offspring will register a festival placing, or for all one knows, one of the entries may even provide this stallion with another festival winner to add to name of ***Holywell***. To me, however, it is like looking for a needle in a haystack. A lot of time and effort for in all probability, little return. Not for me.

Gold Well (GB) – Progeny with Official Rating of 135+

Horses by this sire with an Official Rating of 135 or greater on 9th February 2021. Horses registered with the Irish Horseracing Regulatory Board (I.H.R.B) are shown in *italics*.

					Official Ratings as of 9th February 2021	
Sire	***Horse***	***Age***	***Sex***	***Hurdles***	***Chase***	***Trainer***
Gold Well	*Agusta Gold*	*8*	*f*	*125*	*146*	*Ms Margaret Mullins*
Gold Well	Champagne Well	8	g		136	Fergal O'Brien
Gold Well	Clondaw Cian	11	g	136		Sophie Leech
Gold Well	Dickie Diver	8	g		142	Nicky Henderson
Gold Well	Emitom	7	g		147	Warren Greatrex
Gold Well	*Galvin*	*7*	*g*		*151*	*Gordon Elliott*
Gold Well	*Goose Man*	*9*	*g*		*135*	*T.J. Taaffe*
Gold Well	Lock's Corner	7	g	137	140	Jonjo O'Neill
Gold Well	My Old Gold	11	f		141	Nicky Richards
Gold Well	*Opposites Attract*	*7*	*g*		*136*	*Dermot Anthony McLoughlin*
Gold Well	Palmers Hill	8	g	137	133	Jonjo O'Neill
Gold Well	Pink Sheets	7	f	135		Mick Quinn
Gold Well	*Rebel Gold*	*8*	*g*	*121*	*140*	*Thomas Foley*
Gold Well	Shoal Bay	8	g		137	Colin Tizzard
Gold Well	*Smoking Gun*	*8*	*g*		*135*	*Joseph Patrick O'Brien*
Gold Well	Two For Gold	8	g		149	Kim Bailey

Commentary on selected potential entries for 2021 Festival

Galvin – National Hunt Chase 3m6f (5:30 Tuesday 16th March)

Gold Well hasn't exactly set the world on fire with his festival entries and it is only the impact of ***Holywell*** on the table of statistics that may trick punters into believing that this sire's offspring are perhaps ok. Perhaps I am being over negative on **Gold Well**, after all, one of his progeny, ***Galvin***, may have what it takes to provide this stallion with a 3rd festival success to add to the two victories secured by ***Holywell*** in 2013 and 2014. ***Galvin***, as highlighted earlier, is the first of **Gold Well**'s stock to have produced a festival placing since 2016, so this horse trained by *Gordon Elliott* is certainly going the right way.

Galvin finished 2nd in last year's *Northern Trust Company Novices' Handicap Chase* which means that he has retained his novice status for the 2020-21 season, and hence he sits as 4/1 favourite for the novice event for amateur riders, the *National Hunt Chase*. And albeit the genes inherited by **Gold Well** may not help much, he certainly has other factors in his favour, perhaps the biggest being that he resides at *Longwood, County Meath* with trainer *Gordon Elliott*. The trainer has only ever entered eight runners for the *National Hunt Chase* and providing his entries complete the course, they win. Four managed to complete the course and claim victory. The other four either fell, were unseated or pulled up. *Gordon Elliott* is a huge asset for ***Galvin*** in this race.

Galvin's Official Rating is 151 and in the past decade, a dozen horses have turned up boasting a high rating of 150 or more. Eight went home with their tails between their legs but the other four all won, which is a good record. ***Galvin*** has competed in four novice chases this season and has won all of them and since his last win on 23rd October 2020, *Gordon Elliott* has given him a break. (Anyone would think the trainer knows what he's doing!). Eleven of the past 19 winners of the *National Hunt Chase* finished 1st of 2nd last time out and nine of the last 11 winners had run in a chase before October 31st.

As yet, the trainer has yet to send ***Galvin*** out to race over a distance beyond 3m2f. This is a good move as only 2 winners in the past 20 years had previously gone that far before their *National Hunt Chase* wins. And 7 of the past 11 winners had been to the Cheltenham Festival before and of course we know that ***Galvin*** had that privilege in 2020, but he also finished 6th in the *Ballymore Novices' Hurdle* in 2019. The experience of having already raced over Cheltenham's undulations is clearly an advantage.

I may be talking myself into backing a horse by **Gold Well**. Indeed, I may just do that! But there is one caveat. There's always a 'but'. In the past eleven years, 23 horses lined in the *National Hunt Chase* having contested a Grade 1 chase previously, and of those 23 entries, five won. (***Galvin*** has not contested a Grade 1 chase). If I look down the list of entries and find such a beast who has frequented Grade 1 company and who happens to have a sire that is a little more to my linking than **Gold Well**, then perhaps, I may have to change my mind. It will need careful consideration. After all, the statistic means that 18 of those Grade 1 chasers were beaten. This is a piece of research I'll save for later. In the meantime, I'll whisper it. ***Galvin*** appears to be, on the face of it, a solid bet.

Great Pretender (IRE)

Quote from the 2020 Cheltenham Festival Stallion Guide - "Of the eight **Great Pretender** outsiders that have lined up in their festival races at odds of 22/1 or bigger, four of them have succeeded in registering a top six finish, of which two runners provided supporters with place dividends."

Great Pretender (22-y-o)							
Race Format	*Miles*	*Won*	*Placed*	*Unplaced*	*Total*	*Win %*	*Place %*
Hurdles	About 2m	0	1	7	8	0%	13%
	About 2m 4f	1	2	4	7	14%	43%
	About 3m	0	0	2	2	0%	0%
Chases	About 2m	0	1	3	4	0%	25%
	About 2m 4f	0	0	2	2	0%	0%
	About 3m	0	0	1	1	0%	0%
	About 4m	0	0	2	2	0%	0%
Bumper	About 2m	0	1	0	1	0%	100%
Total	**2011-2020**	**1**	**5**	**21**	**27**	**4%**	**22%**

Many punters who support odds-on shots may have suffered at last year's festival had they supported ***Benie Des Dieux*** (4/6 favourite) to beat *Honeysuckle* (9/4), in the *Close Brothers Mares' Hurdle*. It was a close race that could have gone either way, but in the end, *Honeysuckle* came out on top by ½ length. Despite the defeat and probably a huge number of torn-up betting slips floating around the Cheltenham enclosures, for **Great Pretender**, the sire of the defeated ***Benie Des Dieux***, it was a very satisfactory 2020 Cheltenham Festival. Of the five horses by **Great Pretender** that made the trip to the festival meeting, four secured top six finishes inclusive of three paid place dividends. If one had placed a £10.00 each-way stake on all five of **Great Pretender**'s festival representatives last year, the outcome would have been a small profit of £26.33.

The only other year which would have resulted in a profit backing this stallion's festival entries blind at level stakes would have occurred in 2013. In that year, we witnessed the very first of **Great Pretender**'s offspring to grace a Cheltenham Festival. The horse, named ***Ptit Zig***, had just turned four when he left France to join trainer *Paul Nicholls* in January of that year, winning his very first race on British soil at *Ludlow* in early February. His next outing was in the festival's *Fred Winter Juvenile Handicap Hurdle*, where he finished in 3rd place at 22/1, which would have provided a very satisfactory £45.00 profit for a £10.00 each way bet. ***Ptit Zig*** was the only horse by **Great Pretender** to race at that meeting.

Sixteen horses by **Great Pretender** have competed in 27 festival races, and with the three place positions recorded at the 2020 Cheltenham Festival, the stallion's win & place strike rate has jumped from 14% before last year's meeting to 22% now. What is worrying for the supporters of **Great Pretender**, is that the number of places is five times higher than the number of wins, and when one considers that of the 27 festival outings, ten of the runners lined up at single figure odds, including two odds-on favourites and two joint favourites, a solitary festival victory is a huge disappointment.

The star attraction of **Great Pretender**'s stock is the mare ***Benie Des Dieux***, who has appeared in the past three of the festival's *Mares' Hurdle* races, registered as the *David Nicholson Mares' Hurdle*. Punters will have different opinions about ***Benie Des Dieux*** ranging from over-rated, under-rated, fantastic, unlucky, unfortunate and so on. As for me, I just look at the results. She won the *Mares'*

Hurdle in 2018 at 9/2; crashed out at the final hurdle when looking certain to win in the 2019 renewal, priced at 10/11; and just missed out to *Honeysuckle* in 2020, when priced at 4/6. ***Benie Des Dieux***, therefore, is the sole horse by **Great Pretender** to have recorded a festival victory and is also the horse behind the comment in the previous paragraph that refers to two odds-on favourites.

If we take a moment to return to the 10 occasions at Cheltenham Festivals in which entries by **Great Pretender** lined up at single figure odds, those sharp at arithmetic will note that ***Benie Des Dieux*** accounts for three of those 10 appearances, having recorded one win, one place and one fall. What is rather disheartening is that of the remaining seven occasions upon which a horse by **Great Pretender** lined up at single figure odds, not one of six competitors (***Mr Mole*** failed twice) were able to secure a top three finish. That said, the second festival placing from **Great Pretender**'s progeny at last year's meeting, came from a 5/1 chance, that did manage to secure a place dividend when sneaking into 4th place in the *Johnny Henderson Grand Annual Challenge Cup Handicap Chase*. ***Greaneteen***, trained by *Paul Nicholls*, had been impressive in winning all three of his chasing starts preceding the *Grand Annual* and so was well fancied in the market, starting as the 5/1 second favourite. He may have finished closer had he not blundered two fences out.

Whereas I am of the view that those horses by **Great Pretender** towards the fore of the market have underperformed, rather curiously, I am of the view that the stallion's outsiders have somewhat over-performed. And let's start again with the 2020 Cheltenham Festival and the third entry of the progeny that was successful in securing a place dividend at last year's meeting. Like ***Greaneteen***, ***Cracking Smart*** just sneaked into the place positions when claiming 4th place in the *Coral Cup Handicap Hurdle*. When I say, 'just sneaked in', I mean it literally. The 5th horse was just a nose behind him! ***Cracking Smart*** returned a starting price of 33/1 and hence the profit that materialised had one backed at level stakes all five of **Great Pretender**'s 2020 festival entries, was pretty much down to the nose of the *Gordon Elliott* trained, ***Cracking Smart***.

The one other place dividend alongside ***Benie Des Dieux*** 4/6, ***Greaneteen*** 5/1, ***Ptit Zig*** 22/1 and ***Cracking Smart*** 33/1, came from the easy to pronounce, ***Claimantakinforgan*** who finished in 3rd place at a price of 22/1 in the 2017 *Weatherbys Champion Bumper*. Fourteen of **Great Pretender**'s 27 festival representatives have returned starting prices of 16/1 or greater. Three have been placed and a further four have secured top six finishing positions, including ***Cobra De Mai*** (20/1), who finished in 6th position in last year's first handicap to take place, the 3m1f Grade 3 *Ultima Handicap Chase*.

Whether one decides to back **Great Pretender**'s stock that line up at single figure odds, or those considered outsiders, or those in-between, from a financial perspective, it doesn't make much difference. Had one backed £10.00 each way on all 27 of the sire's festival entries, the losses would amount to £220.68. For the record and to the same staking plan, backing those 10 runners at single figure odds would equate to a loss of £92.18 and backing all entries with starting prices of 16/1 or greater calculates to a loss of £68.50. The three 'in-betweeners', all of whom finished between 8th and 11th priced at 12/1 (twice) and 14/1 contribute £60.00 to the losses.

In conclusion, it is relatively early days with **Great Pretender**, and the results recorded from the 27 festival outings to date, aren't revealing any meaningful green shoots of trends and patterns, and so any solid conclusions are just not possible. That said, 2020 did, just about, represent an upturn in results with four of the five runners securing a top six finish, and three of those paying out on each way bets. My thinking with regards to this stallion's 2021 Cheltenham Festival entries is in three parts. My first recommendation is to maintain a watching brief on the offspring to see if anything more conclusive emerges that may bring about the green shoots of a pattern or trend. That said, if you have carried out a detailed analysis of the runners and riders for a festival race and a horse by **Great Pretender** emerges as your chief fancy, then I wouldn't dissuade you from placing a bet. However, if you are going to place a bet on your **Great Pretender** bred 'fancy', let me offer my last piece of advice. Be cautious if your selection is towards the front of the market – maybe a small wager. And if your selection is an outsider? My advice is be bolder but without being reckless. Best of luck with your decision-making if you end up fancying one of this sire's festival entries!

Great Pretender (IRE) – Progeny with Official Rating of 135+

Horses by this sire with an Official Rating of 135 or greater on 9th February 2021. Horses registered with the Irish Horseracing Regulatory Board (I.H.R.B) are shown in *italics*.

				Official Ratings as of 9th February 2021		
Sire	***Horse***	***Age***	***Sex***	***Hurdles***	***Chase***	***Trainer***
Great Pretender	Al Roc	10	g		152	Dr Richard Newland
Great Pretender	*Benie Des Dieux*	*10*	*f*	*159*		*W.P. Mullins*
Great Pretender	Claimantakinforgan	9	g		144	Nicky Henderson
Great Pretender	Cobra De Mai	9	g		135	Caroline Bailey
Great Pretender	*Cracking Smart*	*9*	*g*	*150*		*Gordon Elliott*
Great Pretender	Elvis Mail	7	g	138	143	N. W. Alexander
Great Pretender	Greaneteen	7	g		161	Paul Nicholls
Great Pretender	Hacker Des Places	4	g	136		Paul Nicholls
Great Pretender	Sao	7	g		138	Rebecca Menzies
Great Pretender	Stoner's Choice	6	g	139		Fergal O'Brien

Commentary on selected potential entries for 2021 Festival

Benie Des Dieux – Close Brothers Mares' Hurdle 2m4f (4:10 Tuesday 16th March)

At the time of writing, it seems clear that *Honeysuckle* will now go to the *Champion Hurdle* rather than go for a second successive win in the *Mares' Hurdle* which I believe will strengthen the chances of ***Benie Des Dieux*** lining up in this race rather than tackle the *Stayers' Hurdle* or new *Mares' Chase*, both of which are sponsored by *Paddy Power*. As of February, the odds available on ***Benie Des Dieux*** were 8/1 for the *Stayers'*, 5/1 for the *Mares' Chase* and 3/1 for the *Close Brothers Mares' Hurdle*. Although the 3/1 available takes into account that she may run in a different event, the price does reflect that ***Benie Des Dieux*** is no 'sure-thing' to win this. In both of the past two renewals of this race, when falling at the last in 2019 and finishing 2nd to *Honeysuckle* in 2020, she has been sent off as the odds-on favourite. Her price when she won the 2018 renewal was 9/2.

Albeit all three mares are showing up in the betting of other races, the head of affairs in the betting for the *Mares' Hurdle* are *Concertista* (6/4 favourite), ***Benie Des Dieux*** (3/1) and *Roksana* (5/1) and I think it is really difficult to split them. The former two are trained by *Willie Mullins*, and so perhaps, he may wish to race ***Benie Des Dieux*** somewhere else. And then there is age to take into consideration. ***Benie Des Dieux*** is now 10 years old, but then again, this race was won by *Quevega* when she was aged 10, although she was rather exceptional, having won this race on six occasions. *Roksana* is a year younger and *Concertista* is the youngest, aged 7.

Here are some of the key trends based upon previous:

1) 10 of the 13 winners had won or placed in a Grade 1 or Grade 2 race against geldings (not just mares). ***(Benie Des Dieux and Roksana are a yes. Concertista – no)***
2) 10 of the 13 winners had already won a Grade 1 or Grade 2. ***(Benie Des Dieux as well as Concertista and Roksana)***
3) The last 12 winners had already won over a minimum of 2m4f. And 6 of the last 10 had won over 2m6f+. ***(Benie Des Dieux and Roksana have won over 2m6f+, whereas Concertista has won over 2m4f)***
4) Of the 13 winners, French bred mares have won nine, Irish 3 and GB 1. ***(Benie Des Dieux and Concertista are French, Roksana Irish)***
5) Last time out winners have won 10 of the 13 renewals. ***(Roksana and Concertista are a yes. Benie Des Dieux – no)***
6) 11 of the 13 winners have been trained in Ireland. ***(Dan Skelton may have to try harder with Roksana!)***
7) Willie Mullins has won 9 of the 13 renewals so far from 24 runners in total. Six of those winners of course were from the fabulous Quevega. ***(Can Dan Skelton win it with Roksana a second time!)***

Other than the fact that ***Benie Des Dieux*** is not getting any younger, my big reservation is that she has been off the track for a whole year, which is the same preparation as how she was prepared when falling at the last in 2019 which let *Roksana* in to win. ***Benie Des Dieux*** was eight years old then and at her peak. Did she fall because she hadn't had a run for a year? Or was she just plain unlucky and actually the preparations were spot on as, without the fall, she would have won easily? This could be argued one way or the other for a long time. At 3/1 for ***Benie Des Dieux*** or 5/1 for *Roksana*, I think I will plump, just, for the latter.

And what about *Concertista*? I like the fact she is aged seven, two years younger than *Roksana*. And she has had a 2nd and 1st in Cheltenham's *Mares' Novices* contest at the past two festivals. That said, in looking through her form, the mares that she has beaten keep cropping up as *Minella Melody* and *Black Tears*, both of whom can be backed at around 25/1 for the 2021 *Close Brothers Mares' Hurdle*. *Roksana*, meanwhile, likes to mix it with the boys and in the past few months, she has been thereabouts with the likes of *Paisley Park* and *Thyme Hill* who are rated in the 160s.

If the three protagonists turn up for this event, and with a certain amount of hesitation, at a price of 5/1, my money will be on *Roksana*.

Hacker Des Places – Boodles Juvenile Handicap Hurdle 2m½f (4:50 Tuesday 16th March)

Four juveniles by **Great Pretender** have tried to win the *Boodles Juvenile Handicap Hurdle* and although all four failed to take the prize, there have been a couple of respectable performances. ***Ptit Zig*** (22/1) recorded a 3rd place finish in the 2013 race and two years later the 13/2 favourite, ***Box Office***, finished 7th. The finishing positions and starting prices are in line with the trend of **Great Pretender**'s festival runners where the outsiders are performing better than those that are well fancied. At the time of writing, ***Hacker Des Places*** is available at around 14/1, so sits somewhere in between.

Following two hurdle outings in France, including one win, ***Hacker Des Places*** is now with trainer *Paul Nicholls*, who has a good record in the *Boodles/Fred Winter*. In the past 11 years, *Paul Nicholls* has sent out 19 horses in this event, of which almost half have rewarded each-way wagers with 3 winners recorded and six being placed. His three winners were all French bred who had raced in France before being transferred to *Paul Nicholls*' stable in Somerset. Another horse with a similar profile who was placed in a *Fred Winter* is the aforementioned ***Ptit Zig*** who had a similar journey to his half-brother

Hacker Des Places. ***Ptit Zig*** also started life in France, before one run with *Paul Nicholls* followed by the *Fred Winter* placing. ***Ptit Zig*** joined *Paul Nicholls* just 42 days before the *Fred Winter*, but with ***Hacker Des Places***, the trainer has more time to work his magic, as this juvenile joined his *Ditcheat* yard in mid-October. ***Hacker Des Places*** was a touch disappointing when losing on his debut UK hurdles outing when as the 4/9 favourite, he was beaten at *Wincanton*. He made up for it on his next outing on heavy ground at *Wetherby* when winning what may have been weaker opposition by a huge margin of 32 lengths.

In looking at the profile of previous winners of this contest, there are some negatives associated with ***Hacker Des Places***, not least the fact that his last outing, at the time of writing, was in 2020. I think there are some stronger contenders, so despite the trainer's credentials in this race, I will be leaving ***Hacker Des Places*** alone.

Footnote:

For further insight to the *Boodles Juvenile Handicap Hurdle*, read the commentary on ***Saint Sam*** by **Saint Des Saints**.

Jeremy (USA)

Quote from the 2020 Cheltenham Festival Stallion Guide - "I anticipate somewhere between 6-10 horses by **Jeremy** to make it to the 2020 Cheltenham Festival, and, on paper, one may consider that one or two have the chance of adding to the progeny's one festival victory, and perhaps 4-5 have opportunities to achieve a place dividend. But that has always appeared to be the case with **Jeremy**'s offspring, where even though the bulk of the stallion's festival entries are typically priced somewhere between 6/1 and 16/1, they don't quite deliver to expectations.

Jeremy (Died as an 11-y-o in 2014)							
Race Format	*Miles*	*Won*	*Placed*	*Unplaced*	*Total*	*Win %*	*Place %*
Hurdles	About 2m	1	2	8	11	9%	27%
	About 2m 4f	0	3	5	8	0%	38%
	About 3m	0	0	2	2	0%	0%
Chases	About 2m	0	0	1	1	0%	0%
	About 2m 4f	0	1	2	3	0%	33%
	About 3m	0	0	2	2	0%	0%
	About 4m	0	1	0	1	0%	100%
Bumper	About 2m	0	1	2	3	0%	33%
Total	2011-2020	**1**	**8**	**22**	**31**	**3%**	**29%**

Jeremy's career as a national hunt stallion is going to be short and sharp. He died young at the age of 11 back in 2014, which means that the youngest of his stock is now six years old. The stallion first appeared in the Cheltenham Festival Stallion Guide in 2020, as with six outings from his progeny at the 2019 festival added to the 14 runs that had gone before, provided just enough data to start carrying out some analysis of how horses by **Jeremy** may fare at forthcoming Cheltenham Festivals. By the time we get to 2025/2026, **Jeremy**'s offspring will all be in the veteran stage and the two or three entries that do make it to a Cheltenham Festival will find it hugely difficult to reward any bets, as horses aged 10 or older don't pick up too many wins and places at festival meetings.

The current age profile of **Jeremy**'s stock probably means that the 2021 Cheltenham Festival provides this stallion with the best opportunity for a record year of festival wins and places. The majority of his festival entries are likely to be at the peak of their careers aged between 6-8 and the only races for which his progeny won't be eligible, will be the two juvenile races, these being the *JCB Triumph Hurdle* and the *Boodles Novices' Handicap Hurdle*. At this year's festival, horses by **Jeremy** can still be competitive in the festival's hurdle events, which won't be the case in a couple of years from now. Indeed, over the next 2-3 years, we will see a gradual shift of more of **Jeremy**'s festival representatives racing in longer distance chases and fewer of progeny entered in the shorter distance hurdle events. It is worth noting that of the 20 festival outings by **Jeremy**'s offspring that took place up to and including the 2019 Cheltenham Festival, three-quarters of them were in hurdle races up to a distance of 2m5f. And as for competing in festival races over fences, horses by **Jeremy** had only tried that twice. The gradual shift from hurdles to chases was initiated at last year's Cheltenham Festival, as five of the eleven entries at the 2020 Cheltenham Festival participated in chases.

Making concrete assertions about how horses by **Jeremy** will fare at the Cheltenham Festival is rather difficult based on just 20 appearances, especially when 17 of them had taken place in hurdle events. That doesn't tell us much about how the progeny will perform in chases. This was the data available to me when writing the 2020 Cheltenham Festival Stallion Guide, and as the quote from last year's

Guide states, I had a general sense that horses by **Jeremy** weren't quite performing to expectations. One year on, and I have another eleven festival appearances to add to the mix, so what does the information and my subsequent analysis tell me now?

Last year I highlighted that of the 20 festival outings by **Jeremy**'s offspring, 14 of the runners lined up at starting prices ranging from 4/1 to 16/1 and even the outsiders weren't 'rank outsiders' – all of them priced between 20/1 and 40/1. Taking into account those starting prices, I considered a return of one win and four places was probably below expectations. So, what happened with the 11 festival contenders that made the trip to Prestbury Park in 2020? Nothing has changed as regards how the punters and bookies consider **Jeremy**'s festival representatives. Nine of the 11 runners at last year's meeting lined up at prices between 15/8 favourite and 14/1, with two outsiders at 25/1 and 50/1. As to the question on whether the progeny performed to expectations, I would suggest maybe or not quite. Four place positions but no festival victory from 11 appearances from horses more to the front of the betting market is perhaps par or just below par. In my view, one would need to be rather generous to think that the stallion exceeded expectations.

The first of **Jeremy**'s entries to be placed at the 2020 Cheltenham Festival was ***Hold The Note***, who I mentioned in last year's Guide to be nicely weighted for the *Northern Trust Company Novices' Handicap Chase*. Another clue to the horse's chances came from the knowledge that ***Hold The Note***'s trainer, *Mick Channon* and owner, *Tim Radford*, had won this race two years earlier with *Mister Whitaker*. ***Hold The Note*** (10/1) couldn't quite repeat the feat of *Mister Whitaker*, but the owner/trainer duo would still have been pleased with ***Hold The Note***'s third place dividend.

Two more of **Jeremy**'s festival entries secured place dividends on the second day of last year's meeting. The *Coral Cup Handicap Hurdle* is always highly competitive, and the 2020 renewal was no different as 22 geldings and 3 mares lined up to compete on the Old course over a distance of 2m5f. Where it mattered, on the run-in after the last, it was down to two of the three mares to fight out the finish and it was *Dame De Compagnie* (5/1 favourite) who ran on best, asserting close home to take the spoils from the **Jeremy** sired ***Black Tears*** (12/1) who claimed the runner-up spot.

The last race on the card, the *Weatherbys Champion Bumper*, would see a horse line up as the shortest priced of all previous festival entries, to date, sired by **Jeremy**. ***Appreciate It***, trained by *Willie Mullins* and ridden by his son, *Patrick*, was the 15/8 favourite for this *National Hunt Flat Race* and was well fancied as a result of a superlative prep run and victory in a Grade 2 *Flat Race* at *Leopardstown* in February. As for the Cheltenham race, *Willie Mullins* won his 10th *Champion Bumper*, but not with ***Appreciate It***, but with the second-string, *Ferny Hollow* (11/1). The winner led inside the final furlong before outpacing the **Jeremy** bred ***Appreciate It***, who finished in second place, 2½ lengths behind the winner.

The last of **Jeremy**'s eleven festival entries to make an appearance at the 2020 Cheltenham Festival was ***Happygolucky*** who was making his handicap debut in the *Martin Pipe Conditional Jockeys' Handicap Hurdle*. Trained by *Kim Bailey*, ***Happygolucky*** put in a great effort to claim a 4th place dividend and at the rewarding odds of 25/1. Being the very last race of the festival, perhaps readers are wondering whether the 25/1 placing, alongside three other place dividends, would be enough to make a profit had one backed all eleven of **Jeremy**'s festival runners blind to level stakes. The answer, sadly, is no. To a £10.00 each-way stake, backing all of **Jeremy**'s runners at last year's meeting would have resulted in a loss of £58.75.

In trying to identify patterns and clues by looking at how horses by **Jeremy** have performed in the various festival races, I did find one aspect which may be of interest to punters, although based on what is still limited data, my hypothesis needs looking at with a healthy degree of caution. I've looked at all the results where horses by **Jeremy** rewarded bets, that is, the solitary victory achieved by ***Our Conor*** in the 2013 *JCB Triumph Hurdle* plus the eight occasions in which **Jeremy**'s offspring secured place positions. What is noticeable is that five of the place positions have been achieved in big field handicap hurdles, races which are highly competitive, rough and where there may be a lot of scrimmaging for position. It may be that horses by **Jeremy** are a tough bunch that give as good as they get and revel in the hustle and bustle of big field handicaps. **Jeremy**'s offspring have had four outings in the *Coral Cup*, three appearance in the *County Hurdle* and a couple of runs in the *Martin Pipe*. In those 9 appearances, **Jeremy**'s entries have recorded five place positions, a greater than 50% place strike rate. I have listed those races below including the number of runners. (Placings are in bold):

Year	Festival Race	Runners	Name of horse	Position	Odds
2020	**Coral Cup Handicap Hurdle (2m5f)**	**25**	**Black Tears**	**2nd**	**12/1**
2017	**Coral Cup Handicap Hurdle (2m5f)**	**25**	**Who Dares Wins**	**3rd**	**33/1**
2018	**County Handicap Hurdle (2m1f)**	**24**	**Whiskey Sour**	**3rd**	**7/1**
2019	**County Handicap Hurdle (2m1f)**	**24**	**Whiskey Sour**	**4th**	**5/1 F**
2020	**Martin Pipe Handicap Hurdle (2m4f)**	**23**	**Happygolucky**	**4th**	**25/1**
2020	Coral Cup Handicap Hurdle (2m5f)	25	Birchdale	8th	14/1
2015	Coral Cup Handicap Hurdle (2m5f)	25	Goodwood Mirage	17th	12/1
2016	Martin Pipe Handicap Hurdle (2m4f)	24	Goodwood Mirage	19th	33/1
2016	County Handicap Hurdle (2m1f)	26	Henry Higgins	21st	20/1

Many would say that all races at Cheltenham are ultra-competitive and that most races have big fields, and I wouldn't disagree with either of those statements, so we shouldn't get too carried away with the above hypothesis. That said, some of the non-handicaps often end up with fields where 95% of punters would say that only 5-6 runners have a real chance of winning, the rest of the field making up the numbers or hoping to sneak a place. And there are some races, where the fields can be a lot smaller, usually in some of the Grade 1 chases at 2 and 2½ miles. In concluding this analysis, I will certainly keep an eye on how **Jeremy**'s offspring fare in this season's forthcoming big field handicaps. As an aside, in the other three contests in which horses by **Jeremy** have registered a place, the smallest number of runners has been 18, when ***Jerrysback*** finished in 3rd place in the 2019 *National Hunt Challenge Cup Amateur Riders' Novices Chase*. As for the other two events, which both happened at the 2020 Cheltenham Festival, I would suggest these were also highly competitive; the second-place finish in a field of 23 for ***Appreciate It*** in the *Weatherbys Champion Bumper* and ***Hold The Note***'s 3rd placing in the 20 strong field competing in the *Northern Trust Company Novices' Handicap Chase*. To complete the picture, 17 runners lined up when **Jeremy**'s progeny recorded their sole victory with ***Our Conor***'s success in the 2013 *JCB Triumph Hurdle*.

To sum up, 19 horses by **Jeremy** have made 31 festival appearances. Eight of those 19 horses have managed to reward bets with the sole victory from ***Our Conor*** as highlighted above, plus eight place dividends recorded by another seven of the offspring. ***Whiskey Sour*** is the only horse by **Jeremy** to deliver a festival placing on more than one occasion, with his 3rd and 4th place finishes in consecutive seasons in the *County Handicap Hurdle*. Based upon the expectations set by the starting prices associated with **Jeremy**'s stock at festival meetings, I consider that the offspring have under-performed, not by much perhaps, but I certainly believe that results could have been better. To support this view, one can look at results from a financial perspective. Had one placed a £10.00 each way wager on all 31 festival appearances of **Jeremy**'s progeny, the outcome would be a £206.25 loss.

As we look forward to the 2021 Cheltenham Festival, I anticipate that there will be somewhere in the region of 10-15 horses by **Jeremy** vying to add to the sole victory secured by ***Our Conor*** back in 2013.

And for this stallion's progeny to avoid the tag of under-performing again next year, it is festival victories that are needed. Where the next win comes from is anyone's guess, but I have a hypothesis that **Jeremy**'s stock isn't concerned about race claustrophobia. Instead, they thrive in the rough and tumble throng of big-field competitive handicaps, where horses need to be battle hardened to jostle for position. My advice to punters is to look out for **Jeremy**'s offspring in the festival's big-field competitive handicaps.

Jeremy (USA) – Progeny with Official Rating of 135+

Horses by this sire with an Official Rating of 135 or greater on 9th February 2021. Horses registered with the Irish Horseracing Regulatory Board (I.H.R.B) are shown in *italics*.

					Official Ratings as of 9th February 2021	
Sire	***Horse***	***Age***	***Sex***	***Hurdles***	***Chase***	***Trainer***
Jeremy	*Appreciate It*	*7*	*g*	*153*		*W.P. Mullins*
Jeremy	Atholl Street	6	g	135		Paul Nicholls
Jeremy	Birchdale	7	g		141	Nicky Henderson
Jeremy	*Black Tears*	*7*	*f*	*147*		*Gordon Elliott*
Jeremy	Bold Plan	7	g		138	Evan Williams
Jeremy	Dr Sanderson	7	g		138	Paul Nicholls
Jeremy	Happygolucky	7	g		147	Kim Bailey
Jeremy	Hold The Note	7	g		138	Mick Channon
Jeremy	*Jeremys Flame*	*7*	*f*		*135*	*Gavin Cromwell*
Jeremy	Jerrysback	9	g		142	Philip Hobbs
Jeremy	Mister Fisher	7	g		162	Nicky Henderson
Jeremy	*The Very Man*	*7*	*g*	*135*		*Gordon Elliott*
Jeremy	Who Dares Wins	9	g	144		Alan King

Commentary on selected potential entries for 2021 Festival

Appreciate It – Sky Bet Supreme Novices' Hurdle 2m½f (1:30 Tuesday 16th March)

As of mid-February, ***Appreciate It*** is a warm favourite (11/8) for the opening event of the 2021 Cheltenham Festival. However, I have a couple of opinions about **Jeremy**'s festival contenders. First, they haven't so far lived up to expectations and secondly, they appear to have performed best in big field handicap battles. If **Jeremy**'s offspring were human, they are the ones that are quite happy fighting for bargains in boxing day sales as soon as the doors open; they are the ones who are quite happy to squeeze into the last available space on a tube train. So, what will the *Sky Bet Supreme Hurdle* be like? It's not quite the *Coral Cup*, or *County Hurdle* or *Grand Annual*. The biggest field of runners for the *Supreme* in the past decade has been 19, and in five of the past ten years, the number of runners has been between 12 and 15. I don't think that's crowded enough to bring out the best in ***Appreciate It***. With that in mind combined with my general feeling that horses by **Jeremy** could have done better at the festival, I think ***Appreciate it*** is no dead cert for the *Supreme Hurdle* and I am willing to oppose him. Take note. Horses by **Jeremy** have lined up in festival races on 31 occasions. Almost 1 in 4 of them have managed a place dividend, but ***Our Conor*** is the only one to date to have secured a victory and that was back in 2013 in the *Triumph Hurdle*, ***Our Conor*** being the first of **Jeremy**'s progeny to line up in a festival event.

Here is a list of what is needed to win the *Supreme Hurdle*.

1) Last time out winners have won 21 of the past 24 renewals. ***(Appreciate It won the Grade 1 Chanelle Pharma Novice Hurdle on 7th February. This has been a great race in which to find the Supreme Winner. 3 of the past 4 winners of the Chanelle that went on to contest the Supreme were victorious in the Supreme – Champagne Fever (2013), Vautour (2014) and Klassical Dream (2019). Asterion Forlonge failed to make it 4 from 4 in last year's Supreme when finishing fourth)***
2) Forty-one horses aged 7 or older have contested the Supreme in the past 20 years, of which just 2 have won. ***(Appreciate It is aged 7)***
3) 10 of the past 12 winners had run 4-5 times over hurdles. ***(Appreciate It has run three times over hurdles, the same as last year's winner Shishkin)***
4) 11 of the past 19 winners of the Supreme had contested a Grade 1 novice hurdle earlier in the season, seven of whom won. ***(Appreciate It has won a Grade 1 novice hurdle)***
5) 12 of the past 13 winners have been in the first six in the market. ***(Appreciate It is the favourite)***
6) Trainer Willie Mullins has won the Supreme on six occasions from 43 runners. ***(Appreciate It is with Willie Mullins at Closutton)***
7) Only two of the past 18 winners were unbeaten over hurdles. ***(Appreciate It is unbeaten over hurdles)***
8) 12 of the past 16 winners had never raced beyond 2m2f under rules. ***(Appreciate It raced over 2m4f in a Leopardstown National Hunt Flat Race in December 2019)***

Appreciate It ticks several boxes, but there are a couple of concerns in the above list, such as age, number of runs, and so on. I think he will miss out to finish 2nd, 3rd or 4th.

Kalanisi (IRE)

Quote from the 2020 Cheltenham Festival Stallion Guide - "Punters need to take on board this clear delineation in results where horses by **Kalanisi** struggle to perform in any festival event when it is expected to travel further than 2m1f. The closest that the offspring have come to achieving a place position in the longer distance races was when ***Barters Hill*** (4/1) finished 4th in the 2016 *Albert Bartlett Novices' Hurdle*. Deeper analysis reveals that on the other eleven runs at 2m4f or further, one horse finished 7th, seven registered finishing positions between 9th and 14th and three were pulled up. These trends are hardly encouraging for the **Kalanisi** sired ***Darver Star***, ***Honest Vic***, ***Imperial Aura***, ***Kalashnikov*** and ***The Conditional*** who are possible entries in this year's festival races of 2½ miles or more".

Kalanisi (25-y-o)							
Race Format	*Miles*	*Won*	*Placed*	*Unplaced*	*Total*	*Win %*	*Place %*
Hurdles	About 2m	0	2	5	7	0%	29%
	About 2m 4f	0	0	5	5	0%	0%
	About 3m	0	0	1	1	0%	0%
Chases	About 2m	0	1	1	2	0%	50%
	About 2m 4f	1	0	3	4	25%	25%
	About 3m	1	0	4	5	20%	20%
	About 4m	0	0	0	0	-	-
Bumper	About 2m	1	0	4	5	20%	20%
Total	2011-2020	**3**	**3**	**23**	**29**	**10%**	**21%**

I like to believe that I am an open, transparent individual and if I make a mistake, then admit it, learn from it and move on. With that in mind, regrettably, I need to point readers in the direction of the quote at the top of the page. I'm not sure I could have been more wrong!

Last year, I engaged in a deep analysis of how horses by **Kalanisi** that had achieved a best Official Rating of 140 or greater had fared at Cheltenham when the horse was required to travel further than 2m1f. The analysis was for all races at the Cheltenham racecourse and not just races at the festival. In total, the study revealed that 14 horses had achieved a best OR of 140+ and that those 14 horses by **Kalanisi** had raced at Prestbury Park on 50 occasions. In races that fell within the 2m category, the progeny had won seven times in 27 appearances. For the record, the winners were ***Barizan***, ***Brain Power***, and five victories from top-rated ***Katchit***. In race events at the course of 2m1f or further, **Kalanisi** sired runners had recorded just one victory in 23 attempts. 16 of those 23 races fell within the 2½m distance range and a further seven in the 3m category. The only victory had been achieved by the *David Bridgwater* trained, ***The Conditional***, who had won the 3m1f *"Matchbook Betting Exchange" Handicap Chase* at Cheltenham on 26th October 2019.

Based on the above analysis, I was convinced that the offspring of **Kalanisi** struggled in any festival race beyond the minimum of around two miles, and the historical results at the festival supported this assertion. Confidently, I penned the words that you can read for yourselves in the quote at the top of this chapter. Let's focus on the last sentence and check on how these horses by **Kalanisi** fared at last year's festival meeting, *"These trends are hardly encouraging for the **Kalanisi** sired **Darver Star**, **Honest Vic**, **Imperial Aura**, **Kalashnikov** and **The Conditional** who are possible entries in this year's festival races of 2½ miles or more".*

Kalashnikov had been ruled out of the Cheltenham Festival in February, but the other four that are mentioned above, all took part in the 2020 Cheltenham Festival, with three of them contesting races on the opening day of the festival. In the 3rd race of the day, the *Ultima Handicap Chase*, ***The Conditional***, priced at 15/2, took no notice of the race distance of 3m1f, the soft ground, or my analysis, as he stayed on really well to beat my fancy, *Kildisart*, by a neck. In the next race, ***Darver Star*** pleased me by running a blinder in the 2m½f *Unibet Champion Hurdle*. I was pleased because I am quite a fan of **Kalanisi**'s offspring in races of around a distance of two miles. By the time we had got to Tuesday's 6th race, the *Northern Trust Company Novices' Handicap Chase* over a distance of 2m4f, I had been telling anyone who were still listening to me that ***The Conditional*** was a 'freak' when it came to **Kalanisi**'s progeny. *"He is the only one of the offspring (rated above 140) to win any race at Cheltenham beyond 2m1f"*, I said, as ***Imperial Aura*** by **Kalanisi**, the joint 4/1 favourite, lined up for the approaching 2m4f *Novices' Handicap Chase*. It was more egg on my face and turning out to be a great day for fans of **Kalanisi**, as ***Imperial Aura*** won comfortably, running on strongly in the soft ground up the Cheltenham Hill to complete the final 100 yards or so of 2½ miles. Wednesday's 3rd event would see the *Henry Daly* trained ***Honest Vic*** become the next of **Kalanisi**'s stock to face a distance beyond 2m1f. The seven-year-old was one of 25 runners for the ultra-competitive *Coral Cup Handicap Hurdle* that would be run over a distance of 2m5f and once again in soft ground. At 33/1, he had no chance, surely. ***Honest Vic*** just missed out on 4th place by a nose. The race report stating, *"He lacked the speed of a few around him ... he may want further in time"*.

There were six horses by **Kalanisi** entered at the 2020 Cheltenham Festival, and the two that remained would both be competing in Friday's 3m2½f *St. James's Place Foxhunter Challenge Cup Open Hunters' Chase*. Based on the results of **Kalanisi**'s previous four festival entries, and after a few pints of Guinness, I was half-way towards convincing myself that the two Hunter Chasers may be worth a saver. The eight-year-old mare, ***Kalabaloo*** was a 40/1 chance and finished in 8th place and the ten-year-old, ***Dylrow*** lined up at 50/1 and finished just behind his half-sister in 10th. There was to be no more success for **Kalanisi**'s stock at this festival – just the two wins, one placing and a 33/1 5th place, for which some bookmakers would have paid out, having offered five places.

Interestingly, all six horses by **Kalanisi** were making their Cheltenham Festival debuts which now means that twenty-three horses by **Kalanisi** have raced on 38 occasions at Cheltenham Festivals, of which four horses have recorded victories and five have registered a placing. **Kalanisi**'s festival statistics table at the top of this chapter does not include festivals that precede 2011 and so doesn't include nine races that took place over a decade ago, in which ***Barizan*** and ***Alaivan*** finished 2nd and 3rd respectively in the 2010 *JCB Triumph Hurdle*. More importantly, also omitted from **Kalanisi**'s festival statistics table are the two festival victories achieved by ***Katchit***. The first of **Kalanisi**'s offspring to appear at a Cheltenham Festival, ***Katchit*** won the 2007 *JCB Triumph Hurdle* at 11/2 and then followed up the following season by securing victory, at a price of 10/1, in the *Smurfit Kappa Champion Hurdle Challenge Trophy*.

If one takes into account the races that took place over a decade ago, where **Kalanisi**'s offspring were represented, the race category that is significantly impacted is the festival's two-mile hurdles, where horses by **Kalanisi** recorded two wins and two places from seven appearances. The remaining two outings of the nine runs involved a 14th place in a 2½m hurdle and an 11th place in a 3m hurdle. The table above shows a 29% place strike rate for 2m hurdle results, but if one includes the seven outings dating back before 2011, the table would read 2 wins, 4 places and 8 unplaced efforts, which would result in a win strike rate of 14% and a win & place strike rate of 43%. The overall total strike rates are also improved from 10% to 13% for the win strike rate and 21% to 26% for the win & place strike rate. Financially, had one placed a £10.00 each-way bet blind to level stakes on all 38 appearances by **Kalanisi**'s stock, the outcome would be a loss of £104.25. Some readers may have anticipated that the outcome of this staking plan would have led to profits, after all, 5 wins and 5 places from 38 outings is a very reasonable festival strike rate. The absence of a profit is largely down to the starting prices of **Kalanisi**'s offspring that win or place. All five victories have been achieved where the winner's odds have been 10/1 or less. As for the five placed efforts, the highest starting price has been 14/1. So far, none of the outsiders by **Kalanisi** that have raced at the festival meetings have troubled the judge with the exception of the previously mentioned ***Honest Vic***, who in finishing in 5th place at 33/1, is the only one of 19 **Kalanisi** sired horses, priced at 16/1 or bigger, to have achieved a top six finishing position.

It is interesting to note how the dynamics surrounding **Kalanisi**'s festival performances have changed due to the results achieved at the 2020 Cheltenham Festival. Prior to last year's meeting, horses by **Kalanisi** had recorded just one top six finish in 12 festival appearances in all races above 2m4f or further, a ratio of 1:12 for a top six finish. Following the 6 outings by **Kalanisi**'s offspring at last year's meeting, where 5 of the 6 **Kalanisi** sired runners were engaged in races of 2m4f or further, which resulted in two victories and a 5th place finish, the ratio for a top six finish now sits at better than 1:3. And the win ratio which didn't exist before last year's meeting is now a 1:8 or 1:9 chance! Four top six finishes, inclusive of two wins in 17 festival outings in races of 2m4f+ sounds a lot healthier than one top-six finish in 12 outings. As for races over the minimum distance of around two miles, as of last year, horses by **Kalanisi** had won 3 and been placed 4 times in 20 events, or a slightly better ratio than the progeny securing a win or place for one in every three appearances. If we include into the mix the sole 2020 two-mile festival result from **Kalanisi**'s stock, which is the 3rd place achieved by ***Darver Star*** in the *Champion Hurdle*, then the win and place strike rate has improved to closer to 2½:1 (3 wins, 5 places in 21 outings at two miles).

In looking at the spread of festival outings by **Kalanisi**'s offspring across the various race disciplines, with the exception of two-mile hurdle races where there is information from fourteen appearances, data in the other categories is sparse where the number of runs falls between 2 and 6 outings. With such limited data, it is somewhat difficult to make any concrete recommendations. If we take all race categories and continue to set aside the 2m hurdle events for the moment, **Kalanisi**'s festival contenders have consistently performed rather poorly with finishing positions to the back of the field, with the odd sporadic winner. I don't think anyone can say that they saw a result coming as a result of previous race performances. If we look at the race categories where there have been somewhere between 4-6 outings from **Kalanisi**'s stock, there is a consistent pattern of one good performance amongst duck eggs which can be observed here showing finishing positions per race category in chronological order: 2½m chases (PP01); 3m chases (0P100); Bumper (00001); 2½m hurdles (000005). Within these race categories, or specifically, in all race categories except for two-mile hurdle races, my suggestion to punters is that if they are keen on one or more of **Kalanisi**'s entries that are due to race in anything other than 2m hurdles, then take a look at the likely starting price of your fancy. If your selection is priced up at single figure odds, then you should probably back your judgement, as outside of two-mile hurdles, the starting prices of the three festival winners of ***Fayonagh***, ***The Conditional*** and ***Imperial Aura***, have all been below 8/1.

As for the festival's two-mile hurdle races, in previous editions of the Cheltenham Festival Stallion Guide, I have always highlighted that punters should take serious note of horses by **Kalanisi** that are entered into races of this discipline. And my advice still stands. In 14 festival appearances within 2m hurdle contests, **Kalanisi**'s offspring have registered two victories and four place dividends. As for the eight others that didn't reward each-way wagers, only one of them has finished outside the top ten, which is an additional pointer to the stock's preference for racing in Cheltenham's 2m hurdle events.

Kalanisi (IRE) – Progeny with Official Rating of 135+

Horses by this sire with an Official Rating of 135 or greater on 9th February 2021. Horses registered with the Irish Horseracing Regulatory Board (I.H.R.B) are shown in *italics*.

				Official Ratings as of 9th February 2021		
Sire	***Horse***	***Age***	***Sex***	***Hurdles***	***Chase***	***Trainer***
Kalanisi	And The New	10	g	140		Johnny Farrelly
Kalanisi	Brain Power	10	g	147		Nicky Henderson
Kalanisi	*Cask Mate*	*8*	*g*	*139*		*Noel Meade*
Kalanisi	*Darver Star*	*9*	*g*		*154*	*Gavin Cromwell*
Kalanisi	Honest Vic	8	g	150		Henry Daly
Kalanisi	Imperial Aura	8	g		163	Kim Bailey
Kalanisi	Kalashnikov	8	g	153	159	Amy Murphy
Kalanisi	The Conditional	9	g		149	David Bridgwater

Commentary on selected potential entries for 2021 Festival

Imperial Aura – Ryanair Chase 2m5f (2:50 Thursday 18th March)

Even if I found information persuading me that horses by **Kalanisi** struggle around Cheltenham at anything above two miles, ***Imperial Aura***, ***The Conditional*** and ***Honest Vic*** all made me eat my words at last year's meeting. ***Imperial Aura*** has been around Cheltenham's 2½ miles and has won. So, he's proven he can handle the distance, so let's look at his chances in the *Ryanair* for which at the time of writing, he can be backed at 6/1.

1) Second season chasers have won 8 of the 16 renewals of the Ryanair. ***(Imperial Aura is a second season chaser)***
2) 8 of the past 10 winners had a win percentage strike rate of between 44% and 67%. ***(Imperial Aura has a win strike rate percentage of 57%)***
3) In the 13 renewals since the Ryanair was upgraded to Grade 1 status, there have only been three winners at prices of 13/2 of bigger. ***(At the time of writing, Imperial Aura is priced at 6/1)***
4) Since becoming a Grade 1, all 13 winners had all previously run at the festival, five of whom were victorious. ***(Imperial Aura scores on both counts)***
5) Since becoming a Grade 1, 10 of the 13 winners had already won at the course (not necessarily at the festival). 8 of those winners succeeded in a novice chase. ***(Imperial Aura won the Northern Trust Company Novices' Handicap Chase at the 2020 Cheltenham Festival)***
6) The past 8 winners had all completed between 2 and 4 races during the season. ***(Imperial Aura has had three outings this season)***

All the above are positive signals for ***Imperial Aura***, but trainer *Kim Bailey* may be concerned about the list below:

1) 5 of the past 10 winners had contested between 8 and 11 chases. ***(At the time of writing, Imperial Aura has had 7 outings)***
2) 7 of the past 11 winners arrived at the Ryanair on the back of a 1st or 2nd placing in Grade 1 company. ***(Imperial Aura has yet to contest a Grade 1 event)***
3) Since the Ryanair was upgraded to Grade 1 status in 2008, 10 of the 13 winners had already won a Grade 1 chase. ***(Imperial Aura has yet to contest a Grade 1 event)***

4) French bred horses have won the past seven Ryanair chases from exactly 50% representation. ***(Imperial Aura is Irish bred)***
5) 9 of the past 10 winners had an Official Rating of 165 or greater. ***(Imperial Aura's OR is 163)***
6) In the past decade, 9 of the 10 winners had achieved a Racing Post Rating (RPR) during the season of 169 or greater. ***(Imperial Aura has achieved 167 in winning a Grade 2 Chase at Ascot in November)***

Looking down the second list, one can't help but believe that ***Imperial Aura*** may be a touch below what is required to win this race. The horse is currently rated below the usual mark for a *Ryanair* winner and the lack of race in Group 1 company is a big concern in my view. Having said that, I do believe that the *Ryanair* is of lower quality this year, so it wouldn't surprise me if a few of those trends in the second list may be broken.

This may be a race that I leave alone.

Kapgarde (FR)

Quote from the 2020 Cheltenham Festival Stallion Guide - "As for the two youngsters of ***A Plus Tard*** and ***Fakir D'Oudairies***, if either can win, I have a slight preference for ***A Plus Tard***. I fear, however, that 2020 may be a year too soon for these two outstanding horses and that they will lose out in a competitive battle in their respective races to more experienced rivals. I can see at least one of them, if not both, finishing in the top three but for either of them to provide **Kapgarde** supporters with a second festival victory may just be out of reach. For this festival anyway."

Kapgarde (22-y-o)							
Race Format	*Miles*	*Won*	*Placed*	*Unplaced*	*Total*	*Win %*	*Place %*
Hurdles	About 2m	0	3	9	12	0%	25%
	About 2m 4f	0	1	8	9	0%	11%
	About 3m	0	1	2	3	0%	33%
Chases	About 2m	0	1	4	5	0%	20%
	About 2m 4f	1	1	7	9	11%	22%
	About 3m	0	0	4	4	0%	0%
	About 4m	0	0	2	2	0%	0%
Bumper	About 2m	0	0	2	2	0%	0%
Total	**2011-2020**	**1**	**7**	**38**	**46**	**2%**	**17%**

As a four-year-old, ***Mr Thriller*** became the first of **Kapgarde**'s progeny to take part at a Cheltenham Festival, and it wasn't too bad a run from the 14/1 chance, finishing in 6th place in the *Fred Winter Juvenile Novices' Handicap Hurdle*. The horse, trained by *David Pipe*, returned to Prestbury Park the following season to race over a mile further in the *Pertemps Handicap Hurdle Final*. This time, ***Mr Thriller*** struggled, trailing home at odds of 33/1 to finish in 15th place. Since those two runs by ***Mr Thriller***, a further 23 horses by **Kapgarde** have tackled the Cheltenham track in mid-March, some with just a single appearance to their name, whilst others, like ***Mr Thriller*** have raced at the track more than once. In total, 24 **Kapgarde** sired horses have appeared at the Cheltenham Festival, making a total of 48 appearances. All bar the first two of ***Mr Thriller***'s three festival outings have taken place in the past decade.

Of those 24 horses by **Kapgarde** that have competed at the festival, only one of them, ***A Plus Tard***, has managed to reward bets on more than one occasion, providing the stallion's only Cheltenham Festival winner in 2019 before returning at last year's meeting to reward backers with a 3rd place dividend. A further six of the offspring have managed to place at the festival. All of them just once. The figures in the table at the top of the page provide a disappointing return for **Kapgarde** supporters, a mediocre win & place strike rate of 17%. And the sole victory providing a dismal 2% win-rate. Had one placed a £10.00 each way bet on all 48 appearances from **Kapgarde**'s progeny, the outcome would be a significant loss of £585.50.

The figures above may surprise some Cheltenham festival devotees, as **Kapgarde** is a highly respected stallion, and his current crop of national hunt racehorses boast some notable names that are in their prime as well as some promising youngsters who will hope to make an impact at both this year's festival and those that follow. With such quality amongst the ranks, it is only a matter of time before there are additions to the sole festival victory by ***A Plus Tard***, but that said, I still consider that **Kapgarde**'s offspring aren't at their best at Cheltenham's left-handed, galloping, undulating and testing track. Not only have horses by **Kapgarde** found it challenging to win races at the Cheltenham Festival, but they have found it difficult to win at any time, especially at the longer distances.

As of 24th January 2021, **Kapgarde**'s progeny had won 282 races in 1976 jump racing appearances in Great Britain, which equates to a pretty good win strike rate of 14.3%. Over the two disciplines of hurdles and chases, the percentage win rates are slightly in favour of chases where 829 runs resulted in 133 victories. Over hurdles, horses by **Kapgarde** have won 120 races in 975 appearances. The remaining 29 wins came from 172 National Hunt Flat runs. Although the results show, without doubt, that **Kapgarde** is a very good stallion for producing National Hunt racehorses, on the basis that only seven of those 282 wins happened at Cheltenham, one can certainly doubt the progeny's suitability to the left-handed undulating ups and downs of Prestbury Park. Listed below, with the most recent first, are those seven victories that have occurred at Cheltenham's racecourse:

Date	Horse	Age	Best OR	Odds	Dist	Race event
12/03/19	A Plus Tard	5	170	5/1 F	2m4f	Close Brothers Novices' Handicap Chase (Listed Race)
26/01/19	Fakir D'oudairies	4	160	4/1	2m1f	JCB Triumph Trial Juvenile Hurdle (Grade 2)
01/01/17	Cap Soleil	4	136	11/8 F	1m6f	EBF Stallions & Cheltenham Pony Club (NHF Listed Race)
15/11/15	Garde La Victoire	6	158	8/15 F	2m	Racing Post Arkle Trophy Trial Novices' Chase (Grade 2)
16/11/14	Garde La Victoire	5	158	10/1	2m½f	StanJames.com Greatwood Handicap Hurdle (Grade 3)
16/04/14	Garde La Victoire	5	158	13/8 F	2m4½f	Citipost Novices' Hurdle
12/11/11	Edgardo Sol	4	157	6/1	2m½f	Ultima Business Solutions Novices' Handicap Hurdle

The data within the above table is enlightening. It is rather interesting to note that all victories have been achieved when these **Kapgarde** sired runners were in their early years showing that 6 of the 7 wins occurred when the runners were either four or five years old and where 5 of the 7 victories took place in novice events. If we ignore the only mare of the seven, ***Cap Soleil***, who was victorious in a 1m6f National Hunt Flat Race, the other six wins were achieved by four high quality geldings that all sit within the all-time top 10 of **Kapgarde**'s stock based on Official Ratings. All four winners performed at a best Official Rating (OR) of 157 or greater within their racing careers.

Five of these course wins were won over the minimum distance of around two miles, three of them in hurdle events, one over fences and one success in a 14-furlong National Hunt Flat race. The remaining two victories were recorded over around 2m4f, one being a chase and the other over hurdles. Every **Kapgarde** sired Cheltenham course winner was towards the front of the betting market at prices of 10/1 or shorter, inclusive of four favourites.

A considerable amount of information is presented within the above table which I suggest provides punters with invaluable insights to help them determine whether or not supporting a festival entry by **Kapgarde** is wise. As a starting point, the data strongly suggests that **Kapgarde**'s younger horses that take part at the Cheltenham Festival are more likely than their older half-siblings to reward punters' each-way bets. Of the seven horses by **Kapgarde** that have, to date, recorded the seven places and one victory at festival meetings, five of them were aged five or younger when they achieved the feat. There were four runners aged five, these being ***A Plus Tard***, winner of the 2019 *Close Brothers Novices' Handicap Chase*; ***Fakir D'oudairies***, runner-up in the 2020 *Racing Post Arkle Challenge Trophy*; ***Cap Soleil***, runner-up in the 2018 *Trull House Stud Mares' Novices' Hurdle*; and ***Edgardo Sol***, runner-up in the 2012 *Vincent O'Brien County Handicap Hurdle*. The 4yo ***Style De Garde*** was also a runner-up when taking part in the *Boodles Fred Winter Juvenile Handicap Hurdle* in 2018. Youth appears to be a key factor for this stallion's offspring to perform at Cheltenham. Six of the seven course winners as shown in the above table (including ***A Plus Tard***'s win at the festival) were aged five or younger. No horse by **Kapgarde** aged older than six has ever won at Prestbury Park and only two have placed at the

Cheltenham Festival, these being the 7yo ***Cuneo*** who finished 4th in the *Pertemps Network Final Handicap Hurdle* and the 8yo ***Ubak*** who was placed 3rd in the 2016 *Coral Cup*. Presented with the above trends, if I have a liking for one of **Kapgarde**'s festival entries, although I may take a chance on one of the younger runners, I will have serious reservations about investing in any horse by **Kapgarde** that is aged seven or older.

Having said that I prefer **Kapgarde**'s younger offspring at Cheltenham Festivals, readers may therefore be slightly perplexed by my quote at the top of this chapter where I was concerned that two highly talented horses in the shape of ***A Plus Tard*** and ***Fakir D'oudairies*** may lose out to more experienced rivals in their respective races. As good as both horses are, my concerns were well-founded, as in my view, both horses were entered in races where their youth would be a disadvantage. Eleven lined up in the *Racing Post Arkle Challenge Trophy Novices' Chase*, but only one was aged five, ***Fakir D'oudairies***. Although two-five-olds had won the *Arkle* this century, both *Well Chief* in 2004 and *Voy Por Ustedes* in 2006 had the benefit of a 5yo age allowance. If ***Fakir D'Oudairies*** had won last season, he would have been the first five-year-old to win the event at level weights. As it was, I consider the 3/1 chance put in an outstanding performance to finish 18 lengths ahead of the 3rd placed horse and just a couple of lengths off the winner, *Put The Kettle On*.

A Plus Tard (7/4 favourite) and *Min* (2/1) were the two front runners for the *Ryanair Chase*. *Min* had experience on his side, being aged nine, whereas the **Kapgarde** bred ***A Plus Tard*** was three years younger, aged six, and the youngest in the race. Like ***Fakir D'oudairies***, he also lost out to the more experienced rival, finishing in 3rd place, behind winner *Min* and the 7yo *Saint Calvados* who finished second. ***A Plus Tard*** did run creditably without a doubt, but I still think that winning the *Ryanair* was a tough ask. Only once has a 6-year-old been victorious, *Taranis* in 2007, which was the year before the race was upgraded to Grade 1 status.

Based upon the results of **Kapgarde**'s offspring at the Cheltenham Festival combined with the record of the seven course winners, not only should punters be wary of the stallion's older festival entries, but also the distance in which the horse by **Kapgarde** is expected to travel. On the seven occasions in which **Kapgarde**'s stock have won at Prestbury Park, only twice has the winner travelled more than 2m1f. Similarly, the record at the Cheltenham Festival shows that four of offspring have finished runner-up in races that are within the 2m race category, consisting of three events over hurdles, and ***Fakir D'oudairies***' 2nd placing in the *Arkle*. The two runs by ***A Plus Tard*** at the festival where he secured both a win and place were both in contests around 2½ miles, and ***Ubak*** registered his placing in the 2m5f *Coral Cup*. No horse by **Kapgarde** has ever won at Cheltenham when asked to travel over 2m4½f and when it comes to the nine festival appearances by the offspring that have tackled contests at three miles or more, none have managed to finish in the first three places, the best performance coming from *Cuneo* when claiming a 4th pace dividend in the *Pertemps Network Final Handicap Hurdle*. The evidence above is strong enough for me to have severe doubts about supporting any horse by **Kapgarde** that is tasked with racing in a festival event at a distance of three miles or more. Indeed, although it would appear that horses by **Kapgarde** can perform in races of around two and a half miles, the historical trends point to the offspring being best suited to races at around two miles.

In summary, the evidence suggests that horses by **Kapgarde** are not best suited to the testing track and undulations of Cheltenham. That said, horses of top quality should be able to win anywhere, and **Kapgarde** has, without doubt, some highly talented racehorses amongst his current stock, two of which, as highlighted, put in outstanding performances at last year's festival. The question that punters must ask themselves is whether their **Kapgarde** sired fancy has the race conditions and necessary quality to overcome the evidence which points to their selection being better suited to a different type of track than that at Cheltenham. And stealing a line from those Marks & Spencer adverts, we should never lose sight of the fact that this *"isn't just any old Cheltenham Meeting, this is a Cheltenham Festival meeting"*.

For the 2021 Festival, I will be on the look-out for top quality entries by **Kapgarde**. Whether I back them or not? Well, that depends. If the horse is highly rated, young and running in a race over two miles, or at a stretch, 2½ miles, then yes, I may well take a chance. On the other hand, will I place a bet on an 8yo **Kapgarde** representative that is all the rage in the betting market when lining up in one of the festival's three-mile chases? I wouldn't touch it with a barge pole.

Kapgarde (FR) – Progeny with Official Rating of 135+

Horses by this sire with an Official Rating of 135 or greater on 9th February 2021. Horses registered with the Irish Horseracing Regulatory Board (I.H.R.B) are shown in *italics*.

				Official Ratings as of 9th February 2021		
Sire	**Horse**	**Age**	**Sex**	**Hurdles**	**Chase**	**Trainer**
Kapgarde	*A Plus Tard*	*7*	*g*		*170*	*Henry de Bromhead*
Kapgarde	Almazhar Garde	6	g		135	Charlie Longsdon
Kapgarde	Clan Des Obeaux	9	g		169	Paul Nicholls
Kapgarde	Dolos	8	g		159	Paul Nicholls
Kapgarde	*Fakir D'oudairies*	*6*	*g*		*162*	*Joseph Patrick O'Brien*
Kapgarde	Flic Ou Voyou	7	g	135		Paul Nicholls
Kapgarde	Garde La Victoire	12	g		140	Tom George
Kapgarde	Kapcorse	8	g		135	Paul Nicholls
Kapgarde	*Sizing Pottsie*	*7*	*g*		*156*	*Mrs John Harrington*
Kapgarde	Solo	5	g	141		Paul Nicholls
Kapgarde	The Wolf	7	g		140	Olly Murphy

Commentary on selected potential entries for 2021 Festival

A Plus Tard – Wellchild Cheltenham Gold Cup 3m2½f (3.30 Friday 19th March)

If you look down all the form, trends and signals that will point you to a *Gold Cup* winner, you will find that ***A Plus Tard*** scores highly, ticking box after box. He is 2nd favourite to *Al Boum Photo* and rightly so. Looking through all the challengers, ***A Plus Tard*** has managed to have a pretty good preparation for the big day and the only entry that could say theirs has gone better is almost certainly the two-time champion himself, *Al Boum Photo*.

As good as ***A Plus Tard*** is, and I do believe he is a very talented racehorse, I have a serious worry that he is by **Kapgarde**. Two years ago, ***Clan Des Obeaux***, who is also by **Kapgarde**, lined up in the 2019 *Gold Cup* as the 5/1 second favourite. I wrote 2-3 pages about his chances and opposed him advising punters that he wouldn't win. He finished 5th, a good performance really, some 11 lengths behind *Al Boum Photo* who claimed the first of his *Gold Cup* victories. ***Clan Des Obeaux*** was rated 173 in that *Gold Cup*, whilst ***A Plus Tard*** is currently rated at 170 (an Irish Rating), so there isn't much between them, although I feel that ***A Plus Tard*** at seven years of age has some more improvement in him.

A Plus Tard was the favourite for last year's *Ryanair* which covers a distance of 2m5f but could only finish in 3rd place. He engaged in that race as a 6yo and that wouldn't have helped his chances. Only one horse in the past 10 years has gone onto win the *Gold Cup* having competed in the previous year's *Ryanair*. That horse was *Don Cossack* who also favourite and also finished in 3rd place in the 2015 *Ryanair* before winning the *Gold Cup* in 2016, aged 9.

The stark fact is this. No horse by **Kapgarde** has ever won at Cheltenham beyond a distance of 2m4½ furlongs, and I'm not talking about winning beyond that distance at the festival, I'm talking about any Cheltenham meeting all year round. I think it is asking a lot of ***A Plus Tard***, aged 7, and in the toughest race that he is ever likely to be involved in, to accomplish something that none of his siblings has ever achieved. If trainer *Henry De Bromhead* can get the best out of ***A Plus Tard***, win the *Gold Cup*, and have a **Kapgarde** bred horse win beyond three miles at Prestbury Park for the very first time, then I would say that would be a tremendous training accomplishment.

Footnote:

For further insight to the *Wellchild Cheltenham Gold Cup*, read the commentary on ***Minella Indo*** by **Beat Hollow**.

Kayf Tara (GB)

Quote from the 2020 Cheltenham Festival Stallion Guide - "***Thyme Hill*** is going into this race most closely matched with the record of *Bobs Worth* before he won this event in 2011. And over the next two years, remember, *Bobs Worth* went on to win the *RSA Insurance Novices' Chase* followed by the *Cheltenham Gold Cup*. I seriously question whether ***Thyme Hill*** will be able to reach the dizzy heights of success that was achieved by *Bobs Worth* and, lest we forget, **Kayf Tara**'s stock has failed to achieve a top three finish in the *Albert Bartlett* from six attempts. ***Thyme Hill***'s record is clean, neat and tidy. 3 wins out of 3 in three high quality Graded Hurdle events. Be that as it may, on Friday 13th March 2020, I shall be opposing ***Thyme Hill***."

Kayf Tara (27-y-o)							
Race Format	*Miles*	*Won*	*Placed*	*Unplaced*	*Total*	*Win %*	*Place %*
Hurdles	About 2m	0	0	14	14	0%	0%
	About 2m 4f	0	2	16	18	0%	11%
	About 3m	1	2	16	19	5%	16%
Chases	About 2m	1	2	12	15	7%	20%
	About 2m 4f	0	0	14	14	0%	0%
	About 3m	3	5	22	30	10%	27%
	About 4m	0	1	10	11	0%	9%
Bumper	About 2m	1	1	3	5	20%	40%
Total	2011-2020	**6**	**13**	**107**	**126**	**5%**	**15%**

Kayf Tara won 2/3rds of his 15 races on the flat which included two victories apiece in Ascot's *Gold Cup* and the *Irish St Leger*. After his second *Gold Cup* success for *Godolphin* on 22nd June 2000, he was retired and sent to *Overbury Stud*, where he has stood for 20 seasons, covering his first book of mares amid the foot and mouth crisis of 2001, which Cheltenham Festival devotees will recall, led to the abandonment of the 2001 Cheltenham Festival. In July of 2020, *Simon Sweeting, Overbury Stud* Manager, announced that **Kayf Tara** had been retired from stud duties due to declining fertility. He added that the son of *Sadler's Wells* was otherwise in tremendous health and would live out his days at the Gloucestershire Farm. Albeit that **Kayf Tara**'s offspring have largely underperformed at Cheltenham Festivals, this sire has nevertheless established himself as one of the best national hunt stallions around, being crowned Britain's champion jumps stallion on eleven occasions. Although **Kayf Tara** may no longer be in service, we will continue to see his offspring at Cheltenham Festivals for many years to come.

Nine horses by **Kayf Tara** have recorded a best Official Rating of 160 or more and when combined together, they have registered three Cheltenham Festival victories and four place positions. The top-rated nine of **Kayf Tara**'s stock is ***Thistlecrack*** at 174, ***Special Tiara*** (168), ***Planet Of Sound*** (166), ***Identity Thief*** (165), ***Edwulf*** (165), ***Tea For Two*** (164), ***Secret Investor*** (162), ***Blaklion*** (161) and ***Thyme Hill*** (160). Further down the Official Ratings can be found a further four of the offspring that rewarded festival wagers at least twice during their racing careers, these being ***Ballyandy*** (157), ***Cantlow*** (152), ***The Package*** (147) and ***Alfie Sherrin*** (144). This quartet's achievement of a combined total of 3 wins and 7 places represents 40% of the win and place results recorded by **Kayf Tara**'s festival entries.

Kayf Tara has been represented at Cheltenham Festivals on 146 occasions, of which 126 runs have taken place within the past decade. The 27-year-old has sired 7 Cheltenham Festival winners, and all seven have been first past the post at a festival just once. Taking all 146 runs into account, the win and place strike rate is 16%, effectively a win or place for one in every six runs. I have already highlighted my view that the progeny of **Kayf Tara** has underperformed at Cheltenham Festivals, and this can be seen by analysing the financial consequences of supporting the stallion's festival representatives. Placing a £10.00 each way bet on all 146 appearances from **Kayf Tara**'s stock calculates into a whopping loss of £1,165.75.

If one looks at the table of statistics at the top of this chapter, punters may well think about being more focused in their betting fancies and determine that a better strategy is to target horses by **Kayf Tara** that are entered in the festival's chase events within the 2m and 3m categories. After all, in the 2m chase contests, a win and place strike rate of 20% equates to a return for 1 in every 5 bets whilst in the 3m chases, one may anticipate a winning bet for better than 1 in 4 races. Unfortunately, it is a flawed strategy because a trio of **Kayf Tara**'s offspring have had an overbearing influence on generating these higher strike rates. In the 33 chase contests over three miles (30 this decade), 66% of the win and place results (3 festival victories and 6 place dividends) have been achieved by two horses highlighted earlier, these being ***The Package*** who registered one victory and three place positions and ***Alfie Sherrin*** who delivered a win and a place. Take these two out, and the 3m chase win & place strike rate drops from 27% to 13%.

As for the win and two places showing in the table for the 2m chase contests, all three results were produced by ***Special Tiara*** in the *Queen Mother Champion Chase*. Incidentally, although it was nice to see ***Special Tiara*** win the contest in 2017 at the 4th attempt, and at the age of 10; with an official rating of 159, he was the lowest rated winner of this prestigious prize this century (Note: Official Rating figures were absent for *Moscow Flyer* in 2003 and 2005, and *Newmill* in 2006). The only other horse by **Kayf Tara** to register a place position in a festival 2m chase event happened over a decade ago when ***Planet Of Sound*** finished in 3rd place in the 2009 *Irish Independent Arkle Challenge Trophy.* **Kayf Tara**'s offspring have made 17 appearances in the festival's two-mile chases, of which 15 have taken place within the past ten years. If we take out the 5 runs by ***Special Tiara***, the 2m chase win & place strike rate drops from 24% to 8%.

Although **Kayf Tara** has been an outstanding National Hunt Stallion, the record of his stock at the Cheltenham Festival, the pinnacle of National Hunt racing, has in the main been disappointing. Profitable Cheltenham Festivals have been hard to find for **Kayf Tara** supporters. Even in 2016, when **Kayf Tara**'s runners broke previous festival trends, anyone backing the stock blind would have made a loss. 2016 was the year in which we witnessed, not just the first, but the first three Grade 1 festival winners from this stallion's offspring. ***Ballyandy*** won the *Weatherbys Champion Bumper* at 5/1; ***Blaklion*** (8/1) won the *RSA Chase*; and ***Thistlecrack*** (Evens favourite) won the *Ryanair World Hurdle.* In 2016, **Kayf Tara** had been rather mob-handed with 25 entries of his stock competing across the festival's total of 28 races, and with just one 3rd placing by ***Special Tiara*** at 16/1 to add to the three victories, staking £10.00 each way on all 25 runners would have delivered a loss of £230.00. Only twice in the past 15 years, in 2009 and 2012, has backing **Kayf Tara**'s festival runners blind to level stakes delivered a profit. To a £10.00 each-way stake, backing all **Kayf Tara**'s runners would have resulted in profits of £110.00 in 2009 and £92.50 in 2012.

It is also interesting to note that in all 146 festival runs by this sire's offspring, only on 10 occasions has a horse by **Kayf Tara** registered a 1st or 2nd placing. Of the seventeen festival place dividends secured by the progeny, (of which 13 have occurred in the past decade), fourteen were achieved by the **Kayf Tara** sired runner registering 3rd or 4th finishing positions. Based on these results, it would be difficult to point to **Kayf Tara** somehow being 'unlucky' in registering just 7 festival victories, with an argument suggesting that the stock has suffered some narrow defeats with numerous runner-up spots. On the contrary, when one of **Kayf Tara**'s representatives secures a place position at a festival, it is usually by virtue of "scraping home" into a 3rd or 4th place dividend.

Eight of **Kayf Tara**'s offspring competed at the 2020 Cheltenham Festival, of which none were able to reward each-way wagers and just two entries managed to register top six placings. The highest placed finisher was ***Thyme Hill*** who was sent off the 4/1 favourite in Friday's *Albert Bartlett Novices' Hurdle*. As referenced in the quote at the top of this chapter, I had opposed ***Thyme Hill*** and wrote a couple of paragraphs in last year's Guide explaining my reasons. Although ***Thyme Hill*** ran well, he didn't have the pace of the front three of *Monkfish*, *Latest Exhibition* and *Fury Road*, all of whom were trained in Ireland. ***Thyme Hill***, the star of *Philip Hobbs' Withycombe* stable, could only finish in 4th place, beaten by 1½ lengths. The other encouraging performance from **Kayf Tara**'s offspring at the 2020 Cheltenham Festival came from ***Edwardstone*** (25/1) who finished in 6th position in the festival's opener, the *Sky Bet Supreme Novices' Hurdle*.

When it comes to looking at the festival entries in early March, I typically ignore horses by **Kayf Tara**. That said, I did advise in last year's Guide, that if I was pressed to come up with some races where a horse by **Kayf Tara** may pop up and reward each-way bets, then I would pick out the *Weatherbys Champion Bumper* followed by the three-mile hurdle events. Looking at the table at the top of this chapter, it is the *Champion Bumper* that shows the best set of statistics. There have been six **Kayf Tara** bred contenders in Cheltenham's National Hunt Flat Race, of which five have appeared in the past decade. The very first participant in this event was the *Gary Moore* trained, ***Megastar*** (25/1) who put in a solid enough performance when registering a 5th place finish in the 2010 renewal, some 18 lengths behind the shock 40/1 winner that was *Cue Card*, who as we all know, went onto considerable further success. Of the other five contenders, it makes sense to ignore the two 'also-ran' outsiders of ***Kayf Moss*** (150/1) in 2013 and ***Spirit of Kayf*** (100/1) in 2016, and instead concentrate on the trio that were shorter in the betting. Competing alongside ***Spirit of Kayf*** in the 2016 renewal was ***Ballyandy*** (5/1), trained by *Nigel Twiston-Davies*, who just got the better of *Battleford* by the shortest of margins, to win by a nose. Three years later, the aforementioned ***Thyme Hill*** secured a 3rd place position at a price of 20/1, beaten by *Envoi Allen* who at this year's festival, is sure to be one of the most popular banker bets. The other *Bumper* competitor by **Kayf Tara** was ***Value At Risk*** (22/1) who had a troubled run before finished in 13th spot in 2014.

As for the three-mile hurdle contests, **Kayf Tara** has been represented on 23 occasions, 19 of which have taken place in the past decade as shown in the table. The stand-out performance, and indeed the horse that has achieved the highest rating of any **Kayf Tara** bred racehorse is ***Thistlecrack***, owned by *John* and *Heather Snook*, who following his authoritative win in the 2016 *Ryanair World Hurdle* was raised 6lb to an Official Rating of 174. The only other horse by **Kayf Tara** to contend the *Stayers Hurdle* is ***Lieutenant Colonel*** who was disappointing in both his performances in 2015 and 2016. In the other non-handicap three-mile hurdle, the *Albert Bartlett Novices' Hurdle*, **Kayf Tara**'s offspring have competed on seven occasions without success, although three runners have managed to finish just outside the places; ***Value At Risk*** finishing in 5th at 8/1 in the 2015 contest; ***Constantine Bay*** (12/1) who was placed 4th in 2017; and ***Thyme Hill*** (4/1 favourite) who also registered a 4th place finish in 2020.

In my view, the most likely chance of reward for **Kayf Tara**'s stock in a long-distance hurdle will arrive in the festival's only three-mile handicap hurdle, the *Pertemps Network Final*. In 13 appearances in this race, the offspring have registered 5 top six finishes, including a win with ***Kayf Aramis*** at 16/1 in 2009, a runner-up with ***Glenloe*** (9/2 fav) in 2018, and a third place with ***Cantlow*** at 33/1 in 2012. Had one staked £10.00 each way blind on all 13 contenders in this race, the outcome would be a profit of £73.75.

It is a rare occurrence for **Kayf Tara**'s offspring to be battling it out with a rival up the Cheltenham Hill in an attempt to claim a festival victory. Having had 146 opportunities, only on ten occasions has a horse by **Kayf Tara** recorded a 1st or 2nd place at Cheltenham Festival meetings. With that in mind, my recommendation is to avoid horses by **Kayf Tara** in your festival betting selections. That said, if you are really tempted by one of the sire's progeny, then perhaps you may have a whiff of a chance if your fancy is lining up in a long distance 3m hurdle event or the *Weatherbys Champion Bumper*. These contests aside, my advice is leave well alone!

Kayf Tara (GB) – Progeny with Official Rating of 135+

Horses by this sire with an Official Rating of 135 or greater on 9th February 2021. Horses registered with the Irish Horseracing Regulatory Board (I.H.R.B) are shown in *italics*.

				Official Ratings as of 9th February 2021		
Sire	***Horse***	***Age***	***Sex***	***Hurdles***	***Chase***	***Trainer***
Kayf Tara	Admiral's Secret	10	g		141	Victor Dartnall
Kayf Tara	*All The Answers*	*10*	*g*		*140*	*Aidan Anthony Howard*
Kayf Tara	Ballyandy	10	g	154		Nigel Twiston-Davies
Kayf Tara	Blaklion	12	g		145	Dan Skelton
Kayf Tara	Dashing Perk	10	g		135	Dr Richard Newland
Kayf Tara	Edwardstone	7	g	146	146	Alan King
Kayf Tara	*Internal Transfer*	*10*	*g*	*110*	*135*	*E. McNamara*
Kayf Tara	Master Tommytucke	10	g		159	Paul Nicholls
Kayf Tara	No Comment	10	g	138		Philip Hobbs
Kayf Tara	Porlock Bay	10	g		137	Will Biddick
Kayf Tara	Relentless Dreamer	12	g		137	Rebecca Curtis
Kayf Tara	Secret Investor	9	g		162	Paul Nicholls
Kayf Tara	Southfield Harvest	7	g	135		Paul Nicholls
Kayf Tara	*The Long Mile*	*7*	*g*		*145*	*J.P.Dempsey*
Kayf Tara	Thyme Hill	7	g	162		Philip Hobbs
Kayf Tara	Yalltari	10	g		135	Venetia Williams

King's Theatre (IRE)

Quote from the 2020 Cheltenham Festival Stallion Guide - *"As favourite for the RSA Insurance Novices' Chase,* it is only right that the final piece in this chapter is about ***Champ***. My prediction? He will run well and be with the leaders as they come into the straight. But he won't win. A second or third place, I think. And in an exciting race."

King's Theatre (Died as a 20-y-o in 2011)							
Race Format	*Miles*	**Won**	**Placed**	**Unplaced**	**Total**	**Win %**	**Place %**
Hurdles	About 2m	0	4	12	16	0%	25%
	About 2m 4f	4	3	24	31	13%	23%
	About 3m	2	3	16	21	10%	24%
Chases	About 2m	1	2	7	10	10%	30%
	About 2m 4f	2	4	18	24	8%	25%
	About 3m	2	3	44	49	4%	10%
	About 4m	2	0	11	13	15%	15%
Bumper	About 2m	0	2	5	7	0%	29%
Total	2011-2020	**13**	**21**	**137**	**171**	**8%**	**20%**

I was wrong. In last year's Guide, I advised that ***Champ*** would not secure victory in the Grade 1 *RSA Insurance Novices' Chase*. To be fair, clearing the last, he looked to have little opportunity of adding to the sixteen festival victories that have been achieved by the stock of **King's Theatre**. I wasn't the only one who believed his chance had gone – he was trading at 720/1 on the betting exchanges. But *Barry Geraghty* rallied ***Champ*** to finish with a rattle, making up eight lengths as *Minella Indo* and *Allaho* both faltered, and going away at the end to win by a length. *Barry Geraghty* announced his retirement from the saddle on July 4th last year and as of that date, he was the fourth most successful British and Irish jump jockey with 1920 winners. Being the second most successful jockey of all time at the Cheltenham Festival, amassing 43 winners in total, he will be sorely missed by festival devotees. *Barry Geraghty* is a super jockey and has enjoyed a great career and he will live in our memories forever, and not just because of his barnstorming finish on ***Champ*** last year.

The very first horse by **King's Theatre** to race in a three-mile chase event at a Cheltenham Festival was ridden by another famous jockey, the powerhouse that was *AP McCoy*. And it was another race in which the **King's Theatre** bred runner needed all the assistance possible from the rider to claim an unlikely victory. Many consider ***Wichita Lineman***'s success in the 2009 *William Hill Trophy Handicap Chase* (now named the *Ultima Handicap Chase*) to be *AP McCoy*'s best ever ride. Throughout the race, ***Wichita Lineman*** ran lazily and made a series of errors at the fences, but his jockey never gave up galvanising his mount to just get up on the line to beat *Maljimar*, who looked the most likeliest winner after jumping the last, evidenced by his in-running price trading as low as 1.06 on the betting exchanges.

Since that win by ***Wichita Lineman*** in 2009, in the past ten years, the offspring of **King's Theatre** have competed in 49 further festival chases within the three-mile chase category, and have secured victory just twice more, with both winners being ridden by the aforementioned *Barry Geraghty*. Sandwiched between the improbable successes of ***Wichita Lineman*** and ***Champ*** is the rather less finger-biting win of ***The Druids Nephew***, who won the 2015 *Ultima Business Solutions Handicap Chase*, the same race as ***Wichita Lineman*** six years previously. It was a straightforward ride for *Barry Geraghty* as ***The Druids Nephew*** (8/1), beat *Grand Jesture* by 3¾ lengths.

I opposed ***Champ*** at last year's festival for two main reasons. First, the win and place festival strike rates for **King's Theatre**'s progeny in the three-mile chase category was the lowest across all seven categories. And I was also put off by ***Champ***'s age. 16 of the past 20 renewals of the *RSA* had been won by seven-year-olds and even though there are more seven-year-olds entries than all other age groups for the event, an 80% win strike rate was still a strong statistic for ***Champ*** to overcome. In claiming victory last year, ***Champ*** became the third 8-year-old winner of the *RSA Insurance Novices' Chase* this century, following the victories of *Rule Supreme* (2004) and *Might Bite* (2017).

At last year's festival meeting, **King's Theatre** was represented by 10 entries of which five competed in 3m chase events. With the exception of ***Champ***, the achievements of the other four **King's Theatre** bred contenders was very much in line with the performances delivered by the previous 44 of the offspring within the 3m chase category. Two of the runners finished in 15th place, one was pulled up and the other, ***Staker Wallace*** priced at 15/2 in the *St. James's Place Foxhunter Challenge Cup Open Hunters' Chase*, finished in 4th place in line with his position in the betting market. As it stands today, if one had placed a £10.00 each way bet on all 50 of **King's Theatre**'s progeny who had appeared in the festival's 3m chase events, the result would be a loss of £644.50. I haven't calculated how much profit the offspring would have delivered had one placed a £10.00 in running bet on the exchanges after the last fence had been jumped!

Ninety-eight horses by **King's Theatre** have appeared at Cheltenham Festivals registering 195 runs between them, of which 24 appearances preceded the 2011 meeting. Within those 195 festival appearances, there have been 17 victories which is the reason why **King's Theatre** has so often been mentioned as a sire to follow at the Cheltenham Festival. The progeny has amassed 13 festival victories in the past decade, which is more than any other National Hunt stallion. And there are some familiar names amongst those winners such as ***Cue Card, Captain Chris, Riverside Theatre, The New One, Balthazar King*** and we can now add ***Champ***.

In last year's Guide, I highlighted that with the death of **King's Theatre** in 2011 and hence the remaining offspring approaching older age, there would be fewer opportunities for the stock to add to their total of festival victories. For 2020, the youngest of **King's Theatre**'s offspring were aged eight and although ***Champ*** achieved a 17th festival victory for this stallion at last year's meeting, it will be even tougher for the progeny at the 2021 Cheltenham Festival now that all entries by **King's Theatre** will be aged nine or in double figures. One will find the majority of older national hunt horses racing over fences rather than hurdles, and more than likely over longer distances too. And it is in these types of contests at the Cheltenham Festival where the progeny of **King's Theatre** will have the best chance of picking up an 18th festival win. If we look at the 10 entries by **King's Theatre** that appeared at the 2020 Cheltenham Festival, nine of them contested chase events, ***L'Ami Serge*** being the sole contender over hurdles, when pulled up in the 3m *Paddy Power Stayers' Hurdle*. Of the 9 who raced over the larger obstacles, seven of them raced over a distance of three miles or more.

If we take the 500 festival races that have been contested this century, 176 of them (35.2%) have been won by horses that are aged 8 or older. Take away the 8yo winners, and victories by horses aged 9 or more is 97 (19.4%). For the 2022 meeting, supporters of **King's Theatre** bred runners should turn their attention to just two races, these being the *St. James's Place Festival Challenge Cup Open Hunters' Chase* and the *Glenfarclas Cross Country Chase* which combined together have provided 17 of the 37 festival victories from horses aged 10 or older.

For this year's festival, where the youngest of **King's Theatre**'s offspring will be nine-years old, it makes sense to turn our attention to the races in which 9yo entries have previously been successful. To that end, I suggest punters focus their attention on the 12 events where horses aged nine or more have won at least 3 of the renewals of those specific races this century. For the record, in the remaining 16 festival events, horses aged 9 or more have won just 8 out of 268 races this century, equivalent to one win in every 33 contests – and the remarkable *Quevega* is responsible for two of those successes, when aged 9 and 10, she won the last two of her six successive victories in the *David Nicholson Mares' Hurdle*.

As highlighted earlier, trainers will typically enter their older horses over fences, which is why of the 12 festival contests which I referred to earlier, ten of them are chase events. The percentage of 9yo plus winners of these races this century is 38% (89 winners from 232 races) and two of the races provided 26 of those victories, these being the *Foxhunters* (fifteen 9yo+ winners from 20 renewals) and the *Glenfarclas Cross Country Chase* (11 wins from 16 renewals). Seven **King's Theatre** bred horses have competed in the 3m *St. James's Place Foxhunter Challenge Cup Open Hunters' Chase* with the best finishing position being at last year's meeting when ***Staker Wallace***'s finished 4th and just out of the places. The record is not strong for this stallion's offspring with the next best placing being 8th, so it is not a race where I will be looking out for **King's Theatre** representatives. As for the 3m6f *Glenfarclas Cross Country Chase*, there have also been 7 appearances from the offspring which have been dominated by three runs each by ***Kingswell Theatre*** and ***Balthazar King***. ***Kingswell Theatre*** finished 10th in 2017, 6th in 2019 and was pulled up last year. His predecessor in tackling this unique course was far more successful. ***Balthazar King*** was victorious in both 2012 and 2014, before falling in 2016 when attempting to win the race for the third time. The other race over this distance of 3m6f is the *National Hunt Challenge Cup Amateur Riders' Novices' Chase*, where 20% of the winners this century have been aged nine or more, including last season's 10yo victor, *Ravenhill* (12/1), ably assisted in the saddle by *Jamie Codd*. **King's Theatre** has been represented in this race by six of his offspring, the best performance coming from ***Perfect Gentleman***, who finished 4th in the 2015 renewal.

Albeit that ***Champ*** prevailed in a 3m chase at last year's meeting, I have already highlighted that the achievements of **King's Theatre**'s runners within the 3m chase category is rather poor, with just 3 wins and 3 place positions recorded out of 50 appearances. The four 3m chase events where older horses have a respectable record are highlighted below with the number of wins for 9yo plus contenders from year 2000 onwards shown in brackets:

Foxhunters - 15 wins from 20 (75%)
Kim Muir – 9 wins from 20 (45%)
Gold Cup – 5 wins from 20 (25%)
Ultima – 5 wins from 20 (25%)

As already highlighted, of the 3 wins achieved by **King's Theatre**'s progeny within the 3m chase category, two of them occurred in the *Ultima Handicap Chase* where ***Wichita Lineman*** and The ***Druids Nephew*** took the prize when both were 8-year-olds. **King's Theatre** has been represented in this event on no less than 17 occasions, and outside of the two victories, only ***King Fontaine*** has managed to deliver a top six finish, when registering fifth position at 16/1 in 2011. In similar fashion to the *Foxhunters*, neither the *Cheltenham Gold Cup* nor the *Fulke Walwyn Kim Muir Challenge Cup Amateur Riders' Handicap Chase* have been fruitful events for the offspring of **King's Theatre**. Of six attempts in the *Cheltenham Gold Cup*, ***Carlingford Lough*** did manage a 4th placing in the 2016 renewal whereas in the *Kim Muir*, none of the eight **King's Theatre** bred contenders have finished higher than 8th.

The record of **King's Theatre**'s progeny within the 2m chase category is respectable with a 30% win and place strike rate in the past decade, and it is perhaps surprising when thinking about the speed at which the runners go at in these contests, to note that older horses have done rather well in this category. Horses aged 9 or greater have won 9 of the past 20 renewals of the *Queen Mother Champion Chase* and 8 of the past 20 renewals of the *Grand Annual Chase Challenge Cup*. That said, the win and 2 places that appear in **King's Theatre**'s performance table were all achieved in the 2m chase event for novices, the *Arkle Challenge Trophy Chase*. **King's Theatre** has only had four of the offspring take their chance in the *Grand Annual* with 100/1 outsider, ***Dick Dundee*** securing the highest placing when 6th in 2015. As for the *Queen Mother*, winning this event requires a classy chaser with the ability to jump at speed. *Special Tiara*, with an official rating of 159, is the only winner in the past decade to have run off a mark below 160. ***Baily Green*** who fell four fences from home in the 2014 renewal is the one and only **King's Theatre** sired runner to have taken his chance in this Grade 1 contest.

Eight festival races have been highlighted above where horses aged 9 or more have won 66 of 156 renewals this century, but the track-record of **King's Theatre** bred contenders in these events is hardly encouraging punters to rush out and place bets on any of the stallion's entries. My advice for supporters of **King's Theatre** is to make the trip to Cheltenham on Thursday. The 4 races yet to be mentioned where 9-year-olds have a respectable record of success, all take place on the 3rd day of the festival meeting. The 2nd and 4th races on the card are three-mile hurdle contests where runners aged 9 or more have won a combined total of 8 races from 40 renewals. The 3rd and 5th races on the Thursday fall within the 2½m chase category, events in which 9yo plus contenders have won 15 of 36 renewals.

If we take the chase events first, the Grade 1 *Ryanair Chase* (Registered as *The Festival Trophy*) was introduced to the Cheltenham Festival in 2005 and horses by **King's Theatre** have won the *Ryanair* twice. In 2012, ***Riverside Theatre*** was victorious for the *Nicky Henderson* stable, beating *Albertas Run*, who had won the previous two *Ryanair* renewals. The following year, ***Cue Card***, who was a shock 40/1 winner of the 2010 *Weatherbys Champion Bumper*, secured his second Cheltenham Festival success when he won with authority to beat *First Lieutenant* by nine lengths. With **King's Theatre**'s offspring having been represented on just seven occasions in this 2m5f chase, this sire's stock has a win strike rate of 29%, but it will take a very classy animal if the progeny is to secure a 3rd *Ryanair Chase* victory. Having been upgraded to Grade One status in 2008, today's winners of the *Ryanair* are of a far higher class than in the early days, as evidenced by last year's winner, *Min* being officially rated at 170, fifteen pounds higher than *Thisthatandtother*'s 2005 success. The past ten winners have all been rated between 161 (*Uxizandre* in 2015) and 176 (*Vautour* in 2016) with the two **King's Theatre** sired victors, ***Cue Card*** and ***Riverside Theatre*** being rated at 165 and 168 respectively.

The 5th race on the card is the Grade 3 *Paddy Power Plate* in which **King's Theatre** has been represented on 11 occasions, most recently by ***Happy Diva*** at last year's meeting. ***Happy Diva***, a 9yo mare, trained by *Kerry Lee*, led at the last but had no more to give when finishing a gallant runner-up to *Simply The Betts*. Past performances from the offspring has also delivered a couple of 3rd place finishes, by ***King's Palace*** (8yo) in 2016 and ***King's Odyssey***, another 9yo, in 2018.

Now to the two 3m hurdle races that take place on the Thursday of the Festival meeting. The *Stayers Hurdle* has been contested on six occasions by the stock of **King's Theatre**, and in the 2012 renewal, it was ***Voler La Vedette*** that came closest to victory when losing out to *Big Buck's* by 1¾ lengths. Next best is ***L'Ami Serge*** who finished 8th in 2018. The *Stayers* is a tough race for nine-year-old horses to win. *Big Buck's* was a 9yo when winning for the 4th time in the aforementioned race, and *Inglis Drever* was also a nine-year-old when winning this event for the second time in 2008. The only other horse aged nine to win the *Stayers* this century is *Solwhit* who was victorious in 2013. There is a better chance of success in the *Pertemps Network Final Handicap Hurdle*, where there have been five 9yo plus winners this century. Nine runners by **King's Theatre** have lined up in this contest of which two battled it out to the line to secure a 1-2 finish in 2014 renewal when ***Fingal Bay*** (9/2 favourite) beat ***Southfield Theatre*** (20/1) by a nose, resulting in an exacta dividend of £121.20. There is usually a big field for the *Pertemps Final*, so it is worth noting that two of the other seven **King's Theatre** representatives finished towards the front of the field, these being ***Regal Encore*** (7th in 2015) and ***Electric Concorde*** (6th in 2017).

Now that the last remaining offspring of **King's Theatre** are in their later years, it is going to be increasingly difficult for this stallion to record an 18th Cheltenham Festival success, where this century, only 1 in 5 festival winners have been aged nine or older. As highlighted in this chapter, if we are selective and focus our attention on just 12 of the 28 festival contests, then the win-rate for the older horses is close to doubling and we can anticipate two in every five races being won by the 9yo plus contingent. That said, the success of **King's Theatre** bred runners in these specific 12 contests is mixed and not especially promising. There is limited data on which to make sensible conclusions as regards to chases over the shortest (2m) and longest (3m6f) distances, and with the exception of the *Ultima Handicap Chase* where the progeny have picked up two wins, it would appear that the offspring have under-performed in the 3m chase category. If I had to stick my neck out, I believe the most encouragement for supporters of **King's Theatre** is in the middle-distance 2½m chases and the 3m hurdle races that take place on the festival meeting's third day.

King's Theatre (IRE) – Progeny with Official Rating of 135+

Horses by this sire with an Official Rating of 135 or greater on 9th February 2021. Horses registered with the Irish Horseracing Regulatory Board (I.H.R.B) are shown in *italics*.

				Official Ratings as of 9th February 2021		
Sire	***Horse***	***Age***	***Sex***	***Hurdles***	***Chase***	***Trainer***
King's Theatre	Acting Lass	10	g		145	Harry Fry
King's Theatre	Bellshill	11	g		153	Sandy Thomson
King's Theatre	Born Survivor	10	g		138	Dan Skelton
King's Theatre	*Cabaret Queen*	*9*	*f*		*147*	*W.P. Mullins*
King's Theatre	Champ	9	g		165	Nicky Henderson
King's Theatre	Cogry	12	g		142	Nigel Twiston-Davies
King's Theatre	Happy Diva	10	f		145	Kerry Lee
King's Theatre	King's Odyssey	12	g		135	Evan Williams
King's Theatre	Kings Temptation	9	g		135	Ben Case
King's Theatre	Kingswell Theatre	12	g		139	Michael Scudamore
King's Theatre	L'Ami Serge	11	g	150		Nicky Henderson
King's Theatre	Minellacelebration	11	g		148	Katy Price
King's Theatre	Monbeg Theatre	12	g		135	Jamie Snowden
King's Theatre	*Mortal*	*9*	*g*	*125*	*150*	*Joseph Patrick O'Brien*
King's Theatre	*Peregrine Run*	*11*	*g*		*155*	*Peter Fahey*
King's Theatre	Regal Encore	13	g		150	Anthony Honeyball
King's Theatre	*Royal Rendezvous*	*9*	*g*		*153*	*W.P. Mullins*
King's Theatre	Royal Vacation	11	g		139	Colin Tizzard
King's Theatre	The Dutchman	11	g	135	145	Tristan Davidson
King's Theatre	Theatre Guide	14	g		135	Colin Tizzard
King's Theatre	William Henry	11	g		151	Sam Thomas

Commentary on selected potential entries for 2021 Festival

Champ – Wellchild Cheltenham Gold Cup 3m2½f (3:30 Friday 19th March)

I was wrong about ***Champ*** in last year's *RSA Insurance Novices' Chase* when I said he wouldn't win. Well, I'm up for more ridicule. I'm going to put my neck on the line and say that ***Champ*** won't win this year's *Cheltenham Gold Cup*, even though 4 of the past 10 winners of the *Cheltenham Gold Cup* had run in the previous season's *RSA Insurance Novices' Chase*.

There are plenty of reasons why I can't be on ***Champ***. The biggest factor is the record of his sire's progeny in the festival's three-mile chases which I have covered at length in the commentary on **King's Theatre**. In 50 festival chases at three miles, horses by **King's Theatre** have won just three times, and on two of those occasions from impossible positions as evidenced by the huge odds available in-running on the betting exchanges. If it wasn't for two brilliant jockeys in the shape of *Barry Geraghty* on board ***Champ*** and *Tony McCoy* who rode ***Wichita Lineman***, then the record would be reading just one victory, that of ***The Druid's Nephew***.

Another concern must be that ***Champ*** hasn't appeared on a racecourse following a wind operation in September or since that brilliant ride by *Barry Geraghty* at last year's festival. He was due to appear at *Newbury*'s *Betfair Hurdle* meeting in February, but the meeting was abandoned. Plans are afoot to rearrange the fixture for 21st February. Even if trainer *Nicky Henderson* does get ***Champ*** to appear at *Newbury*, it is hardly ideal preparation for a *Cheltenham Gold Cup*. Mind you, apart from *Al Boum Photo*, I think most of the other potential *Gold Cup* entries have also had issues with their preparations. If it's not a race meeting being called off, it may be that a *Gold Cup* challenger is withdrawn due to heavy going, or falls, or simply has an off-day and is pulled up. Meanwhile, whilst all this is going on, I have an image of a relaxed *Al Boum Photo* calmly sat at home with his feet up, watching Netflix or replays of the past two *Gold Cups*.

If *Nicky Henderson* can get ***Champ*** to win the *Gold Cup* with such limited preparations, then hats off to him. The trainer is definitely capable as evidenced by *Sprinter Sacre* a few years back. I don't believe ***Champ*** will win the 2021 Cheltenham Gold Cup. Too many question marks for me.

Footnote:

For further insight to the *Wellchild Cheltenham Gold Cup,* read the commentary on ***Minello Indo*** by **Beat Hollow**.

Mahler (GB)

Mahler was not featured in the 2020 Cheltenham Festival Stallion Guide.

Mahler (17-y-o)							
Race Format	*Miles*	*Won*	*Placed*	*Unplaced*	*Total*	*Win %*	*Place %*
Hurdles	About 2m	0	0	2	2	0%	0%
	About 2m 4f	0	0	1	1	0%	0%
	About 3m	0	1	1	2	0%	50%
Chases	About 2m	0	0	2	2	0%	0%
	About 2m 4f	0	0	1	1	0%	0%
	About 3m	0	1	4	5	0%	20%
	About 4m	0	1	2	3	0%	33%
Bumper	About 2m	0	0	1	1	0%	0%
Total	**2011-2020**	**0**	**3**	**14**	**17**	**0%**	**18%**

Fifteen horses by **Mahler** have raced on 17 occasions at Cheltenham Festivals, and all of those 17 appearances have taken place in the past four years. One runner at the 2017 Cheltenham Festival was followed by three more in 2018, six in 2019 and seven at last year's meeting. The number of festival entries are increasing for this young stallion and as a result **Mahler** makes an entry in the Cheltenham Festival Stallion Guide for the first time. Had one placed a £10.00 each-way bet on all seventeen outings to date, the outcome would be a loss of £227.00. This isn't surprising as **Mahler**'s progeny have yet to register a festival winner. That said, it is early days and there have been signs of encouragement as three of **Mahler**'s festival representatives have at least achieved place dividends. There isn't enough data to make any sweeping statements about whether **Mahler** will be a stallion to follow at festivals or not, but in the seventeen performances so far, there are a couple of trends beginning to emerge that are worth highlighting.

In looking at the **Mahler**'s festival statistics table, it is noticeable that the three place positions that have been achieved have all happened in contests that cover a distance of at least three miles, and these have been secured from 10 outings. In races at two miles and 2½ miles, there have been seven unplaced efforts from seven appearances. As this is a very limited number of runs, I carried out a brief analysis of seeing how **Mahler**'s offspring performed at the Cheltenham racecourse at meetings outside of the festival. I didn't do anything especially scientific other than to count how many top three finishes were achieved by **Mahler**'s stock at the course and them split those results into three distance categories of two, 2½ and three miles plus. This study shows that outside of the Cheltenham festival, horses by **Mahler** have recorded top three finishes at the Prestbury Park racecourse on nine occasions. In races at around three miles or more, the offspring have won one race and finished 3rd in another. In races covering a distance of about 2½ miles, horses by **Mahler** have recorded one win, three runner-up spots and another three runners that finished in 3rd. Rather than reinforce the argument that **Mahler**'s progeny may prefer longer distances, with the majority of 1-2-3 positions coming in the middle distance contests, the results are seemingly placing a greater emphasis that perhaps **Mahler**'s offspring aren't speedy enough to win over the minimum distance and races that fall within the two mile categories.

Looking again at the Cheltenham Festival results, no judgements can be based upon just the two runs that have taken place by **Mahler**'s stock in races run over 2½ miles events, and even the five appearances at two miles, where the highest finishing position to date is 8th, are insufficient in being able to make any robust conclusions. Nevertheless, when one adds in the results at Cheltenham outside of the festival, it does tend to raise questions about how well horses by **Mahler** will perform in races at two miles.

As regards the festival results of **Mahler**'s stock in the ten races covering three miles or more, horses by **Mahler** have recorded a finish in the top six places on five occasions, including the three recorded place positions. The first horse by **Mahler** to appear at a festival is one that finished in the top six places. ***Kerrow*** was a 33/1 outsider for the 2017 *JT McNamara National Hunt Challenge Cup Amateur Riders' Novices' Chase*, and despite being well beaten, it wasn't a bad effort to finish in 6th place. Better was to follow for this stallion's progeny in the 2018 renewal of this contest when ***Ms Parfois***, at 11/2, just missed out on victory when beaten ½ length by *Rathvinden*. The mare challenged strongly up the Cheltenham Hill and even led in the final 100 yards, but *Rathvinden* found a little bit extra near the line to prevail. At that same meeting in 2018, **Mahler** supporters celebrated a second runner-up performance in Friday's *Albert Bartlett Novices' Hurdle*, when the oldest runner in the field at the age of eight, ***Ok Corral*** (16/1) stayed on to take second place behind the winner, *Kilbricken Storm*. The final two of the top six places achieved by **Mahler**'s stock were achieved in the 2020 renewal of the *Fulke Walwyn Kim Muir Challenge Cup Amateur Riders' Handicap Chase*, where ***Bob Mahler*** put in a gutsy effort to claim 3rd place at 16/1, and a couple of places behind him to finish in 5th position was his half-brother ***Deise Aba*** at 8/1.

One other interesting aspect of these first 17 festival outings by **Mahler**'s progeny is how the betting market perceives the stallion's entries. In 10 of the 17 festival appearances, **Mahler**'s offspring have lined up at prices ranging from 4/1 to 16/1, with half of these at single figure odds, so generally, horses by **Mahler** tend to be reasonably well considered to perform well. To complete the picture, four horses were sent off at big prices, two at 50/1 and a further two at 100/1.

As we look forward to the 2021 Cheltenham Festival, I anticipate that somewhere in the region of 5-10 horses by **Mahler** will make the trip to Gloucestershire adding to the 17 appearances that have been made to date. With such a small amount of data upon which to base any trends, I think the wise advice is to give **Mahler**'s stock a watching brief and see how the 5-10 runs reinforce or alter any initial and early opinions. My early opinion suggests that if one really does like the look of a **Mahler** sired festival entry come this March, then make sure it is running in a race that covers a distance of 2m4f or more. As for the festival events at a distance of around two miles, until I see something that suggests that **Mahler**'s offspring can perform in races at the minimum distance, then I will leave well alone.

Mahler (GB) – Progeny with Official Rating of 135+

Horses by this sire with an Official Rating of 135 or greater on 9th February 2021. Horses registered with the Irish Horseracing Regulatory Board (I.H.R.B) are shown in *italics*.

				Official Ratings as of 9th February 2021		
Sire	***Horse***	***Age***	***Sex***	***Hurdles***	***Chase***	***Trainer***
Mahler	Annie Mc	7	f		149	Jonjo O'Neill
Mahler	Annual Invictus	6	g	135		Chris Gordon
Mahler	*Atlantic Shore*	*8*	*g*		*136*	*Philip Fenton*
Mahler	Bob Mahler	9	g		135	Warren Greatrex
Mahler	*Brace Yourself*	*8*	*g*		*137*	*Noel Meade*
Mahler	Canelo	8	g		147	Alan King
Mahler	*Chris's Dream*	*9*	*g*		*164*	*Henry de Bromhead*
Mahler	Commanche Red	8	g	137	142	Chris Gordon
Mahler	Deise Aba	8	g		142	Philip Hobbs
Mahler	Glen Forsa	9	g		147	Mick Channon
Mahler	Late Romantic	11	g		137	Oliver Greenall
Mahler	Manofthemountain	8	g		135	Emma Lavelle
Mahler	Notachance	7	g		146	Alan King
Mahler	*Ornua*	*10*	*g*	*133*	*142*	*Henry de Bromhead*
Mahler	*The Big Dog*	*8*	*g*		*136*	*Peter Fahey*
Mahler	*Torygraph*	*6*	*g*	*137*		*Gordon Elliott*

Commentary on selected potential entries for 2021 Festival

Canelo – Ultima Handicap Chase (2:50 Tuesday 16th March)
Diese Aba – Ultima Handicap Chase (2:50 Tuesday 16th March)

Two horses by **Mahler** may turn up in the *Ultima Handicap Chase*, won last year by *The Conditional*. Both horses have pointers that suggest they could run well in this event, but there are also some factors that appear to be against them. I have listed some of the pertinent areas below:

1) 9 of the past 11 winners had all run at Cheltenham during the season. ***(Neither Canelo or Diese Aba have run at Cheltenham this season. Canelo, in fact, has never run at Cheltenham)***
2) 10 of the past 12 winners had raced at a previous festival and 11 of the past 23 winners had finished in the first four places at a previous festival. ***(Diese Aba finished in 5th place in last year's Kim Muir. Canelo has never run at Cheltenham before)***
3) The Conditional won this event with an Official Rating of 139 last year, the lowest rated winner since Golden Chieftain (132) in 2013. In the six renewals between 2014 and 2019, the winner has held a rating (2014) first of 145 146 148 155 142 151. ***(At the time of writing, Diese Aba has a rating of 142 and Canelo 147)***
4) In the past 17 renewals, only one winner had not finished in the first 5 places last time out. 8 of those 17 winners had won last time out. ***(At the time of writing, Canelo had finished 4th on his previous outing, whilst Diese Aba won)***
5) 9 of the past 11 winners had run at least four time during the season. ***(Canelo has made five racecourse appearances this season, whilst Diese Aba had raced on three occasions)***
6) 7 of the past 11 winners had previously had 9 or fewer runs over fences. ***(Canelo has won 3 of 9 chase outings and Diese Aba has won 3 of 8 outings)***

The above trends are all somewhat interesting rather than producing a critical insight as to who will win this year's *Ultima Handicap Chase*. And we only have very limited data on which to suggest that **Mahler**'s offspring are best, maybe, at the festival's 3m chases. The betting market seems to slightly prefer ***Diese Aba*** who, at the time of writing is around 16/1, whilst ***Canelo***'s price is about 22/1. It is also debateable whether either horse will run in this race or even travel to Cheltenham.

I won't be betting on this race until nearer the festival, but of these two horses by **Mahler**, I have a preference for ***Canelo*** and that is primarily as a result of his connections. *J P McManus*, who has won three *Ultima Handicap Chases* with horses in his ownership, is the owner of ***Canelo***. And if one wants to win this race, it usually requires a British trainer to win it. No Irish trainer has won this race since 2006. And to win the *Ultima*, *Alan King* is a pretty good choice. He has won the race twice, most recently with *Bensalem* in 2011. *Bensalem* may well have won in 2010 too if he had not fallen two out when he was travelling ominously well.

Martaline (GB)

Quote from the 2020 Cheltenham Festival Stallion Guide - "My guess is that **Martaline** will once again be well represented at this year's festival with probably 8-12 entries and I'm not especially keen on any of them."

Martaline (Died as a 20-y-o in 2019)							
Race Format	*Miles*	*Won*	*Placed*	*Unplaced*	*Total*	*Win %*	*Place %*
Hurdles	About 2m	0	1	9	10	0%	10%
	About 2m 4f	0	0	7	7	0%	0%
	About 3m	1	0	6	7	14%	14%
Chases	About 2m	0	0	3	3	0%	0%
	About 2m 4f	1	3	4	8	13%	50%
	About 3m	0	1	7	8	0%	13%
	About 4m	0	0	2	2	0%	0%
Bumper	About 2m	0	1	5	6	0%	17%
Total	2011-2020	**2**	**6**	**43**	**51**	**4%**	**16%**

My first prediction was correct. I suggested somewhere between 8-12 horses by **Martaline** would make the trip to last year's Cheltenham Festival and nine turned up. My second comment about *"not being keen on any of them"* was pretty near the mark too. Only one of the nine entries by **Martaline** secured a finish in the top ten places, achieved by ***Thatsy*** in the *Randox Health County Handicap Hurdle* when finishing in 7th place at a price of 8/1.

To be fair, five of **Martaline**'s nine representatives at last year's meeting were outsiders with starting prices ranging between 33/1 and 100/1, so it would be entirely reasonable to anticipate 'also-ran' type performances. But, for the other four of the offspring, one can only suggest that their performances, when taken together, were disappointing. After being held up, ***Thatsy***, trained by *Gordon Elliott*, did make some late headway towards the end of the *County Hurdle*, but all the same, he was never involved in the finish. In the end, his 7th placing was some eleven lengths behind *Saint Roi*, the *County* winner. The other three of **Martaline**'s progeny that were nearer the front, as opposed to the rear of the betting market, were ***Ramses De Teillee*** (12/1) in the *Albert Bartlett Novices' Hurdle*; ***Burrows Edge*** (14/1) in the *Coral Cup Handicap Hurdle*; and ***Elwood*** (18/1) in the *Ultima Handicap Chase*.

Taking the last of that trio first, ***Elwood***'s run in the *Ultima* didn't last too long, as the grey six-year-old fell at the 4th of 20 fences. As for ***Ramses De Teillee***, trainer *David Pipe* said he could offer no explanation for the gelding's performance in the *Albert Bartlett*, which was to trail home by more than 50 lengths to finish 13 of 14 finishers. As regards ***Burrows Edge***, he ran in the typically competitive *Coral Cup Handicap Hurdle*, a race in which the horse's trainer, *Nicky Henderson*, had trained three of the previous 10 winners. *Nico de Boinville*, riding ***Burrows Edge***, positioned the 14/1 chance to track the leaders, but when the race really started, the horse was simply outpaced, finishing some 15 lengths behind the winner in 13th place. As for the trainer's other two contenders, they were both owned by *John P McManus* and both finished ahead of ***Burrows Edge***. *Birchdale*, who was also sent off at 14/1, finished in 8th position, whilst 5/1 favourite, *Dame De Compagnie*, provided *Nicky Henderson* with his 4th winner in 11 years, when running on well after the last to win somewhat comfortably by 2¼ lengths.

The 51 festival appearances from **Martaline**'s progeny highlight disappointing strike rates of 4% for a win and 16% for a win or place, and I'm not keen on supporting a stallion's offspring if I have to watch 24 losers before one of the sire's stock registers a victory. From a financial perspective, supporting all 51 runners to a level £10.00 each way stake show returns of minus £399.75. To some extent, this figure is quite misleading, as the size of losses would be double that amount if it hadn't been for the 33/1 success of ***Very Wood*** in the 2014 *Albert Bartlett Novices' Hurdle*. ***Very Wood***, owned by *Michael O'Leary*, CEO of Ryanair and founder of *Gigginstown House Stud*, recorded the second of four winners on that Friday of 14th March 2014 for the famous *Gigginstown* maroon and white star colours. The 4-timer was kicked off by *Tiger Roll* (10/1) in the *JCB Triumph Hurdle* opener and closed out in the festival's final two races with victories from *Don Poli* (12/1) in the *Martin Pipe Conditional Jockeys' Handicap Hurdle* and *Savello* (16/1) in the *Johnny Henderson Grand Annual*. If you have the calculators out to figure out the odds, let me help. 82,653/1.

Basil Fawlty once said to his wife Sybil Fawlty that if she was on Mastermind, her specialist subject would be, "*stating the bleedin' obvious*", and I'm going down that path when I state that big-priced winners, such as ***Very Wood***'s 33/1 victory, happen far less frequently than winners that return prices of, say, under 5/1. That said, as advised in previous Guides and this one too, there are some stallions where the big-priced outsiders of the stock, seem to have much more regularity of featuring in the sire's list of festival wins and places. This is not the case with **Martaline**, where the small list of festival successes is dominated by those at the very fore of the betting market. Indeed, from the 51 festival outings by **Martaline**'s offspring, the one victory other than ***Very Wood***'s, and four of the six place positions have been recorded by runners with starting prices of between 11/8 and 5/1. The remaining two placed horses by **Martaline** returned prices of 12/1 and 14/1. Returning to the "*stating the bleedin' obvious*" theme, a £10.00 each-way bet on a horse at 5/1 that finishes placed in a non-handicap event is breakeven, £20 returned for a £20 outlay. Perhaps less obvious is the reality that a £10.00 each-way bet on a 16/1 shot in a non-handicap that finishes 2nd, provides the same return as a £20.00 win bet on an 11/10 favourite that wins. For the outsider, a fifth of 16/1 = 3.2, so £10 x 3.2 = £32 plus a stake of £10 = £42 with £20.00 staked (£10 for win and £10 for loss), whereas for the favourite, a £20 win x 11/10 = £42 return (£22 profit plus the £20.00 stake). Both bets incur a £20.00 outlay, returns of £42, and hence a profit of £22.

I mention all of the above, because it emphasises how difficult it has been to date, to win money on **Martaline**'s progeny at the festival. Imagine someone who had placed a £10.00 win bet on all 51 festival runners where **Martaline** is listed as the sire. The individual would have won just twice: £340 for the bet on ***Very Wood*** and £40 for the bet on ***Dynaste***, winner of the 2014 *Ryanair Chase*. Total losses would be £130 (£510 less £380). But horses by **Martaline** have recorded six festival places at the festival, so let's imagine our punter placing £5.00 each-way bets instead, so that the outlay of £510 is the same as for backing just to win. Although our individual would have received 'returns' on eight bets (2 wins and 6 places), he would have actually made a 'loss' on 3 of his place bets where odds on three horses (all in non-handicap races) were 11/8, 3/1 and 4/1. Therefore, our punter would have made a profit on 5 of his 51 bets, these being the two winners, and three each-way bets where the odds returned were 14/1, 12/1 and 5/1, the latter having been placed in a handicap, hence ¼ of the odds. The each-way betting strategy is financially more damaging where total losses amount to £199.87.

In last year's Cheltenham Festival Stallion Guide, I advised punters to leave **Martaline**'s entries out of their betting selections, and based on the festival performances, and indeed the run-up to the 2021 Cheltenham Festival, I don't see any reason why the advice should be altered. Frankly, the older and more experienced of **Martaline**'s progeny appear to be well below the standard needed to make an impression at the festival, and so hopes rest on whether any bright sparks reveal themselves amongst the **Martaline** sired four to five- year-olds. Perhaps the likes of another ***Disko*** or ***Dynaste*** is overdue.

Martaline (GB) – Progeny with Official Rating of 135+

Horses by this sire with an Official Rating of 135 or greater on 9th February 2021. Horses registered with the Irish Horseracing Regulatory Board (I.H.R.B) are shown in *italics*.

					Official Ratings as of 9th February 2021	
Sire	***Horse***	***Age***	***Sex***	***Hurdles***	***Chase***	***Trainer***
Martaline	Agrapart	10	g	144		Mrs Jane Williams
Martaline	*Annamix*	*8*	*g*		*152*	*W.P. Mullins*
Martaline	Arrivederci	6	g	139		Jonjo O'Neill
Martaline	Brinkley	6	g	140		David Pipe
Martaline	Diese Des Bieffes	8	g		135	Paul Nicholls
Martaline	*Diol Ker*	*7*	*g*	*151*		*Noel Meade*
Martaline	Eragone	7	g		137	Micky Hammond
Martaline	Eritage	7	g		137	Paul Nicholls
Martaline	Espoir De Teillee	9	g		138	Tom George
Martaline	Hollywoodien	10	g		139	Tom Symonds
Martaline	Kalooki	7	g		145	Philip Hobbs
Martaline	Malaya	7	f	136		Paul Nicholls
Martaline	*Morosini*	*6*	*g*	*136*		*Mrs John Harrington*
Martaline	*My Sister Sarah*	*7*	*f*	*142*		*W.P. Mullins*
Martaline	Ramses De Teillee	9	g	149	152	David Pipe
Martaline	Snow Leopardess	9	f		138	Charlie Longsdon
Martaline	Terrefort	8	g		152	Nicky Henderson
Martaline	*Vanillier*	*6*	*g*	*137*		*Gavin Cromwell*

Milan (GB)

Quote from the 2020 Cheltenham Festival Stallion Guide - "Although chasers by **Milan** are yet to provide a winner within the 2½m chase category, 70% of **Milan**'s runners have finished in the top six places. Within the 3m and 4m categories, the progeny's top six strike rate is 54% and 55% respectively. With these figures, punters will more often than not get a run for their money by backing **Milan**'s entries in the festival's chase events."

Milan (23-y-o)							
Race Format	*Miles*	*Won*	*Placed*	*Unplaced*	*Total*	*Win %*	*Place %*
Hurdles	About 2m	1	3	4	8	13%	50%
	About 2m 4f	0	0	12	12	0%	0%
	About 3m	2	3	12	17	12%	29%
Chases	About 2m	0	1	6	7	0%	14%
	About 2m 4f	0	4	6	10	0%	40%
	About 3m	2	9	19	30	7%	37%
	About 4m	2	3	9	14	14%	36%
Bumper	About 2m	0	0	9	9	0%	0%
Total	**2011-2020**	**7**	**23**	**77**	**107**	**7%**	**28%**

I will start with the quote at the top of the page where I highlight the top six strike rates for festival chases of 2½ miles or further. Twelve horses by **Milan** participated at the 2020 Cheltenham Festival, and although there were no entries in the 2½ mile chases, seven of the twelve competed in chases of three miles or more, of which five finished in the first five places, thereby maintaining **Milan**'s impressive top six strike rate in chases of three miles plus, which now stands at 57%. Of those five who registered a top five finishing position, two rewarded punters who had backed them, these being ***Milan Native*** (9/1) who beat off the challenge of *Kilfilum Cross* to secure victory in the *Fulke Walwyn Kim Muir Challenge Cup Amateur Riders' Handicap Chase*, and ***Santini*** (5/1), who stayed on at the finish to come within a neck of *Al Boum Photo* to claim the runner-up spot in Friday's *Magners Cheltenham Gold Cup Chase.*

The returns from ***Milan Native***'s victory and ***Santini***'s second placing was as far as it went for **Milan**'s offspring at last year's festival meeting - one win and one placing from 12 runners resulting in a win & place strike rate of 17%, a percentage that is below the typically consistent festival win & place strike rates associated with **Milan**'s stock. Looking back over the previous seven festival meetings from 2013 to 2019, the win & place strike rates, in chronological order, were 29%, 42%, 25%, 33%, 31%, 31% and 29%. That said, at the 2020 Cheltenham Festival, we should take note perhaps that three of **Milan**'s representatives at the 2020 Cheltenham Festival finished just one position outside the places, so one place higher for any of these three would have boosted the win & place strike rate to 25%. The three runners who just missed out were ***Forza Milan*** (12/1) who finished 4th in the *National Hunt Challenge Cup Amateur Riders' Chase*; ***Big River*** (20/1) who was just a neck outside a placing when taking 5th place in *the Ultima Handicap Chase*; and ***Monalee*** (20/1) who finished in 4th place and yet less than 2 lengths away from *Al Boum Photo* and half-brother, ***Santini***, in the *Magners Cheltenham Gold Cup.*

A nose, a neck, a short head. At the end of the day, whatever the margins, the results are what they are, and the offspring's results at the 2020 Cheltenham Festival would calculate into a financial loss had one supported all 12 runners blind to level stakes. And, albeit the strike rates for this stallion held up well at the previous two festival meetings, staking blind to level stakes would also have resulted in financial losses at the 2018 and 2019 Cheltenham Festivals. The outcome was different for the five festivals preceding 2018, where a £10.00 each way stake on all **Milan**'s entries would have delivered a profit at all five festivals, starting with 2013 as follows: £68.00, £120.50, £19.30, £87.50 and £58.50. For comparison, the losses suffered to the same staking plan in the 2018, 2019 and 2020 Cheltenham Festivals, starting with 2018, calculate to - £169.90, -£97.00 and -£87.50.

68 horses by **Milan** have raced on 108 occasions at Cheltenham Festivals, of which all bar one appearance has taken place within the past decade. The festival statistics from this stallion's progeny highlight a win & place strike rate of 28% or at least a minimum of a place dividend for two in every seven occasions in which a horse by **Milan** lines up in a festival event. It is slightly frustrating that **Milan**'s offspring show a record of having won a festival race for approximately one in every 16 runs, whereas securing a place is lot easier, better than 1 in 5 appearances. These strike rates provide the rationale as to why a £10.00 each way stake on all 108 of **Milan**'s festival runners would have produced an overall loss of £194.65, a loss which could so easily have been turned into a small profit had just one or two of those 23 place positions instead resulted in a win.

Another intriguing aspect of the festival results associated with **Milan**'s progeny is that six of those seven victories were in long distance races of three miles plus. Combining this statistic with the stock's data that appears to show an ordinary win strike rate, and yet a strong record of places and top six positions, leads me to the guarded conclusion that **Milan**'s offspring are blessed with stamina reserves, but perhaps lack a finishing kick.

It is interesting to consider the results of **Milan**'s progeny in festival races within the 3m and 4m categories and compare those with the results taken from festival events within the 2m and 2½m race categories. As can be seen from the table below, if one takes all 108 of the festival results achieved by **Milan**'s progeny and categorise them into two camps of (a) races below about three miles in distance and (b) races of about three miles or further, the difference between the two sets of results is striking. The category 'less than about 3m' includes the festival's bumper and all of the chase and hurdle events raced over a distance of up to around 2m5f and highlights a measly win strike rate of 2% thanks to the sole victory from ***Jezki*** in the 2014 *Champion Hurdle*. The win & place strike rate of 19% tells us to expect a return on our festival wagers for one in every five occasions when a horse by Milan doesn't have to race much further than around 2½ miles.

Milan (23-y-o)						
Race Distance (miles)	*Won*	*Placed*	*Unplaced*	*Total*	*Win %*	*Place %*
Less than about 3m	**1**	**8**	**38**	**47**	**2%**	**19%**
about 3m or further	**6**	**15**	**40**	**61**	**10%**	**34%**

By comparison, within the category that includes the festival's three 3m hurdle events and all chases of three miles and more, the win & place strike rate is 34%, which equates to a return on bets for one in every three occasions when a horse by **Milan** appears in one of the festival's longer distance events. From a financial perspective, if one had placed a £10.00 each way bet on all 61 of **Milan**'s offspring to appear in festival races of around three miles or more, the profits returned would be £300.60. To the same staking plan, backing the 47 horses by **Milan** that have appeared in festival races up to and around 2m5f would have resulted in a loss of £495.25.

Based upon the above information, a sensible strategy is to support **Milan**'s festival entries in the longer distance races and ignore them in the shorter and middle-distance events. A sound strategy for sure, but for those interested in delving a little deeper, I shall provide a few additional indicators to help punters ponder a little more before parting with their cash. In the longer distance festival contests, there are three races in which **Milan**'s offspring have recorded the best results. Starting with the two marathon events which are now both competed over a distance of 3m6f, horses by **Milan** have a far superior record in the *Glenfarclas Cross-Country Chase* than what has been achieved in the *National Hunt Chase*. In six appearances in the *National Hunt Chase*, the closest that **Milan**'s progeny have come to registering a place position was at last year's meeting, when ***Forza Milan*** finished in 4th place. That said, I don't believe punters should take any notice of this statistic, as three of the six **Milan** sired horses that lined up in this event were huge outsiders, at odds of 100/1 or bigger. Meanwhile, only three of **Milan**'s stock have competed in the *Glenfarclas Chase*, these being ***Big Shu***, ***Duke of Lucca*** and ***Josies Orders***. Combined together, this trio have tackled Cheltenham's cross-country course at the festival on 8 occasions which has resulted in two wins and three place positions. All 3 horses secured a place position, whilst ***Big Shu*** and ***Josies Orders*** also went one better, when winning their races in 2013 and 2016 respectively. (In 2016, ***Josies Orders*** was promoted to 1st place after it was revealed that *Another Currency* who was first past the post was disqualified as a result of a positive post-race test found traces of a pain killer).

Of the chases run over three miles, **Milan**'s offspring show a strong set of performances in the *Ultima Handicap Chase*, a race in which **Milan** has been represented on ten occasions. Although yet to win the race, horses by **Milan** have finished in the first six positions on six occasions, inclusive of three place dividends. The starting prices have been attractive also, with the place dividends being rewarded at odds of 5/1, 16/1 and 28/1. The trio that finished just outside of the place positions went off at 8/1, 20/1 and 33/1.

In the three hurdle contests that take place over a distance of almost three miles, specifically 2m7f and 213yds, **Milan**'s progeny has the best record in the *Albert Bartlett Novices' Hurdle*. Albeit that **Milan** sired runners have lined up on only five occasions, the offspring can boast an 80% win & place strike rate. Most recently, ***Santini*** lined up as the 11/4 favourite in the 2018 race to finish in 3rd place. Prior to that, in 2017, ***Monalee*** (8/1) took the runner-up spot with ***Tommy Rapper*** finishing 8th. Further back in 2015, anyone who had the foresight to back the two **Milan** sired runners in a forecast would have been absolutely delighted, as ***Martello Tower*** (14/1) just got the better of ***Milsean*** (33/1) to provide forecast backers with an Exacta dividend of £635.60.

As regards the festival races that take place below three miles, despite the figures, it may be a little hasty to just dismiss all entries by **Milan** out of hand. For example, on the eight occasions that the offspring have appeared in hurdle events over two miles, only twice has the **Milan** bred competitor finished outside the first 6 places. ***Darlan*** (7/1) was the runner-up in the 2012 *William Hill Supreme Novices' Hurdle* and ***Jezki*** (5/1) was also placed when finishing third in the following year's renewal. ***Jezki*** went on to win the 2014 *Champion Hurdle* at a price of 9/1 before finishing just outside the places in 4th when attempting to retain his crown in 2015. At that meeting in 2015, another **Milan** sired hurdler, ***Sort It Out*** (17/2) took the runner-up slot in the *Vincent O'Brien County Handicap Hurdle*. Therefore, out of a total of eight 2m hurdle outings from **Milan**'s progeny, the combined results achieved by the *John P McManus* owned trio of ***Darlan***, ***Jezki*** and ***Sort It Out***, of one win and three places, means that **Milan**'s stock has a 50% win & place strike rate in the festival's two-mile hurdle races.

Finally, I should return to the quote at the top of this chapter, where I highlight that although chasers by **Milan** are yet to provide a winner within the 2½m chase category, 70% of **Milan**'s runners have finished in the top six places, including four place dividends out of a total of ten outings. Despite my concerns that **Milan**'s stock may lack a finishing kick or burst of speed, it wouldn't be the greatest surprise for the progeny to pick up a festival victory within this race category.

Based upon the evidence of 108 festival appearances, punters should certainly take **Milan**'s offspring into account when determining their selections for the 2021 Cheltenham Festival and to improve the chances of financial reward, the percentage call is to focus most attention on the longer distance races. Although it may be a little hasty to dismiss **Milan**'s entries in races that are contested below three miles, I have a rather shaky suspicion that **Milan**'s stock is more Mo Farah than Usain Bolt.

Milan (GB) – Progeny with Official Rating of 135+

Horses by this sire with an Official Rating of 135 or greater on 9th February 2021. Horses registered with the Irish Horseracing Regulatory Board (I.H.R.B) are shown in *italics*.

				Official Ratings as of 9th February 2021		
Sire	***Horse***	***Age***	***Sex***	***Hurdles***	***Chase***	***Trainer***
Milan	Acey Milan	7	g		135	Anthony Honeyball
Milan	Big River	11	g		139	Lucinda Russell
Milan	Brewin'upastorm	8	g	155	150	Olly Murphy
Milan	*Dancing On My Own*	*7*	*g*	*136*		*Henry de Bromhead*
Milan	Double Shuffle	11	g		145	Tom George
Milan	*Forza Milan*	*9*	*g*		*136*	*J.A. Nash*
Milan	Hazel Hill	13	g		143	Mrs Melanie Rowley
Milan	If The Cap Fits	9	g		152	Harry Fry
Milan	*Lakemilan*	*9*	*f*	*126*	*141*	*Terence O'Brien*
Milan	Marie's Rock	6	f	138		Nicky Henderson
Milan	Marown	7	g		135	Nicky Richards
Milan	Mcfabulous	7	g	158		Paul Nicholls
Milan	*Milan Native*	*8*	*g*		*147*	*Gordon Elliott*
Milan	Milanford	7	g		140	Nick Mitchell
Milan	*Monalee*	*10*	*g*		*170*	*Henry de Bromhead*
Milan	*Monbeg Notorious*	*10*	*g*		*135*	*Gordon Elliott*
Milan	Mossy Fen	6	g		139	Nigel Twiston-Davies
Milan	My Drogo	6	g	140		Dan Skelton
Milan	One Night In Milan	8	g	140	138	Keith Dalgleish
Milan	*Ordinary World*	*11*	*g*		*149*	*Henry de Bromhead*
Milan	*Roaring Bull*	*8*	*g*		*139*	*Gordon Elliott*
Milan	Santini	9	g		167	Nicky Henderson
Milan	Supremely Lucky	9	g	136	133	Dan Skelton
Milan	Tommy Rapper	10	g	136		Dan Skelton
Milan	Whitehotchillifili	7	f	136		Harry Fry

Network (GER)

Quote from the 2020 Cheltenham Festival Stallion Guide - "Based upon the trends of **Network**'s previous festival contenders, it would appear that providing ***Delta Work*** and ***Easywork*** are sent off at odds of 16/1 or shorter, then they are guaranteed to finish in the first six places and have a more than 50% chance of rewarding each-way supporters. As for any entries by **Network** that are outsiders and priced at anything at 18/1 or bigger, you can forget them."

Network (Died as a 22-y-o in 2019)							
Race Format	*Miles*	*Won*	*Placed*	*Unplaced*	*Total*	*Win %*	*Place %*
Hurdles	About 2m	0	1	3	4	0%	25%
	About 2m 4f	0	2	3	5	0%	40%
	About 3m	1	0	1	2	50%	50%
Chases	About 2m	3	0	2	5	60%	60%
	About 2m 4f	0	1	3	4	0%	25%
	About 3m	0	1	8	9	0%	11%
	About 4m	0	0	1	1	0%	0%
Bumper	About 2m	0	0	0	0	-	-
Total	**2011-2020**	**4**	**5**	**21**	**30**	**13%**	**30%**

I will start with the quote at the top of the page. Both ***Delta Work*** and ***Easywork*** lined up at odds shorter than 16/1. Both finished in the first six places, one of which rewarded punters with a return on each-way bets. I'm happy with that!

Delta Work was making his third visit to the Cheltenham Festival. In 2018, he won by the tiniest of margins, a nose, to gain a 6/1 success in the 2018 *Pertemps Network Final Handicap Hurdle*. Twelve months later, he finished in 3rd place in the *RSA Insurance Novices' Chase*. In my book, that was a fine achievement considering that he was a French-bred six-year-old. Irish bred horses had won 14 of the last 18 renewals at the time (16 of the last 20 as of today) and the record for six-year-old horses in the *RSA* is dire. Since 1978, just three of that age group have been victorious. ***Delta Work*** was just one of three horses by **Network** to take part in the 2020 Cheltenham Festival, and in my view, was one of half a dozen entries that had a chance of lifting what was a very open *Magners Cheltenham Gold Cup*. In the end, his jumping wasn't particularly fluent and so he had far too much to do at the business end of the race, staying on but without the pace to challenge his high-quality and older rivals. ***Delta Work*** finished 5th at 5/1.

Delta Work's connections are well known. The trainer is *Gordon Elliott*, and the owner is *Gigginstown House Stud*, and last year, the same connections sent over another high-quality **Network** sired gelding in the shape of ***Easywork***. On his debut, ***Easywork*** had been set a tough assignment in the *Ballymore Novices' Hurdle*, as if he was to win the race, he needed to beat one of the best national hunt racehorses in training, his stablemate, *Envoi Allen*. Under an excellent ride by jockey, *Rachael Blackmore*, as they turned in, momentarily at least, it looked as if ***Easywork*** (12/1) was going to give the 4/7 favourite, *Envoi Allen*, a decent battle. But a burst of speed and a few giant strides later and *Envoi Allen* showed his class and was away, beating ***Easywork*** by 4¼ lengths.

Sadly, in December 2020, it was announced that ***Easywork*** had died of a heart attack whilst on the gallops. He was only aged six when he died, so we will never know how good he could have been. Before his sad misfortune, he had been a leading contender for the *Brown Advisory Novices' Chase*.

The 3rd horse by **Network** that made the trip to Cheltenham last March was ***Blazer***. It was his second visit to the festival, the previous occasion being way back in 2016, when aged just five, he was sent off at a price of 8/1 when registering a 4th place dividend in the *Coral Cup*. Four years later, and now aged nine, he lined up in the *Brown Advisory & Merriebelle Stable Plate Handicap Chase* for what would be his 12th race over fences. In the green and gold colours of *J P McManus* and trained by *Willie Mullins*, it was a disappointing race for the 11/1 chance, as mid-race, he dropped to the rear after being badly hampered by a faller. ***Blazer*** could never get back into the race after that incident and trailed home to finish in 15th place.

Fifteen horses by **Network** have raced on 30 occasions at Cheltenham Festivals, but only one third of those 15 horses have rewarded punters with winnings. One of **Network**'s progeny turned out to be a 'wonder horse', responsible for five of the stock's 30 festival runs; 3 of the 4 victories; and one of the five places. The horse in question is ***Sprinter Sacre***, who has such a huge bearing on the table that highlights **Network**'s festival statistics, that to include him within an analysis of how the offspring perform at Cheltenham Festivals would be misleading. For example, anyone who looks at the table at the top of this page without any further analysis, could easily believe that horses by **Network** are brilliant in the festival's two-mile chases, whereas the reality is that only one horse by **Network**, other than ***Sprinter Sacre***, has raced in a festival 2m chase. It would be folly to make any judgements based on one 8th placing by a 33/1 outsider, and 3 wins from 4 outings by one superb 188 rated chaser.

I have written quite a lot about ***Sprinter Sacre*** in the past two Cheltenham Festival Stallion Guides, so I will try and keep this paragraph on this great two miler chaser brief and to the point. ***Sprinter Sacre***, trained by *Nicky Henderson*, competed at the Cheltenham Festival on five occasions. Having finished in 3rd place on his festival debut in the 2011 *Stan James Supreme Novices' Hurdle*, he was sent chasing where he made his mark as an exceptional two-miler. On 13th May 2012, in the *Racing Post Arkle Challenge Trophy Chase*, ***Sprinter Sacre*** coasted to victory to beat *Cue Card* by seven lengths, in what jockey *Barry Geraghty* described as the equivalent of a "schooling session". In 2013, as the 1/4 odds on favourite, he beat *Sizing Europe* by 19 lengths to win the *Sportingbet Queen Mother Champion Chase*. After a shock defeat when pulled up in the *williamhill.com Desert Orchid Chase* at *Kempton Park* in December 2013, post-race tests revealed that ***Sprinter Sacre*** was suffering from an irregular heartbeat, and for the next 18 months, a series of injury and health problems continued to plague him and was evidenced when he was pulled up in the 2015 renewal of the *Queen Mother Champion Chase*. His third outing in the *Queen Mother Champion Chase* took place in 2016, where his chief opponent would be the highly impressive 4/6 favourite *Un De Sceaux*. In what was to be his last racing appearance at the Cheltenham Festival, ***Sprinter Sacre***, now aged ten, delivered an impeccable performance to win the *Champion Chase* for the second time, provoking a few tears of joy and a deafening roar from those in the Cheltenham Grandstands.

As advised earlier, to analyse how **Network**'s stock will perform at future festivals, I believe it is necessary to take the brilliant ***Sprinter Sacre*** out of the equation, as his influence on **Network**'s festival statistics is domineering. All of which leaves us with 25 festival appearances from 14 of **Network**'s progeny, and I am going to split those 25 outings into two groups; those that lined up at odds of 18/1 and bigger and those that returned starting prices of 16/1 or shorter.

Starting with the outsiders, of the 25 festival appearances by the progeny, 3 out of every 5 horses by **Network** have set off in their races at a price of 18/1 or bigger. A quick warning. If you are a punter that backs outsiders, then you should avoid **Network**'s big-priced contenders like the plague. Of the 15 horses by **Network** that lined up at a price of 18/1 or bigger, not one of them has recorded a top five finish. In fact, only twice has the offspring's outsiders finished in the first ten. For the record, eight runners failed to complete the race, six of which were pulled up, and as for the seven times that the outsider by **Network** finished the race, the finishing positions from best to worst were 6th 8th 12th 14th 15th 17th and 20th.

Whereas **Network**'s outsiders will do little more than make up the numbers in their festival races, of the ten horses by **Network** that have lined up in their races at a price of 16/1 or shorter, nine of those ten have recorded a top six finish. The only exception was at last year's meeting where I have already highlighted ***Blazer***'s 15th place finish, at a price of 11/1, in the *Brown Advisory & Merriebelle Stable Plate*. Within the ten festival outings from the more fancied contenders by **Network**, one resulted in victory, courtesy of ***Delta Work***'s 6/1 success in the 2018 *Pertemps Network Final Handicap Hurdle*. In addition, four runners have achieved place dividends, these being ***Rubi Light*** (16/1) who finished in 3rd place in the 2011 *Ryanair Chase*; ***Blazer*** (8/1) 4th place in the 2016 *Coral Cup*; ***Delta Work*** (15/8 Favourite) who finished 3rd in the 2019 *RSA Insurance Novices' Chase*; and ***Easywork***, the runner-up in last year's *Ballymore Novices' Hurdle*.

At this year's Cheltenham Festival, I am guessing that, once again, the number of festival entries by **Network** will be low, with perhaps four or five of the offspring making it to Prestbury Park this March. The advice to punters is quite simple. If the **Network** sired runner is an outsider at 18/1 or greater, then keep your money in your pocket. However, if the sire's entry is priced up at anything below 16/1, then take a serious look as there is roughly a 50:50 chance that this more fancied of **Network**'s progeny will secure a finishing position within the first three home.

Network (GER) – Progeny with Official Rating of 135+

Horses by this sire with an Official Rating of 135 or greater on 9th February 2021. Horses registered with the Irish Horseracing Regulatory Board (I.H.R.B) are shown in *italics*.

				Official Ratings as of 9th February 2021		
Sire	***Horse***	***Age***	***Sex***	***Hurdles***	***Chase***	***Trainer***
Network	*Acapella Bourgeois*	*11*	*g*		*155*	*W.P. Mullins*
Network	*Blazer*	*10*	*g*		*135*	*W.P. Mullins*
Network	*Delta Work*	*8*	*g*		*168*	*Gordon Elliott*
Network	Domaine De L'Isle	8	g	121	137	Sean Curran
Network	*Enjoy D'allen*	*7*	*g*	*115*	*136*	*Ciaran Murphy*
Network	*Entoucas*	*7*	*g*		*139*	*Joseph Patrick O'Brien*
Network	*Le Richebourg*	*8*	*g*	*140*	*153*	*Joseph Patrick O'Brien*
Network	Remastered	8	g		138	David Pipe

Commentary on selected potential entries for 2021 Festival

Entoucas – Johnny Henderson Grand Annual Handicap Chase 2m½f (4:50 Wednesday 17th March)

Network's offspring have an excellent record of finishing in a top six place at the festival if they are priced at 16/1 or shorter in the market, which is why I believe I should comment briefly on ***Entoucas*** who may well start around the 12/1 mark for the *Grand Annual*. ***Entoucas*** delivered a fine performance at the *Dublin Festival* in early February finishing 4th of 20 runners in the *Matheson Handicap Chase* which will be great experience should he take part in the *Grand Annual*. Interestingly, in 14 races under rules, ***Entoucas*** has never finished outside the top four finishing places except once, and that was in the one and only graded race in which he has been engaged, the 2019 *Chanelle Pharma Novice Hurdle*, where ***Entoucas*** finished 6th of 7 finishers. The winner of that Grade 1 race incidentally, *Klassical Dream*, went onto win that year's *Supreme Novices' Hurdle*.

I do like the fact that ***Entoucas*** has been engaged in big fields which I think is important for when one has to fight tooth and nail in the competitive *Grand Annual*. In six contests in which ***Entoucas*** has had to compete against anywhere between 17 and 25 rivals, the gelding's finishing positions have been 1st, 2nd, 2nd, 2nd. 3rd and 4th. ***Entoucas*** also boasts good connections. His trainer is *Joseph Patrick O'Brien* who saddled ***Us And Them*** to be 3rd in the 2020 *Grand Annual*. His owner is none other than *J P McManus*, who since 2003 has been the winning owner of the *Grand Annual* victor on four occasions as well as registering six runner-up positions.

The *Grand Annual* is a tough race but ***Entoucas*** certainly looks good for a top six position and looks a solid each-way bet.

Footnote:

For further insight to the *Grand Annual*, read the commentary on ***Zanza*** by **Arcadio**.

Oscar (IRE)

Quote from the 2020 Cheltenham Festival Stallion Guide - "If you are one of those punters that doesn't fancy odds-on favourites, and so will give ***Paisley Park*** a miss, I can advise that there may well be 2-3 other horses by **Oscar** lining up in the *Stayers*, such as ***Lisnager Oscar***, ***Kilbricken Storm*** and ***Not Many Left***. If one takes all runs from this trio at Cheltenham, not just at the festival, the finishing positions recorded are highly respectable, which combined, shows six top 3 finishes from 10 outings. At the time of writing, all three were priced at 33/1 or bigger."

Oscar (27-y-o)							
Race Format	*Miles*	*Won*	*Placed*	*Unplaced*	*Total*	*Win %*	*Place %*
Hurdles	About 2m	1	5	6	12	8%	50%
	About 2m 4f	0	2	13	15	0%	13%
	About 3m	4	6	31	41	10%	24%
Chases	About 2m	0	5	6	11	0%	45%
	About 2m 4f	0	3	15	18	0%	17%
	About 3m	4	4	19	27	15%	30%
	About 4m	1	0	4	5	20%	20%
Bumper	About 2m	0	0	8	8	0%	0%
Total	2011-2020	**10**	**25**	**102**	**137**	**7%**	**26%**

I'm not quite sure why I didn't back the *Rebecca Curtis* trained and **Oscar** sired, ***Lisnager Oscar***, in last year's *Paddy Power Stayers' Hurdle*. I think I was enjoying my Guinness too much. Hindsight is a wonderful thing. I certainly believed that it would be one of **Oscar**'s stock that would be victorious, but like many others, I believed the winner would be the other **Oscar** bred entry in the race, namely the 4/6 favourite, ***Paisley Park***. I had missed the 50/1 winner and after the result, re-read what I had written in the summary section as regards **Oscar** in last year's Cheltenham Festival Stallion Guide. (I have underlined the pertinent points.) "*Historically, the trends point to **Oscar**'s offspring performing best in non-handicaps and in races within the 3m category. In addition, punters can be reassured that **Oscar**-breds won't mind soft ground should the heavens open and neither does the stock of **Oscar** care about their odds; the records show that a large percentage of winners and placed horses line up with SPs that are well into double figures*." I'm not one to back odds-on favourites so I didn't bet in the race. But why not a small fun bet on ***Lisnager Oscar***? I enjoyed the Guinness though ...

Lisnager Oscar became the 16th festival winner to be sired by **Oscar** and following three blank years between 2015 and 2017 when the winners stopped, results have improved considerably at the past three Cheltenham Festivals, where **Oscar**'s offspring have recorded 4 victories to add to the 12 achieved between 2006 and 2014. **Oscar,** who was relieved of his stallion duties in 2015, has been represented by his stock at Cheltenham Festivals on 187 occasions, of which 137 runs have taken place within the past decade. For punters, he has been a stallion to follow at Cheltenham Festivals, where the progeny can usually be relied upon to reward supporters with profit. A punter placing £10.00 each way blind on all of **Oscar**'s offspring to have ever raced at Cheltenham Festivals, would be £552.00 better off, equivalent to a 15% return on investment. It itself, that is some achievement. There aren't too many stallions around where a level stakes profit is achieved simply by backing every single festival appearance that is made by the sire's offspring. That said, with **Oscar**, slightly greater rewards can be gained by being a little more selective and focusing on those factors that I underlined earlier in this chapter; non-handicaps; three miles; and soft ground.

Fourteen of the 16 Cheltenham Festival victories that have been recorded by **Oscar**'s progeny have taken place in non-handicap events. The offspring have lined up in 120 festival non-handicap races and the 14 victories represent a win strike rate of 12%. With a further 18 runs resulting in place dividends, punters can expect a return for slightly better than one in every four bets from an **Oscar** sired entry in one of the festival's non-handicap contests (a win & place strike rate of 27%). A £10.00 each way bet on all 120 of **Oscar**'s non-handicap contenders would have provided a return on investment of 34% and a profit of £827.00. In comparison, backing the 67 of **Oscar**'s representatives in the handicap events to the same staking plan would result in a loss of £275.00. The loss is down to just the two victories, as the 11 places achieved in handicaps equates to 16% which is superior to the 15% recorded in the non-handicap events.

If we analyse how **Oscar**'s stock has performed in festival races over a distance of three miles compared to other race distances, it reveals a similar outcome to results recorded in non-handicaps compared to handicaps. In the 90 festival races in which **Oscar**'s offspring have lined up within the 3m categories (hurdles and chases), the 10 victories and 11 places registered shows a profit of £714.00 to a £10.00 each way stake which equates to a return on investment of 40%. When horses by **Oscar** have appeared in festival events at distances other than three miles, six wins and 18 places have been achieved from 97 contests and highlights a 25% win and place strike rate which is slightly higher compared to 23% achieved in races within the 3m distance categories. But as we all know, when we have a day out at the races, there are two major factors that will typically determine whether we make a profit or not, these being the number or percentage of winning bets and the odds secured on those winning bets. Six wins from 97 races is a win strike rate of 6% and a £10.00 each-way stake on all 97 runners calculates to a loss of £162.00. It is the win strike rate that makes the difference. 6% in non-3m festival races, compared to 11% in the festival's three miles races.

Preceding the 2018 Cheltenham Festival, only 24 races this century had taken place on ground officially described as 'soft', and therefore, I hadn't especially paid attention to the ground conditions previously. The going at the 2018 Cheltenham Festival was highly unusual with the first 5 races of the festival run on ground officially described as heavy and the remainder of the races being run on soft ground. Having had a dearth of soft ground festival races for so long, the rain fell again in 2019 that resulted in all of Tuesday and Wednesday's contests also taking place on soft ground, before conditions changed to be good to soft for the last two days of the meeting. The 2020 Cheltenham Festival welcomed soft ground for the 3rd year in succession, with all bar the three chases on the Friday (that took place on good to soft), taking place on ground officially described as 'soft'. To summarise, of the 84 races that have taken place at the last three festivals, 62 have taken place on 'Soft'; 17 on 'Good to Soft'; and 5 on Heavy, clearly portraying the difference in conditions at the past three Cheltenham Festivals.

Of the 187 festival appearances by **Oscar**'s progeny, 37 of them have taken place on officially soft ground, delivering 3 wins (win strike rate of 8%) and 7 places (27% win & place strike rate). The results suggest that **Oscar**'s progeny perform well on soft going although I believe it is more accurate to state that **Oscar**'s offspring aren't troubled by soft ground. The strike rates on ground other than soft, (and note that none of **Oscar**'s stock has raced at the festival on heavy going) are very much in line with the soft going strike rates as advised above; these are a win strike rate of 9% and a 23% win & place strike rate. Of the 16 victories to date, 3 victories have been won on soft going, six have been won on 'good to soft' and seven have been won on 'good'. That said, from a financial perspective, the majority of wins and places on soft going have been highly rewarding because of the returned starting prices. Had one placed a £10.00 each way bet on all 37 horses by **Oscar** that have lined up in soft going festival races, the outcome would be a profit of £720.00. This return is largely influenced by ***Kilbricken Storm***, who won the 2018 *Albert Bartlett Novices' Hurdle* at a price of 33/1 and last year's 50/1 success by the *Rebecca Curtis* trained, ***Lisnager Oscar***, in the *Paddy Power Stayers' Hurdle*. The majority of the 7 place positions have also come at big odds, with 3 of **Oscar**'s representatives being placed at 25/1 and a 40/1 placing by ***God's Own*** in the 2018 *Betway Queen Mother Champion Chase*. For the record, a £10.00 each-way stake on all 150 appearances by Oscar's progeny on going other than soft would have resulted into a loss of £168.00.

Looking back as regards to the profits delivered by **Oscar**'s progeny in (a) non-handicap races, (b) races over a distance of three miles and (c) soft going, it is important that punters aren't misled, believing that **Oscar**'s offspring should therefore be avoided in races where conditions don't conform to the three criteria as laid out above. The financial losses in handicaps, races at distances other than 3m and on ground that is firmer than soft aren't especially ruinous. For example, hypothetically, let us imagine that the winner of this year's 2021 *Coral Cup* (a handicap race) romps home at 28/1 on good ground and is sired by **Oscar**. The victory would almost certainly be enough to wipe out the 'low hundred' losses that I have highlighted above and would mean that **Oscar**'s offspring would be delivering profits from the 67+ festival handicaps in which they have appeared; and in the 97+ non three-mile events; and in 150+ races where the going wasn't soft.

With such a terrific festival record, and I reiterate, a 15% return on investment had one backed all of **Oscar**'s festival representatives each-way to level stakes, it is perhaps uncharitable to point out to punters the two race categories in which **Oscar**'s progeny have failed to register even a place position. But, if there are races to avoid **Oscar**'s stock, then historic trends would advise us to be cautious of supporting horses by **Oscar** in the festival's 2½m handicap hurdles and non-handicap chases over the same distance. In the latter race category, 6 of the 7 appearances by **Oscar**'s offspring have taken place in the *Marsh Novices Chase*, and four of the runners were quite well fancied in the market, with starting prices ranging from 5/2 favourite to 11/2. But **Oscar**'s representatives haven't lived up to expectations in this race, with ***Felix Yonger***'s 4th place at 7/2 in 2014 being the highest recorded position to date. It may be worth noting that, with the exception of the 2018 festival meeting, no **Oscar** sired chaser has managed to register a place in the festival's 2½m handicap chases either. But results at the 2018 meeting were rather different, where **Oscar**'s four entries in the 2½m handicap chases delivered a runner-up from ***Splash Of Ginge*** (25/1) in the *Brown Advisory & Merriebelle Stable Plate Handicap Chase* and 2nd and 3rd place dividends in the *Close Brothers Novices' Handicap Chase* courtesy of ***Rather Be*** (12/1) and ***Rocklander*** (25/1) respectively. These results in 2018 remain as the only three occasions in 20 attempts where **Oscar**'s stock have registered a place in the festival's 2½m chases.

Turning to the festival's 2½m handicap hurdle contests, ***The Bosses Oscar*** became the 13th of **Oscar**'s offspring to try and secure a place dividend in such events when he lined up in the very last race of the 2020 Cheltenham Festival, the *Martin Pipe Conditional Jockeys' Handicap Hurdle*. Nowadays, some bookmakers are generous enough to pay out on a 5th place in big field festival handicaps, and so some punters may well have been lucky enough to secure a small return as the *Gordon Elliott* trained, ***The Bosses Oscar***, secured 5th place in the race at a price of 11/1. It is the closest that horses by **Oscar** have ever come to recording an 'official' place within this race category. The next highest placing of **Oscar**'s stock in 2½m festival handicap hurdles, occurred in the previous year's renewal of the *Martin Pipe*, when ***Doctor Dex*** (33/1) finished seventh. With a 7th place in 2019 and a 5th in 2020, will **Oscar**'s offspring finally break their duck with a 3rd place in the 2021 *Martin Pipe*? Just in case you are wondering about performances in the festival's non-handicap 2½m hurdle events, horses by **Oscar** are a rather different proposition in comparison to results achieved in the handicaps. Two victories and four place positions from 12 festival appearances in 2½m non-handicap hurdle events translate into a 50% win & place strike rate.

In last year's *Paddy Power Stayers' Hurdle*, I guess many punters would have found the 50/1 starting price on ***Lisnager Oscar*** rather off-putting. However, **Oscar** is one of the few stallions within this Guide, where I strongly advise punters to totally ignore the progeny's starting prices. Taking into account all 187 appearances at the festival, horses by **Oscar** have registered 16 victories and 29 place positions, which equates to a win & place strike rate of 24%. Of those wins and places, around 6 in 10 of the offspring lined up at prices of 10/1 or greater, registering 9 of the 16 wins and 17 of the 29 place positions. ***Lisnager Oscar*** has been the stock's biggest priced winner at 50/1, the next best being ***Kilbricken Storm*** at 33/1 in the 2018 *Albert Bartlett Novices' Hurdle*. A further ten horses by **Oscar** priced up between 25/1 and 50/1 have been placed at the festival. Outsiders at 25/1 or bigger, therefore, are responsible for 27% of all of the progeny's win and place successes at the festival. A further 31% of the offspring's winners and placed horses set off at prices ranging between 10/1 and 20/1 (7 winners and 7 places). It is these rewarding starting prices that have translated into a profit of £552.00 had one placed a £10.00 each way bet on all 187 of **Oscar**'s festival representatives.

If you fancy a festival entry by **Oscar** at this year's Cheltenham Festival, don't be put off should your selection be one of the outsiders or if the heavens have opened and the ground is soft. And perhaps, with money in hand, your confidence will be marginally enhanced if your selection is racing in a non-handicap event and/or in a race run over three miles. If you are bold enough to support your fancy and have kept your concentration by reducing your intake of Guinness, you never know, you may end up cheering home a 50/1 winner in the festival's *Stayers Hurdle* over three miles and on soft ground. Just like in 2020, when you could have been cheering home the success by ***Lisnager Oscar***. Let it go James. Let it go.

Oscar (IRE) – Progeny with Official Rating of 135+

Horses by this sire with an Official Rating of 135 or greater on 9th February 2021. Horses registered with the Irish Horseracing Regulatory Board (I.H.R.B) are shown in *italics*.

				Official Ratings as of 9th February 2021		
Sire	***Horse***	***Age***	***Sex***	***Hurdles***	***Chase***	***Trainer***
Oscar	*Any Second Now*	*9*	*g*	*139*	*151*	*T.M. Walsh*
Oscar	Bags Groove	10	g		147	Harry Fry
Oscar	Clondaw Castle	9	g		154	Tom George
Oscar	Lake View Lad	11	g	147	157	N. W. Alexander
Oscar	*Latest Exhibition*	*8*	*g*		*153*	*Paul Nolan*
Oscar	Lisnagar Oscar	8	g	159		Rebecca Curtis
Oscar	*Minella Times*	*8*	*g*		*144*	*Henry de Bromhead*
Oscar	Oakley	8	g	136		Philip Hobbs
Oscar	Oscar Elite	6	g	138		Colin Tizzard
Oscar	Oscar Rose	9	f		139	Fergal O'Brien
Oscar	Paisley Park	9	g	165		Emma Lavelle
Oscar	Quick Grabim	9	g	144	144	Fergal O'Brien
Oscar	*The Bosses Oscar*	*6*	*g*	*143*		*Gordon Elliott*
Oscar	The Hollow Ginge	8	g		140	Nigel Twiston-Davies
Oscar	Wilde About Oscar	6	g	136		Dan Skelton

Commentary on selected potential entries for 2021 Festival

The Bosses Oscar – Pertemps Network Final (2:10 Thursday 18th March)

When it comes to Cheltenham Festival meetings, **Oscar**'s offspring are far more successful in non-handicaps than handicaps. Horses by **Oscar** have achieved 16 festival wins, but only two of those have occurred in handicaps, one of which was in the *Pertemps Network Final* in 2007, the race won by 14/1 chance, ***Oscar Park***. At the time of writing, this year's favourite for this contest is the **Oscar** sired, ***The Bosses Oscar***, who can be backed at around 7/1.

It is understandable why ***The Bosses Oscar*** is favourite for the 2021 *Pertemps Final*. One reason is that he finished 2nd in the Qualifier that takes place at *Leopardstown*, the qualifying race in which 4 of the past 5 winners of the *Pertemps Network Final* have been found. Of more consequence, perhaps, is that 35-40 minutes after that qualifier, the *Leopardstown Christmas Hurdle* took place. Seven classy hurdlers were to compete for this Grade 1 event, all of whom held Official Ratings between 149 and 158. The field included two previous festival winners; *Sire Du Berlais* who had won the past two *Pertemps Finals* at the Festival and *The Storyteller*, runner-up to *Sire Du Berlais* in the 2020 running of the *Pertemps Final* and also a festival winner himself in 2018 when triumphing in the *Brown Advisory & Merriebelle Stable Plate*. Three horses that had been previously placed at the festival were also in the *Christmas Hurdle*, *Fury Road*, *Bacardys* and *Bapaume*. The outcome of the *Christmas Hurdle* was a victory for *Flooring Porter* (11/1), one of only two entries that had never been to a Cheltenham Festival. Without doubt, this result has had a bearing on ***The Bosses Oscar*** being backed into favouritism for the *Pertemps Final*, as 23 days prior to the *Christmas Hurdle*, in the *eCOMM Merchant Solutions Handicap Hurdle* at *Navan* on 5th December 2020, the 3/1 favourite for the race, ***The Bosses Oscar***, was beaten by a horse priced up at 22/1. That horse is now a Grade 1 winning hurdler, *Flooring Porter* (22/1).

It also wouldn't have gone unnoticed that ***The Bosses Oscar*** is trained by *Gordon Elliott*. In the past five years, all nine of his runners in this event have finished in the first five places, including the past three winners. If there is to be worry for this 6yo gelding come March 18th, then perhaps it will be the lack of a recent run, the last racecourse outing for ***The Bosses Oscar*** being that *Leopardstown Qualifier* on 28th December 2020. It is only a few days away from the turn of the year, admittedly, but nevertheless, only one winner of the *Pertemps Network Final* this century did not have its previous race within the calendar year.

The Bosses Oscar is a worthy favourite for the *Pertemps Network Final* and certainly has a good opportunity to be the third horse by **Oscar** to win a festival handicap and the second to win a *Pertemps Final* since ***Oscar Park***'s success fourteen years ago. That said, it is a tough race to win and I wonder whether when push comes to shove, connections will regret not giving the six-year-old a run since the tail end of December. I've a hunch that ***The Bosses Oscar*** may just miss out and finish in the places instead. We'll see.

Footnote:

For further insight to the *Pertemps Network Final*, read the commentary on ***Unexpected Depth*** by **Shantou**.

Poliglote (GB)

Quote from the 2020 Cheltenham Festival Stallion Guide - "**Poliglote** is likely to be represented by somewhere between 5-10 horses at the 2020 Cheltenham Festival and bearing in mind the progeny's consistency, I fully expect results to be in line with previous trends whereby horses by **Poliglote** will secure a win or place for one in every three festival runs."

Poliglote (Died as a 26-y-o in 2018)							
Race Format	*Miles*	***Won***	***Placed***	***Unplaced***	***Total***	***Win %***	***Place %***
Hurdles	About 2m	1	3	6	10	10%	40%
	About 2m 4f	1	2	4	7	14%	43%
	About 3m	2	0	5	7	29%	29%
Chases	About 2m	1	1	3	5	20%	40%
	About 2m 4f	0	1	6	7	0%	14%
	About 3m	1	2	4	7	14%	43%
	About 4m	0	0	1	1	0%	0%
Bumper	About 2m	0	0	0	0	-	-
Total	**2011-2020**	**6**	**9**	**29**	**44**	**14%**	**34%**

In the 2019 Cheltenham Festival Stallion Guide, I wrote, "*Punters will receive a pay-out for one in every three occasions that a horse by **Poliglote** competes in a festival race.*" At the festival, six horses by **Poliglote** made their way to Prestbury Park and two provided a pay-out, specifically ***Sire Du Berlais*** who won the 2019 *Pertemps Network Final Handicap Hurdle* and ***Politologue*** who finished runner-up in the *Betway Queen Mother Champion Chase*.

Roll on to the 2020 Cheltenham Festival. Déjà vu. At last year's meeting, six horses by **Poliglote** made their way to Prestbury Park and two provided a pay-out, specifically ***Sire Du Berlais*** who won the 2020 *Pertemps Network Final Handicap Hurdle* and ***Politologue*** who won the *Betway Queen Mother Champion Chase*. Not quite déjà vu then. ***Politologue*** going one better in 2020 to claim Wednesday's top prime event, whereas the season before, despite a super performance to finish runner-up, he was no match for the brilliant *Altior*.

For anyone who had backed all of **Poliglote**'s festival representatives to level stakes at both of the past two Cheltenham Festivals, there was a distinct difference. The 6/1 victory by ***Politologue*** in the 2020 *Queen Mother* is clearly more rewarding than securing a runner-up spot at 11/1, as per the outcome of the 2019 renewal. In addition, ***Sire Du Berlais*** was victorious in the 2019 *Pertemps* at a price of 4/1 whereas in the 2020 running, his price was 10/1. To a £10.00 each-way stake, one would have made a loss of £18.00 in 2019, but a £117.00 profit in 2020.

When it comes to **Poliglote**, if one analyses the previous festival results from this stallion's stock, the key message for punters is the recognition that for every six bets placed on **Poliglote**'s offspring at the festival, one can expect a festival victory and another of the progeny to be placed. And the performances by **Poliglote**'s stock have been consistent ever since the first festival runner by **Poliglote**, when ***Liverpool Echo*** (11/1), finished in 9th place in the *Jewson Novices' Handicap Chase* that was won by *King Harald* on 17th March 2005.

Twenty-four horses by **Poliglote** have raced on 49 occasions at Cheltenham Festivals, of which all bar five have taken place within the past decade. Eleven of the 24 horses that have experienced the atmosphere of a Cheltenham Festival have rewarded punters with winnings, with six of the offspring registering wins. Of those six winners, two have been victorious twice at successive festivals. ***Don Poli***, at a price of 12/1, won the 2014 *Martin Pipe Conditional Jockeys' Handicap Hurdle* and then followed up in 2015 when justifying his 13/8 favourite odds when victorious in the *RSA Chase*. The other dual festival winner has already been mentioned, ***Sire Du Berlais***, who has recorded victories in the past two renewals of the *Pertemps Network Final Handicap Hurdle*.

The other four festival winners by **Poliglote** all raced at the Cheltenham Festival more than once. ***Butler's Cabin*** won the 2007 *National Hunt Chase Challenge Cup* at 33/1, returning to the festival two years later when finishing 5th in the 2009 *Fulke Walwyn Kim Muir Challenge Cup Handicap Chase*. ***Spirit River*** (14/1) won the 2010 *Coral Cup* but failed to follow up when falling at the last in the 2012 contest. The mare, ***Let's Dance***, raced at the festival on three occasions, on the first occasion, being one of two mares to tackle the boys when taking 4th place in the 2016 *JCB Triumph Hurdle*. She found it easier on her next visit the following season, when in the second ever running of the *Trull House Stud Mares' Novices' Hurdle*, she was a comfortable winner, quickening clear to reward favourite backers at odds of 11/8. Her form having tailed off after that race, she was a 33/1 outsider when falling mid-race on her 3rd visit to Prestbury Park in the 2018 *Sun Bets Stayers' Hurdle*. And then we come to the already mentioned, ***Politologue***, who having been beaten on his four previous visits to Prestbury Park in March, was finally rewarded with a victory at the 2020 Cheltenham Festival in the *Betway Queen Mother Champion Chase*. It was the grey's 3rd appearance in Wednesday's top race, having finished 4th in 2018 and then taking the runner-up spot behind *Altior* in 2019. It would appear that as ***Politologue*** has matured, he has at last figured out how to deliver strong racing performances going left-handed, although bizarrely, he appears not to be as consistent going right-handed. In his first six chases going right-handed, he won all six of them, but in four further races on right-handed courses since winning at *Ascot* in November 2018, his only victory came more than two years later at *Sandown* in the *Betfair Tingle Creek Chase* on 5th December 2020. In the three right-handed chases preceding the *Tingle Creek*, he hadn't been able to achieve even a front three position. Meanwhile, having only won once going left-handed in his first six chases, he has now not finished outside of the first two in six races since, registering two wins and four runner-up spots.

Looking at **Poliglote**'s festival statistics table at the top of this chapter, it shows a good spread of wins and places pretty much against all race categories. That said, it is worth recognising the impact that ***Sire du Berlais*** and ***Politologue*** have had in the race categories of 3m hurdles and 2m chases respectively. The 29% win and win & place strike rates shown against three-mile hurdles, are wholly down to ***Sire Du Berlais*** and his successive victories in the *Pertemps Network Final Handicap Hurdle*. Next best of the five performances in the festival's 3m contests is 8th. In half a dozen two-mile chase events at the festival, ***Politologue*** has recorded a 1st, 2nd and 4th. The results of the other three contenders have resulted in one horse by **Poliglote** being pulled up, one unseating his rider, and one being placed 14th. In the other chase distances of 2½ miles or more, with a couple of exceptions, **Poliglote**'s offspring are typically registering finishing positions of somewhere between 4th and 8th. The one chase placing at 2½ miles is from ***Top Notch*** in the 2017 *JLT Novices' Chase*, whereas the win and two places shown in the 3m chase category is down to ***Don Poli*** (1st in the 2015 *RSA Chase* and 3rd in the 2016 *Gold Cup*) and ***Wonderful Charm*** (2nd in the 2017 *St. James's Place Foxhunter Challenge Cup Open Hunters' Chase*).

If we take all 49 appearances by **Poliglote**'s progeny into account preceding 2011, it shows that three wins and five place positions have been achieved in the festival's two mile and 2½ mile hurdle events, close to half of the total of seventeen win and place positions. In festival races over two miles, horses by **Poliglote** have finished in the first front five positions on six occasions, including three runner-up spots and one victory. **Poliglote**'s three representatives that have raced in the *Triumph Hurdle* have a

4th placing and two runner-up finishes, so for this year's renewal, punters may wish to look out for any entries from the last remaining four-year-olds from **Poliglote**'s stock.

Horses by **Poliglote** have also performed well in the festival's 2½ mile hurdle races. ***Spirit River*** was victorious in the 2010 *Coral Cup* and in 2013, ***Chatterbox*** (9/1) finished just outside the places when taking 4th place in the progeny's only attempt in what is now called the *Ballymore Novices' Hurdle*. The number one event for **Poliglote**'s offspring, however, has to be the *Martin Pipe Conditional Jockey's Handicap Hurdle*, where in three appearances to date, horses by **Poliglote** have a 100% record of rewarding bets. ***Don Poli*** won at 12/1 in 2014, ***Roi Des Francs*** (3/1 favourite) finished 3rd in 2015 and ***Sire Du Berlais*** (10/1) secured a 4th place dividend in 2018.

The statistics surrounding the progeny of **Poliglote** are highly impressive. Who can argue with picking up either a win or a place dividend for one in every three of **Poliglote**'s festival runners? Taking the results overall, beyond the past decade, a £10.00 each-way bet on all 49 festival runs from **Poliglote**'s progeny equates to a total profit of £383.50. As is typical, there won't be too many festival entries by **Poliglote** at the 2021 Cheltenham Festival, but punters should examine all entries seriously. The stallion's record speaks for itself.

Polilote (GB) – Progeny with Official Rating of 135+

Horses by this sire with an Official Rating of 135 or greater on 9th February 2021. Horses registered with the Irish Horseracing Regulatory Board (I.H.R.B) are shown in *italics*.

				Official Ratings as of 9th February 2021		
Sire	***Horse***	***Age***	***Sex***	***Hurdles***	***Chase***	***Trainer***
Poliglote	Alnadam	8	g		145	Dan Skelton
Poliglote	Capeland	9	g		153	Paul Nicholls
Poliglote	Chirico Vallis	9	g	140		Neil Mulholland
Poliglote	*Class Conti*	*9*	*g*	*142*	*149*	*W.P. Mullins*
Poliglote	Floressa	6	f	143		Nicky Henderson
Poliglote	Katpoli	6	g		137	Dr Richard Newland
Poliglote	Le Patriote	9	g		146	Dr Richard Newland
Poliglote	Politologue	10	g		168	Paul Nicholls
Poliglote	*Sire Du Berlais*	*9*	*g*	*158*		*Gordon Elliott*
Poliglote	Tamaroc Du Mathan	6	g		147	Paul Nicholls
Poliglote	Top Notch	10	g		154	Nicky Henderson

Presenting (GB)

Quote from the 2020 Cheltenham Festival Stallion Guide - "The 2020 Cheltenham Festival will be a tough one for supporters of **Presenting**. In a nutshell, **Presenting**'s stock is lacking in quality at present, so the hope is that some talented youngsters will emerge over the next 2-3 years to add further success to what has been an impressive eighteen years of siring festival winners."

Presenting (Died as a 25-y-o in 2017)							
Race Format	*Miles*	*Won*	*Placed*	*Unplaced*	*Total*	*Win %*	*Place %*
Hurdles	About 2m	0	1	7	8	0%	13%
	About 2m 4f	2	0	18	20	10%	10%
	About 3m	1	1	10	12	8%	17%
Chases	About 2m	0	1	11	12	0%	8%
	About 2m 4f	3	4	18	25	12%	28%
	About 3m	1	6	47	54	2%	13%
	About 4m	0	1	13	14	0%	7%
Bumper	About 2m	0	0	8	8	0%	0%
Total	2011-2020	**7**	**14**	**132**	**153**	**5%**	**14%**

The predominant festival stallion this century is **Presenting**. In total, 126 of his offspring have managed to race at least once at a Cheltenham Festival. Several of the progeny made the trip to Prestbury Park on more than one occasion, most notably ***Denman***, who would prick his ears to the deafening cheers of the festival crowds on every occasion in which he raced up the famous Cheltenham hill in his bid to hit the winning line before his competitors. His festival debut took place in 2006 when he finished 2nd to *Nicanor* in the *Royal & SunAlliance Novices' Hurdle*. Switching to fences the following season, he made no mistake in the 2007 *Royal & SunAlliance Novices' Chase*, storming to the winning line ahead of 16 competitors to win by 10 lengths. In 2008, trainer *Paul Nicholls* celebrated his three *totesport Cheltenham Gold Cup* entries filling the first three places. ***Denman*** was the clear winner, beating runner-up *Kauto Star* by 7 lengths and a short head further away in 3rd, *Neptune Collonges*. Twelve months later and gaining revenge, *Kauto Star* reversed placings with ***Denman*** to take the blue riband prize by 13 lengths. ***Denman*** also found one too good for the next two years, being beaten by 7 lengths on both occasions. In 2010, he was beaten into second by the *Nigel Twiston-Davies* trained *Imperial Commander*, and in the last of his festival appearances, at the grand old age of 11, he didn't have the legs of the youthful six-year-old winner who hailed from *Nicky Henderson*'s yard, the French-bred *Long Run*.

Six festival appearances and never out of the first two. That was ***Denman***. Some record. He wasn't the only Cheltenham Festival 'six-timer' to be sired by **Presenting**. Although ***Drombeag*** was unable to match ***Denman***'s heroics, he still managed to reward each-way bets on three occasions. His debut in 2004 resulted in a 3rd place finish in the four-miler *National Hunt Novices' Chase* and he matched that finishing position when an 11-year-old in another long-distance event, the 2009 *Glenfarclas Handicap Chase Cross Country Chase*. The best of ***Drombeag***'s his six festival performances occurred in the 2007 *Christie's Foxhunter Chase Challenge Cup*, when ridden by *Mr J T McNamara*, he just beat off the challenge of 2/1 favourite *Whyso Mayo* to win the race for trainer *Jonjo O'Neill* and owner *J P McManus* at a price of 20/1.

It is some feat to have 126 of your offspring make it to Cheltenham's top meeting, and all told, **Presenting**-bred horses have made 233 festival appearances, of which 153 have taken place within the past decade. As regards to **Presenting**'s success as a stallion to follow at the Cheltenham Festival, there is no doubt that his stock had a far better festival win strike rate when **Presenting** was younger. Between 2002 and 2010, the first 80 festival outings from **Presenting**'s progeny resulted in 8 victories and 16 place positions, hence a win strike rate of 10% and a win & place strike rate of 30%. Those strike-rates have halved in the past decade where in 153 festival appearances, **Presenting**'s representatives have delivered 7 wins (win-strike rate of 5%) and 14 placed (win & place strike rate of 14%). Converting the above strike rates into financial terms highlights how the festival performances of **Presenting**'s stock have tailed off within the past decade. Had one placed a £10.00 each way bet on all 80 of **Presenting**'s representatives between 2002 and 2010, it would have resulted in a profit of £97.20. The same stake on the offspring's 153 appearances from 2011 onwards delivers a loss of £1,432.25.

There was one **Presenting**-bred winner every year for the five festivals between 2013 and 2017, but since then, the winners have dried up completely. Indeed, the only return on bets placed on **Presenting**'s representatives at the past three festivals has come from the suitably named ***Top Gamble*** (8/1) who finished in 3rd place in the 2018 *Johnny Henderson Grand Annual Challenge Cup Handicap Chase*. It is the one and only occasion in sixteen attempts that **Presenting**'s stock has secured a win or place in the festival's two-mile chase category. ***Top Gamble***'s 3rd place is just one of four top-six finishing positions achieved from 37 outings from the progeny at the past three festivals. ***Ballycasey***, at 33/1, finished 4th in the 2019 *Glenfarclas Cross Country Chase*, and at last year's meeting, two of the six **Presenting** bred representatives came home in 6th place. Only six finished out of the ten starters in last year's *RSA Insurance Novices' Chase* and the *Colin Tizzard* trained ***Slate House*** was the last to cross the finishing line, tailed off and 70 lengths behind winner, *Champ*. The other 6th place finish in the *St. James's Place Foxhunter Challenge Cup Open Hunters' Chase*, was highly respectable given that ***Marcle Ridge*** was sent off as a 100/1 outsider.

There doesn't appear to be anything with the quality of a '***Denman***' within the current crop of **Presenting**'s offspring, but nevertheless, come the spring, there will still be some 5-10 of the progeny bidding to provide this stallion with a 16th Cheltenham Festival victory. To determine which **Presenting** bred entry has the best opportunity for success, I suggest that punters pick out those horses competing in races where the offspring have previously provided punters with lucrative rewards. If we look at how **Presenting**'s hurdlers have performed over the past decade, it is interesting to note that those that lined up at single figure odds have generated a profit, whilst any hurdler at 10/1 or bigger should be avoided at all costs. Since 2011, there have been 40 appearances by **Presenting**'s progeny in the festival's hurdle events, where seven runners lined up at single figure odds. Of those 7, three won, and one was placed, which would have delivered a profit to punters of £179.50 to a £10.00 each-way stake. Of the other 33 runners who were priced up at 10/1 or more, only one of them has recorded a top four placing, when ***Cockney Trucker*** at 33/1 secured 4th place and an each-way return in the 2011 *Vincent O'Brien County Handicap Hurdle*. Betting on outsiders by **Presenting** in the festival's hurdle events is ill-advised. Over the past decade, if one had placed a £10.00 each-way wager on all of **Presenting**'s hurdlers with starting prices of 10/1 or greater, a loss of £567.50 would be the outcome. Having highlighted how the odds on offer on **Presenting**'s festival bound hurdlers have impacted profits, one should note that the last time that a hurdler by **Presenting** turned up at a Cheltenham Festival priced up at single figure odds was in 2016. In fact, there has only been one horse by **Presenting** that has lined up in a hurdle race in the past two years. The horse in question was ***Mount Mews*** in the 2019 *Martin Pipe Conditional Jockeys' Handicap Hurdle*, and when the tapes went up, the 33/1 shot dug his heels in and refused to race.

For those interested in Cheltenham Festival trivia, does anyone recall the name of the horse who lined up as the 4/5 favourite for the 2010 *Supreme Novices' Hurdle*? The horse in question, trained by *Philip Fenton*, finished in 3rd place, beaten by winner *Menorah* and runner-up *Get Me Out Of Here*. The answer is ***Dunguib***, sired by **Presenting**. I mention ***Dunguib***, because horses by **Presenting** have lined up in festival races over a distance of around two miles (chases, hurdles and bumpers) on 47 occasions. Only one has been victorious and that was ***Dunguib*** when he won the 2009 *Weatherbys Champion Bumper*, the year before his 3rd place finish in the *Supreme*. Punters are advised, therefore, to ignore **Presenting**'s progeny when it comes to the festival's shortest races over two miles. But what about the longest two races over, what is now, around 3m6f, the races being the *Glenfarclas Cross Country Chase* and the *National Hunt Amateur Riders' Novices Chase*? **Presenting** has been represented on 26 occasions in these two events; 21 runs (and 2 places achieved) in the *National Hunt Novices' Chase*; and 5 runs (and 1 place achieved) in the *Glenfarclas Chase*. Two out of the three place positions recorded are courtesy of ***Drombeag***, already highlighted at the start of this chapter.

With the recommendation to ignore **Presenting**'s progeny in the two long distance chases as well as races across all disciplines within the 2m race categories, scrutiny should therefore turn to the 2½m and 3m chases. Unfortunately, an analysis of the offspring's performances in three-mile chases underlines how the fortunes of **Presenting**'s stock has turned sour in recent years. Up to and including 2012, chasers by **Presenting** lined up in 29 festival races within the 3m chase category and recorded 7 wins and 7 places, a win & place strike rate of marginally under 50%. Results in the last 8 festivals are radically different. In 44 appearances by **Presenting**'s progeny in 3m chases from 2013 onwards, only three place positions have been achieved, a place strike-rate of just 7%. Against this background, it will take a brave punter to place a bet on **Presenting**-bred 3m chase entries at the 2021 Cheltenham Festival.

So, chases within the 2½m category is all that is left. If we take the same position as the analysis above and look solely at the past 8 festivals, the statistics are somewhat beguiling. In 21 appearances in the festival's 2½m chases, runners by **Presenting** have achieved 3 wins and 3 places which is a win strike rate of 14% and a 29% win & place strike rate. This represents a far better success record than the other chase distances. But it is important to take a look at the four individual races. Nine of the racecourse appearances have taken place in the *Stable Plate Handicap Chase*, where the highest finishing position achieved by a **Presenting**-bred runner was fifth place, recorded by ***Ballycasey*** in the 2016 renewal. If we take out the nine *Stable Plate* outings by **Presenting**'s progeny, then we are left with a 50% win and place strike rate (3 wins and 3 places from twelve 2½m chase appearances). In the past 8 years, eight horses by **Presenting** have lined up in Tuesday's *Listed Novices' Handicap Chase*, sponsored last year by *Northern Trust* but previously known as the *Close Brothers Novices' Handicap Chase*. **Presenting**'s offspring have a particularly strong record in this race, having won it with ***Rajdhani Express*** (16/1) in 2013 and again the following year with ***Present View*** (8/1). ***Gold Present*** (14/1) was runner-up in 2017 when beaten by *Tully East*. Going back further in this event, two other **Presenting** sired chasers also recorded place efforts, courtesy of ***Crescent Island*** (2009) and ***China Rock*** (2010). Regrettably, there is bad news for **Presenting** supporters, as this handicap chase for novices is now discontinued to make way for a new steeplechase for mares. The silver lining is that this new contest will also be raced over 2m4f, so hopefully **Presenting** may be represented by a mare for the inaugural running.

The other two festival chases within the 2½m category are Grade 1 affairs so winners of these contests need to be top class. Perhaps surprisingly, **Presenting** has had very few of his progeny entered in either contest. In the *Marsh Novices' Chase*, **Presenting** has a 100 percent win record having been represented just once, when the quirky ***Yorkhill*** (6/4 favourite) was victorious in 2017. The middle-distance chase with the highest prize money of just short of £200,000 is the *Ryanair Chase*. Once again, **Presenting**'s offspring have a respectable record in this race, albeit from just three appearances. ***First***

Lieutenant finished runner-up in 2013; ***Rajdhani Express*** took 3rd place in 2014; and ***Ballycasey*** was pulled up in 2015. Nine of the past 10 winners of this race went to post with an Official Rating of at least 165.

Presenting's offspring have a very respectable record in the middle-distance festival chases and if this stallion is to record a 16th Cheltenham Festival victory, then I believe it will most likely happen in a chase run over a distance of around 2m4f, even perhaps in the *Stable Plate* where the stallion's record to date is not so strong. The other alternative of achieving a festival winner, although less likely in my view, is if a well-fancied hurdler by **Presenting** lines up in one of the 2½m or 3m hurdle contests.

Presenting (GB) – Progeny with Official Rating of 135+

Horses by this sire with an Official Rating of 135 or greater on 9th February 2021. Horses registered with the Irish Horseracing Regulatory Board (I.H.R.B) are shown in *italics*.

					Official Ratings as of 9th February 2021	
Sire	***Horse***	***Age***	***Sex***	***Hurdles***	***Chase***	***Trainer***
Presenting	*Brahma Bull*	*10*	*g*		*150*	*W.P. Mullins*
Presenting	*Champagne Gold*	*6*	*g*	*138*		*Henry de Bromhead*
Presenting	Chilli Filli	8	f		141	Henry Daly
Presenting	Doing Fine	13	g		135	Neil Mulholland
Presenting	El Presente	8	g		148	Kim Bailey
Presenting	*Gallant John Joe*	*8*	*g*		*149*	*Oliver McKiernan*
Presenting	Give Me A Copper	11	g		147	Paul Nicholls
Presenting	Gold Present	11	g		145	Nicky Henderson
Presenting	Imperial Presence	10	g		147	Philip Hobbs
Presenting	*January Jets*	*7*	*g*		*140*	*Henry de Bromhead*
Presenting	Make Me A Believer	6	g	138		David Pipe
Presenting	*Off You Go*	*8*	*g*		*147*	*C.Byrnes*
Presenting	Present Man	11	g		145	Paul Nicholls
Presenting	*School Boy Hours*	*8*	*g*		*135*	*Noel Meade*
Presenting	Slate House	9	g		148	Colin Tizzard
Presenting	*Snow Falcon*	*11*	*g*		*153*	*Noel Meade*
Presenting	Time To Get Up	8	g		138	Jonjo O'Neill
Presenting	Yorkhill	11	g	142	147	Sandy Thomson

Commentary on selected potential entries for 2021 Festival

Champagne Gold – Martin Pipe Handicap Hurdle 2m4½f (5:30 Friday 19th March)
Make Me A Believer - Martin Pipe Handicap Hurdle 2m4½f (5:30 Friday 19th March)

I haven't spent much time in analysing the runners for this event. There are usually so many entries that also hold engagements in other festival races that it is difficult to know who will end up racing in the 28th and last race of the festival. However, I have come across two horses by **Presenting** that are both in the betting at around 12/1 for the *Martin Pipe Conditional Jockeys Handicap Hurdle*, so to be that price, I'm assuming that they must have shown something in their form.

Champagne Gold is a 6yo trained in Ireland by *Henry De Bromhead* whose last outing was a very satisfactory 2nd place to ***Drop The Anchor*** in the Grade B *Ladbrokes Hurdle* at *Leopardstown* on February 6th in which 22 ran. That looks like a sound prep race for the *Martin Pipe* so we shall see if he makes the trip over to Cheltenham. ***Make Me A Believer***, also aged six is trained by *David Pipe*. He was last engaged in a Grade 2 event at *Warwick* where he finished a close-up 3rd to *Adrimel*. My one concern with *David Pipe*'s runners is that, as yet, they have been wholly unsuccessful in this race, when one may expect the trainer to lay one out to win the race named in honour of his father. Maybe ***Make Me A Believer*** will be the one. As of now, *David Pipe* has entered 20 horses in the *Martin Pipe* without success.

Keep a look-out for how these two fare in the betting market before the off. If you look back through **Presenting**'s commentary, you may note that on the seven occasions in which **Presenting**'s hurdlers at Cheltenham Festivals have been sent off at single figure odds, three of them have won. So, if either horse is 9/1 or less, do what I do and place a win bet. Be brave if the horse is 10/1 or bigger – don't be tempted. Keep your money in your pocket!

Saddler Maker (IRE)

Quote from the 2020 Cheltenham Festival Stallion Guide - "In looking at the potential entries by **Saddler Maker** for the 2020 Cheltenham Festival, some of the offspring, such as ***Eglantine Du Seuil***, ***Discorama***, ***Apple's Jade*** and ***Janika***, appear as if they may end up in races where they may simply be outclassed by some of their rivals. If this quartet all take their chances against top quality opposition in top quality races, then I think it is going to be very difficult for the progeny as a whole to maintain its festival win & place strike rate which currently stands at an incredulous 54%."

Saddler Maker (Died as an 18-y-o in 2016)							
Race Format	*Miles*	*Won*	*Placed*	*Unplaced*	*Total*	*Win %*	*Place %*
Hurdles	About 2m	1	2	4	7	14%	43%
	About 2m 4f	1	4	3	8	13%	63%
	About 3m	0	1	2	3	0%	33%
Chases	About 2m	0	0	1	1	0%	0%
	About 2m 4f	0	4	1	5	0%	80%
	About 3m	0	2	5	7	0%	29%
	About 4m	0	1	1	2	0%	50%
Bumper	About 2m	0	0	0	0	-	-
Total	2011-2020	**2**	**14**	**17**	**33**	**6%**	**48%**

Every so often, Germany (I'm talking about the country, not the stallion) will have a less than satisfactory World Cup Football tournament, but it doesn't happen that often, and they usually bounce back. **Saddler Maker** is one of the flag-bearers for those, like me, who believe that breeding is highly influential to a horse's performance when competing at the Cheltenham Festival. Over the years, the stallion's offspring have consistently produced strong performances in early Spring racing over what is one of the most challenging and testing courses in the country. Bearing in mind the high standards set by this sire, horses by **Saddler Maker** had a disappointing 2020 Cheltenham Festival, not that it was entirely unexpected.

Saddler Maker was represented by just five of his stock at last year's meeting, four of which had made the trip to the festival in previous years. Added together, these four experienced runners had raced at the festival on ten occasions and had registered a top three finish eight times, one of which was a victory. However, in the build-up to last year's meeting, three of this quartet were out of form and one other was entering a race where he would almost certainly be out of his depth. I had mentioned all four horses in last year's Guide, where I had written, *"Since her victory, **Eglantine Du Seuil** hasn't exactly set the world alight ... she could easily dent her sire's superb record in festival races over 2½ miles"*; and on ***Apple's Jade***, *"For the first time in three years, she won't be going off as the favourite in whatever race she tackles at the 2020 Cheltenham Festival and her price will probably be in double figures should she appear in the Paddy Power Stayers' Hurdle."*; *"I should point out that connections of **Bristol De Mai** might consider the competition is too hot in the Gold Cup, and so potentially divert the grey to the Ryanair Chase, although I'm not convinced his chances would be any better."*; and *"In which race **Discorama** is entered, is anyone's guess, but based on his rather disappointing performances so far this season, he is likely to line up at a big price."*

The last of the four horses mentioned above, ***Discorama***, would race at the 2020 Festival against another **Saddler Maker** sired runner, in the *Ultima Handicap Chase*. I was rather annoyed to see that trainer *Venetia Williams* had decided that ***Cepage***'s debut at the Cheltenham Festival would be over three miles in the *Ultima Handicap Chase*, as I had placed a sizeable ante-post bet on ***Cepage*** in Thursday's 2m4½f *Brown Advisory & Merriebelle Stable Plate*. *Venetia Williams* knows far more about racehorses than I shall ever know, but I had risked a wager in the 2½m contest based on three things: (1) In 12 festival races at around 2m4f, runners sired by **Saddler Maker** had finished in the first three positions on nine occasions; (2) ***Cepage*** won a handicap chase on 25th January 2020 which 12 months earlier had been won by the 2019 winner of the *Stable Plate*, *Siruh Du Lac* and (3) *Venetia Williams* has a great record in the *Stable Plate*, having won it three times with *Idole First* (2007), *Something Wells* (2009) and *Carrickboy* (2013). As we all know, ante-post betting is a risky business. Sometimes we can benefit from far bigger odds than what is available on the day of the race but built into those odds is the chance that our selection may not compete. My wager on ***Cepage*** went down the pan.

I didn't back ***Cepage*** in the *Ultima Handicap Chase* for the simple reason that all three influences that made me want to back ***Cepage*** in the *Stable Plate* no longer applied. ***Cepage*** was stepping up to a distance of three miles for the first time in his career in the *Ultima*, and although he pulled his way through to lead at around half-way, in the end, his stamina ran out and the 14/1 chance ended up some eight lengths behind the front four to finish in seventh. As for the *Paul Nolan* trained ***Discorama***, he was well-backed for this race and lined up as the joint 11/2 favourite. Having been placed in his two previous visits to the Cheltenham Festival, despite losing his right-fore show, ***Discorama*** made it 3 places from 3 festival starts when finishing in 3rd.

Having been the surprise 50/1 winner of the 2019 *Mares Novices' Hurdle*, the **Saddler Maker** sired ***Eglantine Du Seuil*** hadn't won a race since, so it was no surprise when the *Willie Mullins* trained mare made no impression in Wednesday's *Coral Cup Handicap Hurdle* when finishing in 11th spot at a price of 16/1. The second mare by **Saddler Maker** to be entered for the 2020 Cheltenham Festival, ***Apple's Jade***, had also been a previous Cheltenham Festival winner, when winning the 2017 *OLBG Mares' Hurdle*, a year after her festival debut when finishing runner-up in the *JCB Triumph Hurdle*. Her entry in the 2020 *Paddy Power Stayers' Hurdle* would mark her fifth festival appearance. In this 3m event, connections were hoping that their audacious plan to have ***Apple's Jade*** lead at a fast pace from the front in first-time blinkers would pay off. An innovative attempt, maybe, but ultimately the plan failed. ***Apple's Jade*** set off at an unsustainable gallop before wilting considerably at the final bend. After the race, *Gordon Elliott* later announced that the mare was to be retired, but that hasn't stopped ***Apple's Jade*** from making headlines. Having won 11 Grade 1 races plus four others from her 28 starts, ***Apple's Jade*** fetched a record 530,000 Euros at *Kildare Paddocks* sale ring in December 2020. In foal to *Coolmore* stallion, *Walk In The Park*, she smashed the previous record for a National Hunt mare sold at public auction and was purchased by *Noel* and *Valerie Moran* of *Bective Stud* in County Meath.

The last of **Saddler Maker**'s five offspring to make it to last year's festival meeting was ***Bristol De Mai***, who was making his 3rd appearance in the *Cheltenham Gold Cup* and his 4th visit to the festival in total. On his festival debut, the grey had finished runner-up to *Black Hercules* in the *JLT*, now known as the *Marsh Novices' Chase*. Ever since, his sole target has been the *Gold Cup*. His best performance was in the 2019 renewal, when priced up at 18/1, he cruised into the race over the last ½ mile but without the strength of his two rivals when it mattered up the Cheltenham Hill. It was an improvement on his *Gold Cup* debut in 2017 where he could only finish in seventh. In last year's contest, ***Bristol De Mai*** led for the first two thirds of the race before being outpaced and weakening as they approached the Cheltenham hill finish. Although it was unlikely that ***Bristol De Mai*** would match his effort of twelve months ago, in truth, it was almost certainly the most disappointing of his four festival appearances.

Just 14 horses by **Saddler Maker** have raced on 33 occasions at Cheltenham Festivals, and only 5 of those 14 have failed to finish in the top three places to register a festival win or place position. Had one placed a £10.00 each-way stake on all 33 festival outings by **Saddler Maker**'s offspring, the outcome would be a profit of £505.75. Although wins have been rare, just the two, horses by **Saddler**

Maker have hit a place position on 14 occasions. The win & place strike rate of 48%, which translates to a return on a festival wager of almost one in every two festival appearances made by one of the stallion's progeny is, quite simply, phenomenal. And one more interesting statistic is that only on three occasions at a Cheltenham Festival has a horse by **Saddler Maker** failed to complete the course in the race in which it started. ***Chef Des Obeaux*** lined up in two festival events and was pulled up in both of them, whilst ***Bouvreuil***, who could already boast three festival places to his name, was just plain unlucky when brought down at the 2nd fence in the 2018 *Grand Annual*.

The sweetest spot for the stock of **Saddler Maker** would appear to be in festival races that are contested within the 2½m categories. In 13 outings in races of around 2½ miles, the offspring have recorded one victory, four that have finished runner-up and a further four that have claimed 3rd position. With just four of the 13 runners failing to secure a win or a place, the strike-rate is an incredible 69%, which is perhaps why some readers may understand my frustration that ***Cepage***'s festival debut was in a three-mile event, instead of 2½ miles!

When a stallion can boast such an outstanding festival strike rate, it makes it all the more difficult to maintain it. For example, with just one placing to show for the five outings by **Saddler Maker**'s offspring at the 2020 Cheltenham Festival, the win & place strike rate dropped 6 points from 54% to 48%, whereas one placing in five runs for a stallion with a poor festival record may result in a strike-rate improvement! With such a high standard of festival success, I think that **Saddler Maker** is entitled to have one sub-standard season. The question is, can he bounce back? I hope so, and especially if, come the 2021 Festival, there are a few more entries in races at 2½ miles.

Saddler Maker (IRE) – Progeny with Official Rating of 135+

Horses by this sire with an Official Rating of 135 or greater on 9th February 2021. Horses registered with the Irish Horseracing Regulatory Board (I.H.R.B) are shown in *italics*.

					Official Ratings as of 9th February 2021	
Sire	***Horse***	***Age***	***Sex***	***Hurdles***	***Chase***	***Trainer***
Saddler Maker	*Alpha Des Obeaux*	*11*	*g*		*149*	*Gordon Elliott*
Saddler Maker	Bristol De Mai	10	g	162	169	Nigel Twiston-Davies
Saddler Maker	Cepage	9	g		158	Venetia Williams
Saddler Maker	*Chef Des Obeaux*	*9*	*g*		*149*	*W.P. Mullins*
Saddler Maker	*Discorama*	*8*	*g*		*149*	*Paul Nolan*
Saddler Maker	Eglantine Du Seuil	7	f	145		Paul Nicholls
Saddler Maker	Janika	8	g	145		Nicky Henderson
Saddler Maker	*Larquebuse*	*7*	*f*	*135*		*Gordon Elliott*
Saddler Maker	Messire Des Obeaux	9	g		150	Alan King

Saint Des Saints (FR)

Quote from the 2020 Cheltenham Festival Stallion Guide - "I am far more optimistic about the festival results that horses by **Saint Des Saints** are likely to achieve at this year's meeting compared to 2019. Although it is difficult to specifically pin down those entries that will reward their supporters' wagers, in my view, the offspring's 2020 festival runners overall, offer far better ammunition than in the past few years to make an impact."

Saint Des Saints (23-y-o)							
Race Format	*Miles*	*Won*	*Placed*	*Unplaced*	*Total*	*Win %*	*Place %*
Hurdles	About 2m	0	6	4	10	0%	60%
	About 2m 4f	1	1	5	7	14%	29%
	About 3m	0	1	5	6	0%	17%
Chases	About 2m	0	0	4	4	0%	0%
	About 2m 4f	1	1	5	7	14%	29%
	About 3m	0	3	6	9	0%	33%
	About 4m	0	1	0	1	0%	100%
Bumper	About 2m	0	1	1	2	0%	50%
Total	**2011-2020**	**2**	**14**	**30**	**46**	**4%**	**35%**

In last year's Cheltenham Festival Stallion Guide, I advised that as far as festival performances went, **Saint Des Saints** was on a bad run. In the three festivals between 2017 and 2019, the stallion's festival runners had recorded just one placing in 16 runs. This compared with 19 contenders at the previous five festivals achieving 2 wins and 8 places. The critical question to be asked was which period of time, 2012-2016 or 2017-2019, was an irregularity from the norm? My conclusion was the latter and the quote at the top of the page predicted that **Saint Des Saints'** stock had far better chances to make an impact last year than at the previous three festivals. My judgement was correct.

Ten horses by **Saint Des Saints** made the trip to Prestbury Park last March and half of them finished in the front three securing five place positions. The three horses that finished as runner-up and the two 3rd placed runners were, unfortunately, unable to go that one step forward to record a victory. The outcome of five places from ten runners undoubtedly translates into a successful festival, but the absence of a victory certainly has a somewhat cruel impact financially. Had one placed a £10.00 each-way bet blind on all ten of last year's festival entries by **Saint Des Saints**, the result would be a loss of £22.00. The financial returns once again emphasising that it is winners that deliver profits, whereas placed horses either reduces the financial losses or gets your stake money back.

Forgive me, but I feel reasonably smug and quite pleased with my chapter on **Saint Des Saints** in last year's Guide. Of the five horses that secured places, I highlighted three of them. This is what I wrote about ***Elfile***, who finished 3rd in last year's Grade 1 *Close Brothers Mares' Hurdle*, *"I quite like **Elfile**, whose race reports always appear to suggest that the mare is giving it her all in her races. Looking at the Official Ratings, she has it all to do in the Mares' Hurdle at Cheltenham, but then again, she was only beaten by 5½ lengths in both of her defeats to Honeysuckle and Stormy Ireland. If she puts in a personal best, I can see this highly likeable mare perhaps snatching a place."* And snatch a place is exactly what ***Elfile*** did, finishing some half dozen lengths behind the front two in the market when outpaced, but nevertheless, rewarding each-way backers, including myself, with a 16/1 starting price. I was pleased with my bet as I believed it represented value, especially as I couldn't make up my mind on who would come out on top out of *Benie Des Dieux* (4/6 Favourite) and *Honeysuckle* (9/4). It was the latter that did.

In the 2020 *Boodles Juvenile Handicap Hurdle (Registered as the Fred Winter)*, I was very keen on one of *Saint Des Saints'* younger offspring, in the shape of the *Gordon Elliott* trained, ***Saint D'oroux***, so much so that I had placed an ante-post bet on the four-year-old at a price of 33/1. My confidence was based upon the rationale that not only do horses by **Saint Des Saints** have a great record in the festival's juvenile races, but so does *Gordon Elliott* who had trained four juvenile winners at previous festivals, split two apiece across the *Triumph* and the *Fred Winter*. In last year's Guide, I highlighted ***Saint D'oroux*** as follows: *"As of early January, he is a big outsider for either the Triumph or the Fred Winter, but then again three horses by* ***Saint Des Saints*** *have already achieved big-priced placings in both races already."* In the race itself, ***Saint D'oroux***, 14/1 on the day, looked a big threat when he led the field turning into the home straight but couldn't find any extra as they approached the last, and he came home in 3rd place, four lengths behind stablemate and winner, *Aramax*. *Gordon Elliott* saddled five runners in last year's *Boodles Juvenile Handicap Hurdle*, resulting in finishing positions of 1st, 3rd, 4th, 8th and 9th. The trainer clearly likes this race.

On the Thursday of the 2020 Cheltenham Festival, entered amongst the eight runners in the *Ryanair Chase* was the seven-year-old **Saint Des Saints** sired ***Saint Calvados***, who lined up at a price of 16/1. Here it what I said about his chances last year, *"Both* ***Saint Calvados*** *and trainer Harry Whittington are a year older and wiser and the experience and knowledge gained by the duo in the 2018 Arkle and 2019 Champion Chase can only be of benefit. The Ryanair will have a high-quality field and it will no doubt be a challenge for* ***Saint Calvados*** *to trouble the leaders and perhaps sneak into a place. Win or lose, if he takes his chance in the 2020 Ryanair, my hunch is that* ***Saint Calvados*** *will experience his best festival performance to date."* **Saint Calvados** did a little more than just sneak into a place in last year's *Ryanair*, he kept on well towards the finish to lose to the 'all out' *Min* by just a neck.

The three horses by **Saint Des Saints** that I highlighted in last year's Guide all secured their place dividends at the quite rewarding odds of 14/1 and 16/1 twice. Not bad. The other two place positions that were registered at the 2020 Cheltenham Festival were both at shorter odds. ***Lord Du Mesnil***, at 11/2, and trained by *Richard Hobson*, finished runner-up to *Ravenhill* in the *National Hunt Challenge Cup Amateur Riders' Novices' Chase*, the front two more than 28 lengths away from the 3rd placed horse to finish, *Lamanver Pippin*. And the one remaining horse to secure a place was the mare, ***Dolcita*** (9/1), who was well beaten when finishing runner-up to stablemate, *Concertista*, in the *Daylesford Mares' Novices' Hurdle (Registered as the Dawn Run)*. The *Dawn Run* is the festival's newest race and in the five renewals to date, *Willie Mullins* has saddled all five winners. Last season, his four mares that were entered finished 1st, 2nd, 4th and 5th.

In total, thirty horses by **Saint Des Saints** have raced on 50 occasions at Cheltenham Festivals, of which 46 have occurred within the past decade. From a financial perspective, had one placed a £10.00 each way wager at level stakes on all 40 runners, the result would be a loss of £157.75. Taking the past decade only, the stallion boasts an excellent win & place strike rate of 35%, or 32% if including the four unplaced festival runners preceding 2011. However, the win strike rate alone of 4% is disappointing with just 2 wins to show from the offspring's 50 appearances. To date, horses by **Saint Des Saints** get placed at the festival seven times more often than when they win, and in half of those 14 placed efforts, the stallion's representatives have finished as the runner-up. If one or two of those runner-up spots had instead been victories, then we would no doubt be reporting an overall festival profit for this stallion rather than a loss.

With ***Lord Du Mesnil*** securing a placing in the 3m6f *National Hunt Chase*, which falls within the 4m chase category within the festival statistics table, the stock of **Saint Des Saints** has now recorded at least one placing in all race categories, with the one exception which is the 2m chase category. There is no reason to suggest that the progeny has any trouble with this discipline, after all, horses by **Saint Des Saints** have only ever contested four festival two-mile chases.

To provide a steer on specific races, punters should definitely look out for any juveniles by **Saint Des Saints** that hold entries in either the *JCB Triumph Hurdle* or the *Boodles Juvenile Handicap Hurdle*. Two horses by **Saint Des Saints** have contested the *Triumph Hurdle* and three others have competed in the *Fred Winter*. ***Connetable*** was unable to finish in the first three places in the 2016 *Triumph Hurdle*, but three years previously in the 2013 renewal, ***Sametegal*** returned a starting price of 33/1 when he finished third and some seventeen lengths behind the runaway winner, *Our Conor*. The progeny of **Saint Des Saints** holds a 100% place record in the *Boodles Juvenile Handicap Hurdle*. In the 2015 running of the contest, ***The Saint James*** (33/1) finished in 3rd place behind the *Paul Nicholls* trained duo of *Qualando* and *Bouvreuil* who finished 1st and 2nd respectively. *Paul Nicholls* was at it again in the 2016 *Fred Winter*, securing a 1-2 for the second year in a row when stablemates *Diego Du Charmil* and ***Romain De Senam*** fought out a tight finish. It was so very close at the line as the **Saint Des Saints** bred ***Romain De Senam*** (20/1), ran on strongly in the last 100 yards, but just failed to catch *Diego Du Charmil* by a head. One or two more yards and ***Romain De Senam*** would have won. And at last year's 2020 Cheltenham Festival, I have already highlighted the 3rd place showing by ***Saint D'oroux*** (14/1).

For the 2021 Cheltenham Festival, I am once again optimistic about the fortunes of **Saint Des Saints'** offspring. I consider there to be some talented racehorses amongst the current stock, and if one or two of the festival entries this March could achieve a victory rather than a 2nd or 3rd placing, then in next year's Guide, instead of places and small losses, I'll be writing about wins and profits.

Saint Des Saints (FR) – Progeny with Official Rating of 135+

Horses by this sire with an Official Rating of 135 or greater on 9th February 2021. Horses registered with the Irish Horseracing Regulatory Board (I.H.R.B) are shown in *italics*.

					Official Ratings as of 9th February 2021	
Sire	***Horse***	***Age***	***Sex***	***Hurdles***	***Chase***	***Trainer***
Saint Des Saints	Aux Ptits Soins	11	g	150		Dan Skelton
Saint Des Saints	*Burrows Saint*	*8*	*g*	*149*	*156*	*W.P. Mullins*
Saint Des Saints	Dolcita	6	f	136		Fergal O'Brien
Saint Des Saints	Fabulous Saga	9	g	140	140	Paul Nicholls
Saint Des Saints	Fidelio Vallis	6	g	138	138	Paul Nicholls
Saint Des Saints	*Fils D'oudairies*	*6*	*g*	*130*	*142*	*Joseph Patrick O'Brien*
Saint Des Saints	Fusil Raffles	6	g		152	Nicky Henderson
Saint Des Saints	*Gaillard Du Mesnil*	*5*	*g*	*150*		*W.P. Mullins*
Saint Des Saints	Kobrouk	10	g	140	145	David Cottin
Saint Des Saints	Lord Du Mesnil	8	g	135	149	Richard Hobson
Saint Des Saints	Magic Saint	7	g		158	Paul Nicholls
Saint Des Saints	Monmiral	4	g	143		Paul Nicholls
Saint Des Saints	Protektorat	6	g		152	Dan Skelton
Saint Des Saints	Romain De Senam	9	g		148	Dan Skelton
Saint Des Saints	Saint Calvados	8	g		167	Harry Whittington
Saint Des Saints	*Saint D'oroux*	*5*	*g*	*135*		*Gordon Elliott*
Saint Des Saints	*Saint Sam*	*4*	*g*	*136*		*W.P. Mullins*
Saint Des Saints	Saint Sonnet	6	g		143	Paul Nicholls
Saint Des Saints	Sametegal	12	g		139	Paul Nicholls

Commentary on selected potential entries for 2021 Festival

Saint Sam – Boodles Juvenile Handicap Hurdle 2m½f (4:50 Tuesday 16th March)

Juveniles by **Saint Des Saints** have a great record at the Cheltenham Festival. Three of the offspring have previously participated in the *Boodles* (or *Fred Winter* as it is typically known) and all three have been placed; ***The Saint James*** (33/1) 3rd in 2015; ***Romain De Senam*** (20/1) 2nd in 2016; ***Saint D'oroux*** (14/1) 3rd in 2020. In the *Triumph Hurdle*, ***Sametegal*** (33/1) finished 3rd in 2013. The only one of the progeny who has failed to register a placing in a festival juvenile race is ***Connetable*** (14/1) who finished 11th in the *Triumph Hurdle* of 2017.

At the time of writing, ***Saint Sam*** is the current favourite for the *Fred Winter* and can be backed at around 8/1. In this contest, there are several trends that point to this *Willie Mullins* trained gelding being a super each-way bet and these are listed below:

1) 4 of the past 5 winners of the *Fred Winter* held an Official Rating of 133+. ***(Saint Sam's OR is 136)***
2) 5 of the past 10 winners began their racing career in France and all 5 competed in at least two French races. ***(Saint Sam took part in 3 hurdle races in France)***
3) 3 of those 5 winners that started life in France, three of them competed in their first hurdle race in April or May. ***(Saint Sam's first race in France took place one day after May on 1st June 2020)***
4) In the past 10 years, 4 winners of the Fred Winter took part in a Grade 1 or Grade 2 last time out, but without winning. ***(At the time of writing, Saint Sam's last race was in the Grade 1 Tattersalls Ireland Spring Juvenile Spring Hurdle on 7th February)***
5) 14 of the past 16 winners had all raced within the previous 37 days. ***(See (4) above - Saint Sam's last run was on 7th February 2021)***

My one niggling worry is that ***Saint Sam*** is trained by *Willie Mullins*. Bizarrely, the brilliant *Willie Mullins* has saddled 14 runners in the *Fred Winter* and a solitary 3rd place is the best that he has achieved. His record in the *Triumph Hurdle* wasn't too good either until *Burning Victory* provided him with his first success in that event last year. Preceding that win, his record stood at 0-20 in the *Triumph*. I'm hopeful that *Willie Mullins* can break his duck in the 2021 *Boodles Juvenile Handicap Hurdle* and win the race with ***Saint Sam***.

Saint Sam does hold entries in both the *Ballymore Novices' Hurdle* (50/1) and the *JCB Triumph Hurdle* (25/1). I very much doubt that he will end up in the *Ballymore*, for which he has no chance in my view. As for the *Triumph*, I guess connections could potentially place him here, buoyed by his performance in the *Tattersalls Ireland Spring Juvenile Spring Hurdle* on 7th February, where he finished runner-up to *Quilixios*. 29 horses beaten in the *Spring Juvenile* have contested the past 9 *Triumph Hurdles* and four have won. I consider that ***Saint Sam*** does have a chance in the *Triumph Hurdle*, but nowhere near as good as the opportunity in the *Boodles/Fred Winter*.

I hope connections enter him for the Boodles. My each-way bet has already been placed.

Galliard Du Mesnil – Ballymore Novices' Hurdle 2m5f (1:30 Wednesday 17th March)

As of early February, ***Galliard Du Mesnil*** by **Saint Des Saints** is the current favourite for the *Ballymore Novices' Hurdle* and is available at around 3/1. The good news for fans of ***Galliard Du Mesnil*** is that within the past decade, four favourites have won this contest. And even if the grey doesn't start favourite on the day, three other winners were priced at 9/2 or shorter. This race is usually won by horses at the front of the market.

There are no major pros and cons as regards the performances of **Saint Des Saints**' stock in festival races of 2½ miles, where from eight outings, the record currently stands as one winner from ***Aux Ptits Soins*** (9/1) in the 2015 *Coral Cup* and a 3rd place finish by *Elfile* in last year's *Close Brothers Mares' Hurdle*. ***Quel Esprit*** is the only horse by **Saint Des Saints** to compete in a *Ballymore Novices' Hurdle*, but the 5/1 chance didn't last long in the 2010 renewal. He fell at the 2nd hurdle.

Irish trainers have won 6 of the past 7 renewals, and ***Galliard Du Mesnil***'s trainer, *Willie Mullins*, has won this race on four occasions. That said, in the last 9 years, he has run 23 horses to collect 2 wins (*Faugheen* in 2014 and *Yorkhill* in 2016). In the last 6 years, his record is one win from 17 runners.

There are several signals to suggest that ***Galliard Du Mesnil*** is a worthy favourite, but several of these factors also point towards his main rivals. Some of the key ingredients required to win the *Ballymore* are advised below:

1) 5 of the past 7 winners were unbeaten over hurdles. ***(Galliard Du Mesnil has won 2 out of 3)***
2) 10 of the past 12 winners have been top-rated or 2nd top-rated on official BHA ratings. ***(Too early to know, but Galliard Du Mesnil will be somewhere within the top 3-4)***
3) Only 16 horses rated 150 or higher have contested the Ballymore in the past 12 years. Six have won. ***(Galliard Du Mesnil's current rating is 150)***
4) 9 of the past 12 winners had all previously won a graded hurdle. ***(as has Galliard Du Mesnil)***
5) The last 11 winners had all won at least one Bumper. ***(Galliard Du Mesnil won 1 out of 6 Bumpers)***
6) 12 of the past 13 winners have been returned at single figure odds. ***(Galliard Du Mesnil will be priced at single figure odds)***

I believe the winner of this race will come from ***Galliard du Mesnil*** or one of his two main rivals, *Bravemansgame* or *Bob Olinger*. It's a close call, but my preference is for *Bob Olinger*, sired by *Sholokhov* (who incidentally is the sire of last year's *Supreme* winner, *Shishkin*). Many of the above factors point to all three contenders at the front of the market, but I like the fact that *Bob Olinger* contested one Point-to-Point and won it; contested one Bumper and won that; and then contested one Grade 1 Hurdle race and won that too. Only 14 horses in the past 12 renewals of this contest have won a Point-to-Point, a Bumper and a graded novice hurdle, and yet 5 of those 14 horses were victorious in the *Ballymore*. The Grade 1 novice hurdle that *Bob Olinger* won was the *Lawlor's of Naas*, the same race won by *Envoi Allen* before he won last year's *Ballymore*. *Bob Olinger* will be stepping up to 2m5f for the first time over hurdles, but that shouldn't be a concern, as 9 of the past 13 winners of this race have done just that. *Bob Olinger* for me. Just.

Shantou (USA)

Quote from the 2020 Cheltenham Festival Stallion Guide - "**Shantou** is the name of a Chinese city, on the eastern coast of *Guangdong*, so when we consider whether **Shantou**'s offspring can deliver yet another year of success, perhaps we should beware of the Chinese proverb, "Of all the stratagems, to know when to quit is the best". On the other hand, if **Shantou**'s representatives can register a level stakes profit at the 2020 Cheltenham Festival, it will make it eight years in succession."

Shantou (28-y-o)							
Race Format	*Miles*	*Won*	*Placed*	*Unplaced*	*Total*	*Win %*	*Place %*
Hurdles	About 2m	0	0	7	7	0%	0%
	About 2m 4f	0	2	5	7	0%	29%
	About 3m	0	4	9	13	0%	31%
Chases	About 2m	0	1	1	2	0%	50%
	About 2m 4f	3	0	7	10	30%	30%
	About 3m	1	8	5	14	7%	64%
	About 4m	0	1	3	4	0%	25%
Bumper	About 2m	1	0	0	1	100%	100%
Total	**2011-2020**	**5**	**16**	**37**	**58**	**9%**	**36%**

Shantou's offspring have an incredible record at Cheltenham Festivals. Betting blind to level stakes on all horses by **Shantou** to have raced at the festival between 2013 and 2019 has delivered a profit every year for seven consecutive festival meetings. Like many readers of the Cheltenham Festival Stallion Guide, I was hoping that the 2020 Cheltenham Festival would result in an eighth year of profits, but sadly it wasn't to be. As the proverb at the top of the page says, *"Of all the stratagems, to know when to quit is the best."* 2020 turned out to be the year to quit.

With the progeny of this stallion failing to muster a profit at the Cheltenham Festival for the first time in 8 years, it was decided, perhaps somewhat spookily, that **Shantou** himself had had enough, as late last year, it was announced that **Shantou** was to be retired from covering duties at the age of 27. At *Burgage Stud, Victor Connolly* advised, *"We're going to let **Shantou** retire gracefully and enjoy his health for as long as he's comfortable. He's been wonderful and you couldn't have asked for better."* As far as previous readers of this Guide are concerned, **Shantou** definitely has been wonderful, and although he will now enjoy his retirement, be in no doubt, his offspring will continue to deliver festival success for a few more years yet.

Although from a financial perspective, it was the worst festival yet for **Shantou**'s stock, I still consider that there were a number of positives from the 'squad' of nine entries that participated at the 2020 Cheltenham Festival, and certainly encouraging enough to believe that profitable festivals from the stallion's runners may be just around the corner.

The table below provides an annual profit and loss breakdown of backing all fifty-nine of **Shantou**'s progeny blind to a £10.00 each way stake. The total profit since 2007 equates to £505.50.

Year	*Won*	*Placed*	*Unplaced*	*Profit*
2007	0	0	1	-£20.00
2012	0	0	2	-£40.00
2013	1	1	1	£283.75
2014	1	1	4	£78.00
2015	0	3	2	£22.00
2016	0	3	5	£38.00
2017	1	1	7	£115.00
2018	1	3	3	£142.50
2019	1	2	6	£26.50
2020	0	2	7	-£140.25
Totals	**5**	**16**	**38**	**£505.50**

Thirty-two horses by **Shantou** have raced on 59 occasions at Cheltenham Festivals, of which all bar one appearance took place within the past decade. Of those thirty-two to have made the trip to Cheltenham in March, fourteen of them have either won or been placed, accounting for the achievement of five victories and sixteen places. To date, **Shantou**'s festival representatives have produced a win or place position for better than 1 in every 3 times in which they have competed in a festival race. That is a strong statistic.

Six of the nine entries by **Shantou** at last year's meeting were sent off as outsiders, consisting of a 25/1 chance, two at 33/1, two at 66/1 and 1 at 100/1. Expectations were therefore low, but amongst these runners, there were some highly respectable performances. The traditional curtain-raiser on Tuesday saw the first of **Shantou**'s runners, ***Allart***, trained by *Nicky Henderson*, take part in the *Sky Bet Supreme Novices' Hurdle*. Having prepared for the race by winning two modest class 4 novice hurdles at *Ludlow* and *Doncaster*, ***Allart*** wasn't particularly well fancied and lined up at 33/1. On the final home turn in the race, ***Allart*** was up there with his two more fancied stablemates, *Shishkin* (the eventual winner) and *Chantry House* (3rd), before being outpaced to be beaten into 5th position by 15 lengths, and less than two lengths behind the 4th placed horse and favourite for the race, *Asterion Forlonge*. It was a very good performance from ***Allart***, especially as **Shantou**'s progeny have typically struggled in the festival's two-mile hurdle events. If we include the run by **Shantou**'s very first festival contender, ***De Valira***, in the 2007 *Supreme Hurdle*, then ***Allart*** became the 8th horse by **Shantou** to tackle the festival's 2m hurdle discipline and the first to secure a top six finishing position.

The opening event of day two of the festival, saw another strong performance from a **Shantou** sired outsider, this time in the shape of 100/1 shot ***Shan Blue***, who was taking on the 4/7 odds on favourite, *Envoi Allen*, in the *Ballymore Novices' Hurdle*. ***Shan Blue*** exceeded expectations when finishing in 6th place, a very solid run considering he jinked right having landed awkwardly two hurdles from home.

In the build up to last year's festival meeting, many festival devotees were looking forward to the *Betway Queen Mother Champion Chase*, anticipating a thrilling contest between *Altior, Chacun Pour Soi* and *Defi Du Seuil*. But we were to be disappointed as first *Altior* (through injury) and then *Chacun Pour Soi*, due to a foot abscess, were withdrawn from the race. As they lined up, *Defi Du Seuil* looked a surefire winner and he was priced up accordingly at 2/5 odds on. But we were all to be surprised as *Defi Du Seuil* fluffed his lines and put in a poor showing to finish 4th. With it being clear that the favourite wasn't going to win, I was hopeful that my small each-way bet on ***Bun Doran***, the **Shantou** sired 33/1 outsider of the five runners, may provide some reward. My selection ran well but perhaps a little enthusiastically as his challenge wilted as they approached the last fence. In the end, he was well beaten into 3rd place and, with only five runners in the race, outside the places.

The **Shantou** sired ***Death Duty*** was all the rage back in 2017 when 13/8 favourite for the *Albert Bartlett Novices' Hurdle* but failed to deliver and was well beaten before unseating his rider at the last. His second visit to Cheltenham came last year where he was heavily backed down to 8/1 from double that price just before the off in Thursday's *Brown Advisory & Merriebelle Stable Plate Handicap Chase*. In the race, he travelled really well for the first three quarters of the event and then suddenly started to struggle and weakened to finish some way back in 10th. Disappointing.

The two shortest priced of **Shantou**'s nine participants last year were both placed, and I may have uttered some sort of swear word or two when my nap of last year's meeting, ***The Storyteller***, was beaten by stablemate *Sire du Berlais* in last year's *Pertemps Network Final Handicap Hurdle*. ***The Storyteller***, priced up as the 11/2 joint favourite for the race, cruised through to lead at the last, but as they battled to the line in the last 100 yards, I just knew that *Sire Du Berlais* was going to win. In truth, I think the winner is just a better horse.

The last chance saloon for **Shantou**'s offspring to claim, what would be a sixth festival winner, came in Friday's fifth race, the *St. James's Place Foxhunter Challenge Cup Open Hunters' Chase*, where ***Shantou Flyer*** was lining up for his 4th Cheltenham Festival race. In 2016, ***Shantou Flyer*** was one of a quartet of six-year-olds who was racing in the *National Hunt Chase Challenge Cup*. Three of these four youngest horses would end up filling 3 of the first 4 places, *Minella Rocco* beating runner-up *Native River* with *Southfield Royale* coming home just outside the places in 4th position. ***Shantou Flyer*** at 25/1, and the only one of the six-year-old contenders not to hold a single figure starting price, fell at the 18th of 25 fences. Two years later and at a price of 14/1, ***Shantou Flyer***, now an 8yo, kept on well towards the end of the 2018 *Ultima Handicap Chase*, but just failed by a neck to reach *Coo Star Sivola*, and so had to settle for 2nd place. In 2019, trainer *Richard Hobson* entered ***Shantou Flyer*** for the *St. James's Place Foxhunter Chase* and once again, connections had to settle for the runner-up position yet again. In January 2020, before the 2020 running of the *Foxhunter*, ***Shantou Flyer*** was moved to the stables of *Mrs Rose Loxton*, but the change of scenery appeared to have minimal impact, as ***Shantou Flyer*** was once again placed, this time at a price of 3/1.

Looking at the table that highlights **Shantou**'s Cheltenham Festival record, punters will no doubt focus their attention on chases within the 3m category, where **Shantou**'s offspring have historically demonstrated that they are more likely to secure a top four finish than not doing so. Indeed, within this discipline, and in 14 festival appearances, there have only been five occasions when horses by **Shantou** have failed to secure a top four finish. That said, I suggest that punters approach **Shantou**'s entries in three mile chases with a small degree of caution as seven of those nine win and place positions have been attributable to just three horses: ***Shantou Flyer***, as covered earlier has secured three place positions; ***Morning Assembly*** has two place positions to his name, a 3rd placing in the 2014 *RSA Chase* and a 4th place finish in the 2016 *Ultima Handicap Chase*; and ***Beware The Bear*** who claimed victory in the 2019 *Ultima Handicap Chase* and a 4th place dividend in the same race in 2018.

Within the 2½m chase category, all three victories have come in the festival's handicap chases, two in the *Brown Advisory and Merriebelle Stable Plate* and one in the now defunct *Close Brothers* or *Northern Trust Novices' Handicap Chase*, which is to be replaced this March with the *Mrs Paddy Power Mares' Chase*.

As for the festival's hurdle contests, it is noticeable that **Shantou**'s progeny is yet to secure a festival win over the smaller obstacles. In 15 appearances in hurdle contests within the 2m and 2½m race categories, only twice have horses by **Shantou** registered a placing. ***Polly Peachum*** (9/1) finished a head in 2nd behind *Glens Melody* in the 2015 *OLBG Mares' Hurdle*, a race most famous for the last flight fall of *Annie Power*, whilst in 2016, ***Tully East*** (50/1) secured a 4th place dividend in the *Martin Pipe Conditional Jockeys' Handicap Hurdle*.

The hurdle race for **Shantou** supporters to focus upon at the Cheltenham Festival is the *Pertemps Network Final* over a distance of three miles. In seven runs in the race, **Shantou**'s offspring have collected four place positions. We have already highlighted ***The Storyteller***'s near-miss in last year's *Pertemps* when the 11/2 joint favourite, but the other three place dividends were secured at big prices. ***The Tourard Man*** competed in the *Pertemps Final* twice and on both occasions successfully secured a place dividend. He finished 3rd at a price of 20/1 in the 2015 renewal before returning as an unfancied 66/1 outsider in 2017. At eleven years old, he was the oldest horse in the race, but it didn't stop him securing a 4th place dividend. The other **Shantou** sired outsider to claim a 4th place spot was ***Taj Badalandabad*** (40/1) who kept on up the run-in to reward backers in 2018.

Interestingly, in one of the other 3m hurdle contests, the Grade 1 *Albert Bartlett Novices' Hurdle*, in five outings by **Shantou**'s progeny, three of the stallion's runners were sent off as the outright favourite for the race, but not one of the three managed to finish the race. After winning the 2013 *Weatherbys Champion Bumper*, ***Briar Hill*** was the 2/1 favourite for the 2014 *Albert Bartlett* but fell at the 7th hurdle. Two years later in 2016, ***Shantou Village*** (7/2 favourite) disappointed when pulled up before the last, and in 2017, as already mentioned, ***Death Duty*** (13/8 favourite) was well beaten when unseating at the last. The highest finishing position in this race has come from ***Shantou Bob*** in the 2015 renewal, when finishing in 6th place at a price of 25/1.

Anyone who backed all of **Shantou**'s entries blind to level stakes made a loss at the 2020 Cheltenham Festival, but it followed seven consecutive years of annual profit-taking. Does the 2020 Cheltenham Festival represent a change in fortune for **Shantou**'s progeny? Or is it just a blip in the success of **Shantou** as one of the best stallions to follow at Cheltenham's blue riband March meeting? I'm inclined to believe the latter. Let's see what happens.

Shantou (USA) – Progeny with Official Rating of 135+

Horses by this sire with an Official Rating of 135 or greater on 9th February 2021. Horses registered with the Irish Horseracing Regulatory Board (I.H.R.B) are shown in *italics*.

					Official Ratings as of 9th February 2021	
Sire	**Horse**	**Age**	**Sex**	**Hurdles**	**Chase**	**Trainer**
Shantou	Allart	7	g		152	Nicky Henderson
Shantou	*Ashdale Bob*	*6*	*g*	*146*		*Mrs John Harrington*
Shantou	Beware The Bear	11	g		153	Nicky Henderson
Shantou	Bun Doran	10	g		150	Tom George
Shantou	Champagne Mystery	7	g		135	Nicky Henderson
Shantou	*Death Duty*	*10*	*g*		*144*	*Gordon Elliott*
Shantou	Dolphin Square	7	g	139	137	Philip Hobbs
Shantou	*Drop The Anchor*	*7*	*g*	*141*		*P.A.Fahy*
Shantou	*Line Out*	*9*	*g*	*130*	*136*	*John E. Kiely*
Shantou	*Myth Buster*	*8*	*g*		*136*	*Henry de Bromhead*
Shantou	*Pencilfulloflead*	*7*	*g*		*151*	*Gordon Elliott*
Shantou	Portrush Ted	9	g	144		Warren Greatrex
Shantou	*Run Wild Fred*	*7*	*g*		*140*	*Gordon Elliott*
Shantou	Sevarano	8	g		147	Oliver Sherwood
Shantou	Shan Blue	7	g		152	Dan Skelton
Shantou	Shantou Flyer	11	g		136	Paul Nicholls
Shantou	The Mighty Don	9	g		140	Nick Gifford
Shantou	*The Storyteller*	*10*	*g*	*153*	*165*	*Gordon Elliott*
Shantou	*Unexpected Depth*	*7*	*g*	*145*		*Oliver McKiernan*
Shantou	Whatsupwithyou	7	g	136		Ben Pauling
Shantou	*Zero Ten*	*8*	*g*		*147*	*Emmet Mullins*

Commentary on selected potential entries for 2021 Festival

Dolphin Square – Pertemps Network Final (2:10 Thursday 18th March)
Portrush Ted – Pertemps Network Final (2:10 Thursday 18th March)
Unexpected Depth – Pertemps Network Final (2:10 Thursday 18th March)

As advised in the commentary of this stallion, in seven runs in the *Pertemps Network Final*, horses by **Shantou** have been placed on four occasions, and the offspring have a great chance of further success in the 2021 renewal with one or more of ***Dolphin Square***, ***Portrush Ted*** or ***Unexpected Depth***. At the time of writing, ***Portrush Ted***, trained by *Warren Greatrex* is priced up at 33/1, ***Dolphin Square*** under the tutelage of *Philip Hobbs* is around 20/1 and *Oliver McKiernan* is the trainer of ***Unexpected Depth*** at around 16/1. Of the three, the one I like best is ***Unexpected Depth***, who returned from a 431-day absence off the track to win at *Punchestown* in early December. He has had two runs since then, finishing 3rd in the *Leopardstown Qualifier* on 28th December, before another fine effort when taking second placing in a Grade B handicap hurdle at *Leopardstown* on 7th February.

Those three fine performances have raised the Official Rating (OR) of ***Unexpected Depth*** from 130 before his win at *Punchestown* to a rating now of 145. The *Pertemps Network Final* is a handicap so some may believe that lining up for this event on the back of three top-3 placings may not have been a wise move, but I take the opposite view in this horse's case. Looking over the past ten renewals of the *Pertemps*, the top weight Official Rating has ranged from 147 to 157 and the bottom weight from 131 to 137. What is interesting to analyse is where the winner has come from within the weight range, and, intriguingly, that would appear to be either near to the top weight or alternatively close to the bottom weight. In the past 10 *Pertemps Finals*, four horses have won when weighted between 0-3lb off top weight. The other six winners have all been within 3-5lbs off the bottom weight. The BHA handicapper has the daunting task of aligning the form of British and Irish horses which often results in the Irish ratings being raised a few pounds when racing at the Cheltenham Festival, so I would anticipate that ***Unexpected Depth*** may end up with a rating just below 150, which could see him within 3lb of the top weight.

For the *Pertemps*, and indeed for some other festival races, I am also on the look-out for horses that have performed well in big fields, which is what the majority have to contend with at the festival. ***Unexpected Depth*** ticks this particular box as his three prep races for the *Pertemps* have been in fields of 18, 20 and 22. The middle of those three races was the *Leopardstown Pertemps Network Handicap Hurdle Qualifier*, and in the past five years, it has easily been the best guide for finding the winner of the *Pertemps Final*. Four of the past five festival winners competed in the *Leopardstown* contest with finishing positions of 4th, 5th, 6th and 9th.

The *Pertemps* is a tough race to win, but I think ***Unexpected Depth*** has the necessary qualities to trouble the judge and I consider an each-way bet could be rewarding, with perhaps a small saver on *Dolphin Square* and *Portrush Ted*!

<u>Footnote:</u>

For further insight to the *Pertemps Network Final*, read the commentary on ***The Bosses Oscar*** by **Oscar**.

Shirocco (GER)

Shirocco was not featured in the 2020 Cheltenham Festival Stallion Guide.

Shirocco (20-y-o)							
Race Format	*Miles*	*Won*	*Placed*	*Unplaced*	*Total*	*Win %*	*Place %*
Hurdles	About 2m	2	0	1	3	67%	67%
	About 2m 4f	0	0	6	6	0%	0%
	About 3m	0	2	2	4	0%	50%
Chases	About 2m	0	0	0	0	-	-
	About 2m 4f	0	0	0	0	-	-
	About 3m	0	1	2	3	0%	33%
	About 4m	1	0	0	1	100%	100%
Bumper	About 2m	0	1	2	3	0%	33%
Total	**2011-2020**	**3**	**4**	**13**	**20**	**15%**	**35%**

At the 2013 Cheltenham Festival, only one horse by **Shirocco** would make an appearance at the Cheltenham Festival. The horse was named ***Lac Fontana***, trained by *Paul Nicholls*. And he was the very first of **Shirocco**'s progeny to grace the stage of a Cheltenham Festival. ***Lac Fontana*** was a juvenile and made his appearance in the *JCB Triumph Hurdle* where he finished in 8th position at a price of 25/1. Over the next few years, there would be better results, not just for ***Lac Fontana***, but for **Shirocco**'s offspring too.

Horses by **Shirocco** never travelled to the Cheltenham Festival mob handed, three runners being the most that would compete at a festival meeting until, that is, the 2020 Cheltenham Festival, when for **Shirocco**'s stock, a record number would arrive. Five. The five horses by **Shirocco** that took part at last year's meeting took the total number of festival outings from this stallion's offspring to 20 and the decision to include the stallion in the Cheltenham Festival Stallion Guide for the very first time.

Twelve horses by **Shirocco** have been responsible for the twenty Cheltenham Festival appearances and up until last year, the best results, wins and places were dominated by three of the progeny, these being ***Lac Fontana***, ***Annie Power*** and ***Minella Rocco***. As of now, these three horses are responsible for 55 percent, or eleven, of the 20 festival appearances by **Shirocco**'s stock. The remaining nine of the progeny have made a single appearance each.

Having been the first horse by **Shirocco** to race at a Cheltenham Festival in 2013, ***Lac Fontana*** returned twelve months later to provide a signal as to the likely success or otherwise of **Shirocco**'s progeny at future festivals, when winning the 2014 *County Handicap Hurdle* at a price of 11/1. ***Lac Fontana*** was one of three horses by **Shirocco** to take part at the 2014 festival meeting, and as far as the betting markets were concerned, the least likely to win. Second favourite for the *Neptune Investment Management Novices' Hurdle* was ***Red Sherlock*** at 7/2, but he weakened in the straight to finish in 9th place, and the mare ***Annie Power***, priced up as the 11/8 favourite, ran in the first of her three festival appearances when finishing in 2nd place behind *More Of That* in the *Ladbrokes World Hurdle*.

Lac Fontana and ***Annie Power*** were two of three entries sired by **Shirocco** that would depart from the 2015 Cheltenham Festival empty-handed, but it should have been very different. ***Annie Power*** was odds-on favourite for the *OLBG Mares Hurdle* but famously fell at the very last flight when well clear. The mare made amends twelve months later when comfortably winning the *Stan James Champion*

Hurdle Challenge Trophy. She was again priced up as the favourite, this time at 5/2. Another couple of **Shirocco**'s offspring competed in 2016, one of which, ***Rock The Kasbah*** (15/2 favourite) flopped when tailed off in the 2016 *Coral Cup*. The other contender, however, ***Minella Rocco***, made it 2 out of 3 for **Shirocco**'s 2016 festival representatives when winning the *National Hunt Chase* at a price of 8/1.

With ***Annie Power*** retired and becoming a broodmare, the two entries by **Shirocco** for the 2017 Cheltenham Festival were ***Lac Fontana***, making his 4th and final festival appearance, and ***Minella Rocco***. The former would bow out with a 16th place finish in the *Martin Pipe Conditional Jockeys' Handicap Hurdle*, whilst ***Minella Rocco*** (18/1) ran a blinder to finish runner-up in the *Cheltenham Gold Cup*. 2018 and 2019 were disappointing festivals as far as this stallion's supporters were concerned. Only one horse travelled to Prestbury Park in 2018 to finish 8th in the *Weatherbys Champion Bumper* and just two would race at the 2019 Cheltenham Festival, including the 2017 *Gold Cup* runner up, ***Minella Rocco***, who was pulled up in the *Ultima Handicap Chase*.

With this stallion's festival contenders drying up and the days numbered for ***Lac Fontana***, ***Annie Power*** and soon, ***Minella Rocco***, I thought that was it as far as this stallion was concerned. Then suddenly, five horses by **Shirocco** turn up at last year's Cheltenham Festival and I'm pretty certain, it will be about the same number or possibly more, that will take their chance at the 2021 meeting. I think the 2020 Cheltenham Festival was the start of a new era for **Shirocco**'s national hunt offspring. The first seven years of **Shirocco**'s festival entries had been dominated by ***Lac Fontana***, ***Annie Power*** and ***Minella Rocco***, but those days are now over, and some new younger blood has arrived, of which two horses very much made their presence felt at last year's meeting, namely ***Third Wind*** and ***Queens Brook***.

Third Wind, trained by *Hughie Morrison*, had won four of his five hurdle starts when he lined up in last year's *Pertemps Network Final Handicap Hurdle*, running well against older rivals to claim a 4th place dividend at a price of 12/1. He is seven years of age so I'm hopeful he will return to Cheltenham for this year's festival meeting. A year younger than ***Third Wind*** is the *Gordon Elliott* trained, ***Queens Brook***, who in receipt of a 7lb mares' allowance, ran well to take 3rd place, at 6/1, in last year's *Weatherbys Champion Bumper*. I would expect her also to be at this year's Cheltenham Festival to line up in one of the festival's novice hurdles.

Third Wind and ***Queens Brook*** have been the first horses by **Shirocco** to reward each way bets since ***Minella Rocco*** finished runner-up in the 2017 *Gold Cup*, and the last-named veteran made his 4th Cheltenham Festival appearance in the 2020 *St. James's Place Foxhunter Challenge Cup Open Hunters' Chase*. Since that super performance in the *Gold Cup* of 2017, eleven races had been contested by ***Minella Rocco*** without success, indeed not even a top three finish, until January 2020 when he won the *Schiaparelli Willoughby De Broke Open Hunters' Chase* at *Warwick* against three rivals. Just over a week later, the *Jonjo O'Neill* trained 10-year-old put himself right in the picture for Cheltenham's *Foxhunter* when beating the 2019 *Foxhunter* winner, *Hazel Hill*, by 1½ lengths in a *Wetherby* Hunters' Chase. ***Minella Rocco*** was a well-fancied 3rd favourite for the 2020 *Foxhunter Chase* and also had the assistance of the excellent amateur jockey *Derek O'Connor* in the saddle, but in the end came up short and finished a well beaten 5th, 25 lengths off 66/1 winner, *It Came To Pass*. It will be interesting to see if ***Minella Rocco***, now aged eleven, returns for another tilt at this race in 2021.

The other two **Shirocco** sired entries at the 2020 Cheltenham Festival were both big-priced outsiders. ***Lieutenant Rocco*** (33/1) was pulled up in the *Albert Bartlett Novices' Hurdle* and ***Good Time Jonny*** (66/1) finished 9th behind half-sister ***Queens Brook*** in the *Champion Bumper*. Whilst writing about ***Good Time Jonny***, it is well worth noting that he lined up as the longest priced of all other horses by **Shirocco** that have appeared at Cheltenham Festivals. Of the other nineteen festival representatives by **Shirocco**, two have been priced up at 33/1, but the remainder have all been at shorter prices, including eight entries that lined up at single figure odds. Generally, the betting market would appear to consider that horses by **Shirocco** that make it to the festival have a reasonable chance of success and that is borne out by the statistics in **Shirocco**'s festival statistics table that shows a win strike rate of 15% and a win & place strike rate of 35%. Albeit these figures are based on limited data of just 20 festival outings, these are very good strike rates.

The three festival winners by **Shirocco** have been priced at 5/1, 8/1 and 11/1 whilst the four placed horses have rewarded punters at prices between 11/8 and 18/1. The odds returned, combined with the healthy strike rates, means that backing **Shirocco**'s offspring blind at level stakes at Cheltenham Festivals would be a profitable strategy. Had one placed a £10.00 each-way stake on all 20 festival appearances, the outcome would be a profit of £44.25.

I think a new era is beginning with **Shirocco**'s progeny and we await to see if the quality of festival contenders matches the likes of ***Annie Power***, ***Lac Fontana*** and ***Minella Rocco***. The early signs are certainly encouraging and although I would prefer to make judgements based on a larger number of festival outings, for the 2021 Cheltenham Festival, I suggest that **Shirocco**'s offspring are more than capable of maintaining the current healthy win and win & place strike rates.

Shirocco (GER) – Progeny with Official Rating of 135+

Horses by this sire with an Official Rating of 135 or greater on 9th February 2021. Horses registered with the Irish Horseracing Regulatory Board (I.H.R.B) are shown in *italics*.

					Official Ratings as of 9th February 2021	
Sire	***Horse***	***Age***	***Sex***	***Hurdles***	***Chase***	***Trainer***
Shirocco	Casablanca Mix	9	f		143	Nicky Henderson
Shirocco	Cheddleton	6	g		149	Jennie Candlish
Shirocco	Highway One O Two	6	g	141	141	Chris Gordon
Shirocco	Lieutenant Rocco	6	g		147	Nick Mitchell
Shirocco	One For The Team	7	g		140	Nick Williams
Shirocco	Rock The Kasbah	11	g		146	Tom George
Shirocco	Silver Hallmark	7	g		145	Fergal O'Brien
Shirocco	Third Wind	7	g	146		Hughie Morrison

Stowaway (GB)

Quote from the 2020 Cheltenham Festival Stallion Guide - "On paper, there are several talented racehorses by **Stowaway** that will be competing this March, and I'm certain that at least two or three of them will make their presence felt."

Stowaway (Died as a 21-y-o in 2015)							
Race Format	*Miles*	*Won*	*Placed*	*Unplaced*	*Total*	*Win %*	*Place %*
Hurdles	About 2m	1	0	4	5	20%	20%
	About 2m 4f	1	1	7	9	11%	22%
	About 3m	1	1	3	5	20%	40%
Chases	About 2m	1	3	4	8	13%	50%
	About 2m 4f	0	1	6	7	0%	14%
	About 3m	0	0	10	10	0%	0%
	About 4m	0	0	2	2	0%	0%
Bumper	About 2m	1	0	3	4	25%	25%
Total	**2011-2020**	**5**	**6**	**39**	**50**	**10%**	**22%**

As each festival passes, more data is collected about how horses by **Stowaway** perform at Cheltenham's showpiece March meeting. **Stowaway**'s offspring have appeared at Cheltenham Festivals on 50 occasions, and the majority of those lined up at the past two festivals, with 13 runners in 2019 and a further 16 participants taking part at last year's meeting. The rapidly increasing amount of data helps to solidify my thoughts upon which races or race categories are punters most likely to gain reward in backing the sire's runners.

The 2020 Cheltenham Festival proved to be a good one for the progeny of **Stowaway**, where ten of the 16 entries were towards the front or middle of the betting market with prices ranging from 5/1 to 16/1. The six outsiders that were priced from 33/1 upwards largely performed according to their odds, although one could argue that ***Julies Stowaway*** (40/1) put in a reasonable effort when finishing in 7th place in the *Weatherbys Champion Bumper*. Of the ten more fancied runners, two were victorious and another couple secured 3rd place dividends. Backing all of **Stowaway**'s offspring at last year's meeting blind to level stakes, and inclusive of the six outsiders, would have been profitable, where to a £10.00 each way stake, the outcome is a £27.00 profit. Ignoring the six outsiders would naturally increase the profits to £147.00.

It was a mare trained by *Henry De Bromhead* that provided **Stowaway** supporters with their first festival win since ***Champagne Classic****'s* 2017 success in the *Martin Pipe Conditional Jockeys' Handicap Hurdle*. The long-awaited victory was secured in the festival's second race of the meeting, the *Racing Post Arkle Challenge Trophy Novices' Chase*, where ***Put The Kettle On*** jumped superbly well throughout the race and stayed on gamely up the hill to comfortably get the better of *Fakir D'oudairies*, who ended up being her only serious challenger. Although ***Put The Kettle On*** had already won over course and distance in the *Racing Post #responsiblegambling Arkle Trophy Trial Novices' Chase* at Cheltenham's November meeting, where she was the outsider of 4 runners, she still wasn't particularly fancied to follow up in the *Arkle* and I was as guilty as most punters in underestimating her. ***Put The Kettle On*** became the first mare since 1980 to win the *Arkle*, no doubt helped by the 7lb mares' allowance. Those that backed this likeable mare would have been delighted to have been rewarded with a 16/1 starting price.

With ***Put The Kettle On***'s appearance in last year's *Arkle*, **Stowaway** has now been represented in this two-mile Grade 1 event for novice chasers on four occasions. A total of four runs is hardly significant on which to make any concrete conclusions, but so far, **Stowaway**'s offspring have performed really well in this race, with the victory of ***Put The Kettle On*** following up on two runner-up positions. At the 2019 Cheltenham Festival, trainer *Henry De Bromhead* had entered another **Stowaway** bred chaser in the *Arkle* in the shape of the ***Paloma Blue***, who had finished 4th in the 2108 *Sky Bet Supreme Novices' Hurdle*. ***Paloma Blue***'s jumping was rather sketchy throughout the contest, and he made no real impression in the race, coming home 27 lengths behind the winner to finish in 6th place at a price of 10/1. Slightly less fancied in the market was the second **Stowaway** sired entry, ***Us And Them*** (14/1), trained by *Joseph Patrick O'Brien*. ***Us And Them*** had finished runner-up in his previous two races to stablemate, *Le Richebourg*, who, leading up to the race, had been the ante-post favourite for the 2019 *Arkle* before an injury ruled him out. With *Le Richebourg* absent, some punters may have hoped for ***Us And Them*** to go one better, but it wasn't to be, as ***Us And Them*** stayed on past tiring runners to take the runner-up spot behind the runaway winner *Duc Des Genievres*. The other *Arkle* runner-up by **Stowaway** was the highly talented ***Champagne Fever***. He was the first of **Stowaway**'s stock to race at the festival when winning the 2012 *Weatherbys Champion Bumper*. The following year, the grey achieved his second festival victory in the *William Hill Supreme Novices' Hurdle* and was very close to making it three from three in the 2014 *Racing Post Arkle Challenge Trophy Chase*, before being collared at the finish by *Western Warhorse*, who beat him by a head. Admittedly, it is only four runs in the *Arkle*, but a record of two runner-up spots and a victory is hard to ignore and would have been financially lucrative if one had backed all four runners blind to level stakes. Specifically, to a £10.00 each-way stake, the result is a profit of £185.50.

Having looked at the above commentary about how horses by **Stowaway** have performed in the *Arkle*, some readers may have glanced at the table at the top of this chapter to check on **Stowaway**'s overall record in the 2m chase race category which shows 1 win, 3 places and 4 unplaced from 8 appearances. So far, **Stowaway** has been unrepresented in the *Queen Mother Champion Chase* so the other four runs within this category have taken place in the festival's only two-mile handicap chase, the *Grand Annual*. Both horses by **Stowaway** that contested the 2019 *Arkle* took their chance in last year's *Johnny Henderson Grand Annual Challenge Cup Handicap Chase*, and as in the previous year's *Arkle*, ***Us And Them*** (10/1) lined up at a bigger price than ***Paloma Blue*** (17/2). Despite the market's take on the two runners, the half-brother to back was once again ***Us And Them*** who made late headway to take 3rd place, thus rewarding his supporters with a place dividend for the second year running.

The second victory from **Stowaway**'s offspring at the 2020 Cheltenham Festival came in Friday's *Albert Bartlett Novices' Hurdle*, where two well-fancied **Stowaway** sired six-year-olds, ***Monkfish*** and ***Fury Road***, both lined up at odds of 5/1. They would be up against 17 other entries, including two highly respected contenders who were just ahead of the **Stowaway** bred pair at the head of the betting, the 4/1 favourite *Thyme Hill* and 9/2 chance *Latest Exhibition*. No doubt, the remaining 15 bigger priced runners would have had their supporters too. After all, since *At Fishers Cross*, at 11/8, won this event in 2013, every winner afterwards has come in at odds ranging from 11/1 to 50/1. With that in mind, it was perhaps a little surprising then, that in the 2020 running of the *Albert Bartlett*, the first four places were taken by the front four in the betting, with ***Monkfish*** taking the honours, followed by *Latest Exhibition* (2nd), ***Fury Road*** (3rd) and *Thyme Hill* (4th). The quartet were separated by just 1½ lengths with a gap of more than 10 lengths back to the 5th placed horse, *Janadil*.

There is a part of me that regards the victory by ***Monkfish*** to be recompense for what may have been for another **Stowaway** bred horse that competed in the *Albert Bartlett Novices' Hurdle* of 2017. In this renewal, ***The Worlds End*** was making rapid headway three from home, in contention alongside the leaders, when he fell two out. We will never know where the *Tom George* trained 10/1 chance would have finished had he stayed on his feet but based upon his victory at *Aintree* three weeks later in the

Doom Bar Sefton Novices' Hurdle, in my view, he certainly would have gone close. Bearing in mind, the 1st and 3rd recorded by ***Monkfish*** and ***Fury Road*** alongside the unfortunate fall of ***The Worlds End***, and even though there is even less data than the *Arkle* to go on, it has to be said that the progeny of **Stowaway**, so far, have performed with credit in this Grade 1 three-mile event for novice hurdlers.

Having highlighted how horses by **Stowaway** have performed so admirably in the *Arkle* and the *Albert Bartlett*, it is only fair that I should also inform punters that they may wish to be a little less bullish about the offspring's chances in chases within the three-mile category. To date, **Stowaway**'s stock has made four appearances in the *RSA Insurance Novices' Chase*, three runs in the *Fulke Walwyn Kim Muir Challenge Cup Amateur Riders' Handicap Chase*, two outings in the *Cheltenham Gold Cup* and one run in *Ultima Handicap Chase*. Taking together, only four of the ten **Stowaway**'s three-mile chase entries managed to finish their races, and not one of them able to register a top six finish. Of the remaining six contenders, one fell and the other 5 were pulled up. To be fair, four of the ten participants were priced between 33/1 and 50/1, but then again, five of the ten were priced between 4/1 and 16/1, including two favourites. With the offspring having been successful in the festival's three-mile hurdle category, there is no obvious rationale as to why, to date, the progeny has performed so poorly when tackling the larger obstacles over the same distance. Bearing in mind the obvious limitations of making any precise judgements based upon just ten outings, I looked beyond the festival meeting to see whether **Stowaway** sired runners had enjoyed better luck in chases over a distance of around three miles at Cheltenham's other meetings. The analysis showed that two horses by **Stowaway** had been successful in winning at Prestbury Park in three-mile chases, the winners being the aforementioned ***The Worlds End*** and ***Pym***. Interestingly, they both won the same race that takes place at Cheltenham's December meeting, the race being currently named the *International Decorative Surfaces Novices' Chase* over 3m1½f. ***The Worlds End*** was the 7/4 favourite when winning the 2018 renewal by 26 lengths and twelve months later, ***Pym*** (2/1 favourite) took the honours when beating *Imperial Aura*, the runner-up returning to Cheltenham to race over a half mile shorter to claim victory in the listed *Northern Trust Company Novices' Handicap Chase*. ***Pym***, meanwhile, was pulled up on his visit to the 2020 Cheltenham Festival when, at a price of 33/1, he took on the leading three-mile novice chasers in the Grade 1 *RSA Insurance Novices' Chase*.

In conclusion, taking into account all 50 festival outings by **Stowaway**'s progeny, the offspring have registered five wins and six place positions, representing a win strike rate of 10% and a 22% win & place strike rate. Financially, had one placed a £10.00 each-way stake on all 50 festival appearances, the outcome would be a small loss of £75.00. More than half of those 50 runs have taken place at the past two Cheltenham Festivals, and I anticipate another dozen or more entries will make the trip to Prestbury Park for the 2021 meeting. In last year's Guide, I advised that **Stowaway** had several talented racehorses amongst his stock that would make their presence felt at the 2020 Cheltenham Festival and so it proved. Many of those talented horses are still in training preparing for their return to Cheltenham, alongside some highly capable festival debutants, in which case, I can't see any reason why the 2021 festival won't result in further successes for this stallion's offspring. In next year's Guide, when I add in the 2021 festival runners to the 50 runs that have gone before and calculate the profit/loss of backing all the stock's appearances blind to level stakes, that small loss of £75.00 highlighted above may well turn into a profit. Let's see what happens.

Stowaway (GB) – Progeny with Official Rating of 135+

Horses by this sire with an Official Rating of 135 or greater on 9th February 2021. Horses registered with the Irish Horseracing Regulatory Board (I.H.R.B) are shown in *italics*.

				Official Ratings as of 9th February 2021		
Sire	***Horse***	***Age***	***Sex***	***Hurdles***	***Chase***	***Trainer***
Stowaway	Another Venture	10	g		140	Kim Bailey
Stowaway	Any News	6	g	143		Neil Mulholland
Stowaway	*Blackbow*	*8*	*g*		*153*	*W.P. Mullins*
Stowaway	*Bridge Native*	*10*	*f*	*119*	*135*	*Mrs D.A.Love*
Stowaway	Cadzand	6	g	140		Dan Skelton
Stowaway	*Champagne Classic*	*10*	*g*		*151*	*Gordon Elliott*
Stowaway	Champagne Platinum	7	g	138		Nicky Henderson
Stowaway	Coconut Splash	6	g		137	Evan Williams
Stowaway	Fiddlerontheroof	7	g		148	Colin Tizzard
Stowaway	*Fury Road*	*7*	*g*	*151*		*Gordon Elliott*
Stowaway	*Go Another One*	*9*	*g*	*145*	*139*	*John C. McConnell*
Stowaway	*Goodbye Someday*	*7*	*g*	*140*		*John E. Kiely*
Stowaway	Highway One O One	9	g	132	135	Chris Gordon
Stowaway	Johnbb	7	g		137	Tom Lacey
Stowaway	King Roland	7	g	140	140	Harry Fry
Stowaway	Leapaway	9	g		135	Philip Hobbs
Stowaway	Mind's Eye	9	g		135	Claire Dyson
Stowaway	*Monkfish*	*7*	*g*		*163*	*W.P. Mullins*
Stowaway	Ofalltheginjoints	7	g		143	Colin Tizzard
Stowaway	On The Blind Side	9	g	153		Nicky Henderson
Stowaway	Outlander	13	g	137	137	Richard Spencer
Stowaway	*Paloma Blue*	*9*	*g*		*148*	*Henry de Bromhead*
Stowaway	Phoenix Way	8	g		145	Harry Fry
Stowaway	*Put The Kettle On*	*7*	*f*		*154*	*Henry de Bromhead*
Stowaway	Pym	8	g		153	Nicky Henderson
Stowaway	Seddon	8	g		135	Harry Whittington
Stowaway	Soupy Soups	10	g		137	Neil Mulholland
Stowaway	*Stattler*	*6*	*g*	*143*		*W.P. Mullins*
Stowaway	Tea Clipper	6	g	141		Tom Lacey
Stowaway	*The Shunter*	*8*	*g*	*134*	*135*	*Emmet Mullins*
Stowaway	The White Mouse	7	f	135		Lucy Wadham
Stowaway	The Worlds End	10	g	149	139	Olly Murphy
Stowaway	*Trainwreck*	*9*	*g*		*137*	*Henry de Bromhead*
Stowaway	Umbrigado	7	g	141	139	David Pipe
Stowaway	*Us And Them*	*8*	*g*		*143*	*Joseph Patrick O'Brien*

Commentary on selected potential entries for 2021 Festival

Monkfish – Brown Advisory Novices' Chase 3m½f (2:10 Wednesday 17th March)

Just to help those who may be confused, the *Brown Advisory* company who used to sponsor the *Stable Plate*, now sponsor this race which used to be called the *RSA Insurance Novices' Chase*. It took me a little while to get my head around it too.

At the time of writing, following his fabulous performance in the *Flogas Novice Chase* at the *Dublin Festival*, ***Monkfish*** is now odds-on to win the *Brown Advisory Novices' Chase*. This is one of those occurrences when a horse produces such a breath-taking prep race that it is difficult for anyone to believe that the horse will be beaten come the big day at the festival. In my mind, there is no such thing as a 'dead-cert' in horse-racing, and if one looks at the make-up of all the previous winners of this race in recent years, ***Monkfish*** ticks most of the boxes. But there are one or two factors which may create a niggling doubt about his chances of winning. There just may be a couple of cracks in his armour that may cause punters concern. But some trends, some unexplainable, are there to be broken and ***Monkfish*** certainly looks like he has the quality to become the exception that proves the rule. I think his current price of 8/11 is about right.

Before I highlight those factors that may concern those that believe ***Monkfish*** is unbeatable, below are a list of trends that reinforce his position as the odds-on favourite:

1) In the past 14 years, 68 contenders of this race had previously won a Grade 1 or Grade 2 Chase. Nine of them won. ***(Monkfish has won two Grade 1 chases)***
2) In the past 12 years, 23 horses had won a Grade 1 chase before lining up for this race. Three of those 23 won this race. ***(Monkfish's last win was the Grade 1 Flogas Novice Chase)***
3) 9 of the past 10 winners had all previously raced between 3-5 times over fences. ***(Monkfish has had three races over fences)***
4) Irish bred horses have won 8 of the past 10 renewals. ***(Monkfish is Irish bred)***
5) 7 of the past 10 winners had all won on their first or second ever race. ***(Monkfish won his second race, a Point-to-Point at Stowlin)***
6) Horses that had two full seasons over hurdles are 0/84 since 1993. And all 11 runners this century that recorded a Racing Post Rating (RPR) over hurdles of more than 160 have been beaten. ***(Monkfish had one year over hurdles and achieved a Hurdles RPR rating of 154)***
7) 16 of the past 21 winners have been aged seven. ***(Monkfish is a 7yo)***
8) 8 of the past 10 winners appeared in a festival hurdle race at the previous year's festival of which five finished either 1st or 2nd. ***(Monkfish won the Albert Bartlett Novices' Hurdle)***
9) 8 of the past 10 winners were 1st or 2nd last time out. ***(Monkfish won the Flogas Novice Chase)***
10) Every winner since 1997 had made their chase debut before January 1st. ***(Monfish had his first chase run on 28th November 2020)***
11) Trainer Willie Mullins has won this contest 4 times from 26 contenders. ***(Willie Mullins trains Monkfish)***
12) Since 2005, 25 horses have lined up in this event, having previously contested the Albert Bartlett Novices' Hurdle in the previous year. 5 of those 25 won. 2 won the Albert Bartlett, 1 finished 4th and 2 were pulled up. ***(Monkfish won the Albert Bartlett)***
13) 3 winners of this event in the past 11 years also finished 1st or 2nd in the Neville Hotels Novice Chase. ***(Monkfish won the Neville Hotels Chase)***
14) 4 winners of this race in the past 12 years also finished in the first 3 places in the Flogas Novice Chase. ***(Monkfish won the Flogas Novice Chase)***

It is a very long list of positives. Here are those factors that may cause odds-on backers some concern:

1) Along with his 4 winners of this race, trainer Willie Mullins has also seen nine of his 26 contenders fall or unseat their jockey. ***(Monkfish is trained by Willie Mullins)***
2) This century, 30 horses lined up who were unbeaten over fences. Only two have won. ***(Monkfish is unbeaten after three starts. It is perhaps a little more comforting to know that the two unbeaten contenders were both favourites in the betting, priced at 13/8 and 6/5)***
3) 7 of the past 11 winners were beaten on their chasing debut. ***(Monkfish won on his chasing debut)***
4) 9 of the past 10 winners all won in their first race discipline, whether hurdles, national hunt flat race or Point-to-Point. ***(Monkfish was pulled up in his first ever race, a Point-to-Point race at Cragmore)***
5) 8 of the past 9 winners had previously raced between 3-5 times over fences, but none of those 8 had won more than two chases. 4 had won twice, 3 had won once, and one was still a maiden. ***(Monkfish has won 3 from 3)***

For those readers who have read my commentary on **Stowaway**, they can probably guess as to my biggest concern. In short, horses by **Stowoway**, of which ***Monkfish*** is one, have a terrible record at the Cheltenham Festival in chase events over a distance of three miles. In ten festival chase events, only four of **Stowaway**'s offspring have finished their races, and none of them have finished in the top six places. Of the other six participants, one fell and the other 5 were pulled up. If we look specifically at this race, the *Brown Advisory Novices' Chase*, three of the offspring have been pulled up and one other finished last of those that managed to complete the course. The record of **Stowaway**'s offspring in three-mile chases at the Cheltenham racecourses generally, away from the festival, isn't that great either. Just two horses by **Stowaway**, ***The Worlds End*** and ***Pym***, have been successful in winning at Prestbury Park in three-mile chases, and they both won the same race in successive years for which they were both favourites.

Not only have punters witnessed a super performance by ***Monkfish*** in February's *Flogas Novice Chase*, but there are also several key pointers suggesting that ***Monkfish*** will triumph in the newly named *Brown Advisory Novices' Chase*. Those who believe he won't win can point towards some of those niggling issues that I have listed, yet I believe the biggest concern for punters should be the record of **Stowaway**'s stock at Cheltenham, and at the festival in particular, in chases covering a distance of three miles. ***Monkfish*** has all the qualities to overcome the doubters and if he was a bigger price, perhaps I may take a chance on him, but I won't take that chance at odds-on. This is where I, along with some other festival devotees, will look at the other contenders and try and find some value in an each-way bet.

Voix Du Nord (FR)

Quote from the 2020 Cheltenham Festival Stallion Guide - "I suggest you skim through the runners for the festival's hurdle events. Entries by **Voix Du Nord** will be few and far between, but if one is found, take a serious look at the horse's credentials. Remember, two out of every five bets on the progeny's hurdlers have historically delivered either a win or place."

Voix Du Nord (Died as a 12-y-o in 2013)							
Race Format	*Miles*	*Won*	*Placed*	*Unplaced*	*Total*	*Win %*	*Place %*
Hurdles	About 2m	2	1	5	8	25%	38%
	About 2m 4f	1	2	5	8	13%	38%
	About 3m	0	1	2	3	0%	33%
Chases	About 2m	0	0	4	4	0%	0%
	About 2m 4f	2	0	12	14	14%	14%
	About 3m	0	0	4	4	0%	0%
	About 4m	0	0	1	1	0%	0%
Bumper	About 2m	0	0	0	0	-	-
Total	**2011-2020**	**5**	**4**	**33**	**42**	**12%**	**21%**

Horses by **Voix Du Nord** that have competed in the Cheltenham Festival's hurdle events, have registered three wins and four place positions from a total of 19 outings. That is a very good record and calculates to a win strike rate of 16% and a 37% win & place strike rate. Had one placed a £10.00 each bet on all 19 outings by **Voix Du Nord**'s festival hurdler contenders, the outcome would be a profit of £35.42.

The picture isn't quite as rosy when we analyse how horses by **Voix Du Nord** have performed when competing in the festival's chase contests, where in 23 outings, the offspring have claimed two victories and no places. This calculates to a win and/or win & place strike rate of 9%, equivalent of a **Voix Du Nord** chaser rewarding bets once in every 11 festival outings. Had one placed a £10.00 each bet on all 23 outings by **Voix Du Nord**'s festival chase competitors, the outcome would be a loss of precisely £300.00.

The statistics point to **Voix Du Nord**'s progeny delivering better festival performances over hurdles than over fences, and unless fortunes improve soon for this stallion over the bigger obstacles, than I fear that any further festival wins and places for **Voix Du Nord**'s offspring are going to be few and far between or worse still may completely disappear. My concerns are based upon the fact that **Voix Du Nord** died in 2013 and hence as we go into the 2021 Cheltenham Festival, his remaining stock of potential festival entries are aged eight or older. When national hunt racehorses become older, they tend to race over fences rather than hurdles, and also are more likely to tackle longer distances too. And when it comes to the Cheltenham Festival, this century, there have been precisely 500 races, of which 176 or 35.2% have been won by horses aged eight or older. Of those 176 wins, 139 have been over the bigger obstacles and just 37 over hurdles. So, at the past 20 festival meetings, 37 hurdle contests have been won by horses aged eight or more, equivalent to roughly two wins per festival. Based on those statistics, it will be very difficult for horses by **Voix Du Nord** to add to the current tally of three festival hurdle wins at the 2021 Cheltenham Festival. And it will be even tougher in 2022, as only 15 festival hurdle races have been won by hurdlers aged nine and older since year 2000. With **Voix Du Nord**'s stock of racehorses becoming older, and festival winning opportunities reducing, this stallion's offspring have it all to do.

At last year's festival meeting, just five horses by **Voix Du Nord** made the journey to Prestbury Park and none of the quintet were able to add to the tally of wins and places. The most disappointing performance was from ***Defi Du Seuil*** who flopped in the *Betway Queen Mother Champion Chase.* Trained by *Philip Hobbs* and ridden by *Barry Geraghty*, the odds on 2/5 favourite, looked a dead cert following the withdrawals of first *Altior* and then *Chacun Pour Soi*, but he never travelled like a dead cert and was soon beaten, finding little after the final turn.

As a sign of things to come, with **Voix Du Nord**'s remaining progeny becoming older, three of the five **Voix Du Nord** entrants at last year's meeting tackled the bigger obstacles over a distance of three miles or more. Prior to the 2021 Cheltenham Festival, only two of the offspring had ever competed in a festival chase over three miles or more, and neither runner had covered themselves in glory. Both horses lined up in the Cheltenham *Gold Cup*. ***Bachasson*** at 33/1, trained by *Willie Mullins*, lined up in the 2018 *Gold Cup*, but fell at the 2nd fence. The following season, it was the turn of ***Kemboy*** to compete in Cheltenham's blue riband event. He didn't get as far as ***Bachasson***. ***Kemboy*** fell at the first.

2020 would see ***Kemboy*** return to Cheltenham and once again, the *Magners Cheltenham Gold Cup Chase*. On this occasion, ***Kemboy*** completed the course and finished in 7th place, staying on at the end but never in the race having made a couple of mistakes at the later fences. As it stands, ***Kemboy*** is the only horse by **Voix Du Nord** to complete a long-distance festival chase as the other two **Voix Du Nord** bred chasers were unable to complete their races. ***Quarenta*** (28/1) was brought down at the 4th fence in the *Ultima Handicap Chase* and ***Arlequin D'Allier*** (33/1) became the first of the progeny to contest one of the festival races within the 4m race category when pulled up in the 3m6f *Glenfarclas Cross Country Chase*.

Of the five of the offspring to take their chance at last year's festival, my view is that the best performance came from ***Bachasson***, the only one of the five entries last year to line up in a hurdle event. Trained by *Willie Mullins*, ***Bachasson*** ran in the *Coral Cup Handicap Hurdle*, and was just beginning to make headway between the last two hurdles when he was denied a clear run. Whether or not the interference denied ***Bachasson*** a place position, we will never know, but all the same, it was an encouraging run from the 33/1 outsider to finish in 6th position, less than 1½ lengths from a 4th place dividend.

Looking at **Voix Du Nord**'s festival statistics table, the majority of the stallion's chasers have raced around Cheltenham in the 2½ mile category, which has resulted in two festival victories and twelve defeats. Both wins have come in the *Marsh Novices' Chase*, with ***Taquin Du Seuil*** successful at 7/1 in 2014 and the 3/1 favourite for the 2019 renewal, ***Defi Du Seuil***, taking the prize five years later. ***Kemboy*** also raced in this event in 2018 but finished just outside the places when taking 4th spot at a price of 15/2. Ignoring the two wins for the moment, of the 12 defeats by the offspring in festival chases at a distance of 2½ miles, ***Kemboy***'s 4th placing in the *Marsh Novices' Chase*, is the highest finishing position that has been achieved. Horses by **Voix Du Nord** have made four appearances in the *Ryanair*, where the highest placed effort was recorded by ***Taquin Du Seuil*** when he finished in 6th place in 2016. In the 2m4½f Grade 3 Paddy Power *Stable Plate Handicap Chase*, runners by **Voix Du Nord** have struggled with just one top ten finish from ***Azzerti*** who finished in 7th at a price of 20/1 in the 2019 running.

The stock of **Voix Du Nord** is now aged eight or more and with age comes more entries in the festival's long-distance chases of three miles or more. With the stallion having had only five of his offspring compete in festival chases that are at a distance of three miles or more, it is rather difficult to assess how horses by **Voix Du Nord** will perform in these longer distance chase events in future, albeit to date, there have been five largely forgettable outings. Being curious about the success or otherwise of **Voix Du Nord**'s progeny at future Cheltenham Festival meetings, I looked to see how many chases at 24f or more had horses by **Voix Du Nord** won at any course whether in Great Britain or Ireland. The result of my analysis doesn't fill me with great confidence. ***Kemboy*** has won four chase events at three miles or more, winning at *Aintree*, *Leopardstown*, *Limerick* and *Punchestown*; ***Quarenta*** has also won four 3m plus chases, successful at *Ascot*, *Fontwell* and *Warwick* twice; ***Val De Ferbet*** won twice at three miles at *Cork* and *Limerick*; ***Django Django*** won at 2m7½f at *Newbury*; and ***Vujiyama*** won in a 3m chase at *Southwell.*

The analysis establishes that five of **Voix Du Nord**'s progeny have won a total of 12 races at distances between 2m7½f and 3m2f. The victory by ***Quarenta*** at 3m2f in a 3-runner event at *Fontwell* is the longest distance victory by any horse sired by **Voix Du Nord**. Next best is ***Kemboy*** winning at *Aintree* over 3m1f. If one analyses the courses where these five horses by **Voix Du Nord** have been victorious, it is apparent that most of them could be described as flat tracks or sharp/tight, rather different from the galloping, testing, undulating challenge that Prestbury Park brings. It is also worth highlighting that ten of the 12 victories were in fields of 8 or fewer runners. Indeed, the highest number of runners in which **Voix du Nord**'s chasers claimed a 3m chase victory was 11 encountered by ***Kemboy*** at *Leopardstown* and ***Quarenta*** at *Ascot*. In short, the progeny of **Voix Du Nord** have never won a three-mile chase at Cheltenham at any time, and where the offspring have been successful at this distance, the type of track and number of runners is rather different than what is typical when it comes to a Cheltenham Festival three-mile chase event. We should also take note that horses by **Voix Du Nord** haven't won any chase event beyond 3m2f, which doesn't bode well for the chances of any of the stallion's entries in either the *Glenfarclas Cross-Country Chase* or the *National Hunt Chase*.

In summary, it doesn't look too good for supporters of **Voix Du Nord**. As the stallion's older horses turn their attention to the festival's three-mile chases, it would seem that the progeny may not be suited to Cheltenham's galloping, undulating and testing track along with the likely bigger fields. Historically, the offspring have been very successful in the festival's hurdle events, but now that the stallion's remaining stock is aged eight or more, the chance of further success over hurdles is diminishing. That said, perhaps **Voix Du Nord**'s last swan song will be an entry by one or more of the offspring in either the *Pertemps*, *Stayers*, *Coral* or *County* Hurdle contests. These four events, where on occasion, horses aged eight or more have been successful, may be the best hope for **Voix du Nord**'s remaining stock to sign off with a sixth Cheltenham Festival win. With such a strong record in the festival's hurdle events, it's certainly not out of the question.

Voix Du Nord (FR) – Progeny with Official Rating of 135+

Horses by this sire with an Official Rating of 135 or greater on 9th February 2021. Horses registered with the Irish Horseracing Regulatory Board (I.H.R.B) are shown in *italics*.

				Official Ratings as of 9th February 2021		
Sire	***Horse***	***Age***	***Sex***	***Hurdles***	***Chase***	***Trainer***
Voix Du Nord	*Bachasson*	*10*	*g*	*148*	*160*	*W.P. Mullins*
Voix Du Nord	Cap Du Nord	8	g		142	Christian Williams
Voix Du Nord	Defi Du Seuil	8	g		165	Philip Hobbs
Voix Du Nord	Destrier	8	g		140	Dan Skelton
Voix Du Nord	*Djingle*	*8*	*g*	*137*	*143*	*John Queally*
Voix Du Nord	*Kemboy*	*9*	*g*		*169*	*W.P. Mullins*
Voix Du Nord	Quarenta	9	g		141	Jonjo O'Neill
Voix Du Nord	Voix Du Reve	9	g	149		Iain Jardine

Commentary on selected potential entries for 2021 Festival

Bachasson – Paddy Power Stayers' Hurdle 3m (3:30 Thursday 18th March)

In the commentary on **Voix Du Nord**, I highlighted that the best performance from **Voix Du Nord**'s festival entries at last year's meeting came from ***Bachasson***. He was engaged in the *Coral Cup* and was just beginning to make headway between the last two hurdles when he was denied a clear run. He may have secured a place position.

Whether ***Bachasson*** runs in the *Paddy Power Stayers' Hurdle* or has another go in the *Coral Cup*, I will place a small each way wager on him, because I think he is going to register a place at the 2021 Cheltenham Festival, despite all the trends in either contest suggesting he has no chance. I won't back him until I know what race he is going to run in as he should still be a big price come the day of the race. I am hoping that he goes for the *Stayers' Hurdle* but won't be over-concerned if ends up in the *Coral Cup*.

For information, here is a list of trends to find the winner of the *Stayers' Hurdle*. To be clear, I think ***Bachasson*** will find it very difficult to win this race, but if he stays on his feet, I'm convinced he will put in a great performance and hopefully enough to give me a place dividend.

1) 6 of the past 7 winners of the Stayers' were second season hurdlers. ***(Not Bachasson)***
2) 5 winners this century had not previously raced beyond 2m5f, and we shouldn't forget that six renewals were won by previous winners, such as Big Buck's and Inglis Drever, so this is an interesting statistic. ***(Bachasson has had 24 races under rules, of which he has raced beyond 2m5f on three occasions. He won a four-runner 2m6f chase at Thurles in November 2017; he unseated his rider at the last in the 2016 Albert Bartlett Novices' Hurdle (3m); and he fell at the 2nd fence in the 2018 Cheltenham Gold Cup (3m2½f)***
3) No beaten horse in a Stayers Hurdle has gone on to win a subsequent renewal since Iris's Gift in 2004. ***(Bachasson has not previously raced in the Stayers' Hurdle)***
4) 14 of the past 24 winners had won or been placed at a previous festival – inclusive of those 6 renewals won by multiple winners. ***(Bachasson has not won or placed at a previous festival)***
5) Since the race was reformed in 1972, the only winner to be older than 9 to win the race was Crimson Embers in 1986. ***(Bachasson is aged 10)***
6) The last winner to have run within 45 days of this race was My Way De Solzen in 2006. ***(At the time of writing, Bachasson last raced on 31st January, so it will be 46 days come the Stayers' Hurdle)***
7) 8 of the past 10 winners had a win strike-rate over hurdles of 45% or greater. ***(Bachasson has a win strike rate percentage over hurdles of 54%)***

Well, at least he meets the criteria of bullet points '6' and '7'.

Although ***Bachasson*** is now aged 10, he is a very good horse, and his stallion's offspring have a very strong record over hurdles at the Cheltenham Festival. I think his age may be to his advantage too, as I believe his previous festival experiences may well help him. ***Bachasson*** is trained by *Willie Mullins* who has sent him out racing for 21 of his 24 races under rules. His first three races were in France in three national hunt flat races over 1m4f. He finished 6th of 9 on his debut, 9 lengths off the winner. After winning his next two races, he headed off to Ireland and *Willie Mullins*.

In his 21 outings with *Willie Mullins*, he has won 12 races, been placed 3 times, fell or unseated on 3 occasions, and finished unplaced in the remaining three outings finishing somewhere between 8-12 lengths behind the winner. All that is a reasonable record in my book. Reading about his defeats are interesting. He unseated his rider at the last in the 2016 *Albert Bartlett Novices' Hurdle* – if he stayed on his feet, he would have finished 5th or 6th; He fell on his chase debut at *Thurles*, again at the last when a close 3rd and under pressure; He finished 4th of 6 runners in the Grade 2 *Boyne Hurdle* at *Navan* (Feb 2019) where the vet reported that he was making a respiratory noise post-race; And in a Grade 1 Novice Hurdle at *Leopardstown* in December 2015, whilst going well and a close 2nd, he suddenly emptied before the last and weakened to finish 8th or 9. And he was good enough, albeit at 33/1, to be entered in the 2018 *Cheltenham Gold Cup*, only to fall at the 2nd flight.

He is in very good form at the moment and is unbeaten in four races since his 6th place finish in last year's *Coral Cup*. After winning the *Clonmel Oil Chase* over 2m4f, the write-up advised, "*This was a career-best from **Bachasson** who jumped well throughout and was always holding a 163-rated rival*". ***Bachasson***'s last outing was in the Grade 3 *Limestone Lad Hurdle* at *Naas* on 31st January, where he once again received a glowing report, "*made all and was never likely to be caught. The drop back to a distance of little short of 2m was not an issue for him, the testing ground probably helping him, and his jumping was mostly quick slick.*" And "*There will be plenty of options for him, a straightforward and sound-jumping horse with a considerable engine.*"

Bachasson is getting old, admittedly, but he seems in the form of his life. He deserves a change of luck at the festival and I hope he gets it. Whichever race connections decide is best for him, that will be good enough for me to have a small each-way flutter.

Footnote:

For further insight to the *Coral Cup*, read the commentary on ***Benson*** by **Beat Hollow**.

Westerner

Quote from the 2020 Cheltenham Festival Stallion Guide - "In the past three Cheltenham Festivals, not one of **Westerner**'s 44 representatives have managed to register a top three finish and the only horse to provide a return on bets placed is ***Eamon An Cnoic***, courtesy of a 4th place finish at 10/1 in last year's *Brown Advisory and Merriebelle Stable Plate Handicap Chase.*"

Westerner (22-y-o)							
Race Format	*Miles*	*Won*	*Placed*	*Unplaced*	*Total*	*Win %*	*Place %*
Hurdles	About 2m	0	1	5	6	0%	17%
	About 2m 4f	0	1	11	12	0%	8%
	About 3m	1	1	19	21	5%	10%
Chases	About 2m	2	0	4	6	33%	33%
	About 2m 4f	1	1	10	12	8%	17%
	About 3m	0	0	15	15	0%	0%
	About 4m	0	0	5	5	0%	0%
Bumper	About 2m	1	0	4	5	20%	20%
Total	2011-2020	**5**	**4**	**73**	**82**	**6%**	**11%**

It is difficult to provide any advice to punters on how to approach **Westerner**'s progeny that make their way to the Cheltenham Festival. The 2016 Cheltenham Festival was rather unusual in that very few outsiders won. Indeed, the two biggest priced winners were ***Empire Of Dirt*** at 16/1 in the *Brown Advisory & Merriebelle Stable Plate* and ***Solar Impulse*** at 28/1 in the *Johnny Henderson Grand Annual Chase Challenge Cup*. Both horses were sired by **Westerner**. And if anyone had backed, at £10.00 each way, all 30 of Westerner's offspring that had appeared at Cheltenham Festivals up to and including ***Solar Impulse***'s win in the very last race of the 2016 meeting, they would have been sitting on a huge profit of £716.50.

In the three festivals that followed, 44 additional appearances were made by **Westerner**'s offspring, but not one of them managed to register a top three finish and the only horse to provide a return on any bets placed was ***Eamon An Cnoic***, who secured a 4th place dividend in the 2019 *Brown Advisory and Merriebelle Stable Plate Handicap Chase*. If there had been a punter sitting on £716.50 who continued to place £10.00 each way wagers on every **Westerner** bred festival entry through to the end of the 2019 Cheltenham Festival, the profits would have disappeared, and turned into a loss of £128.50.

Come the 2020 Cheltenham Festival, eight horses by **Westerner** turned up at *Prestbury Park*. The odds offered for the eight contenders were 8/1, 11/1, 50/1, 66/1 (twice) and three horses at 100/1. With those starting prices and on the back of 44 consecutive appearances whereby horses by **Westerner** have failed to muster a top three position, I was confident that the advice that I had provided in the 2020 Cheltenham Festival Stallion Guide was sound. I had written, *"Taking into consideration that dismal record of results and the absence of any **Westerner** bred 2m chaser that takes my fancy, then the advice to punters is straightforward. Make sure to strike a line through all horses by **Westerner** entered for the forthcoming 2020 Cheltenham Festival."*

Here are how the eight entries by **Westerner** fared at the 2020 Cheltenham Festival. Three were pulled up, two finished in 16th place, one unseated, one finished sixth and the 11/1 chance won the *Weatherbys Champion Bumper*. The trainer of the winner was, you guessed it, *Willie Mullins*. He does have a rather good record in the *Bumper*. Ten winners from 77 contenders. ***Ferny Hollow*** by **Westerner**, who won the race in the same *Cheveley Park Stud* colours as the 2019 winner, *Envoi Allen*, was ridden by *Paul Townend* who beat stablemate and favourite, *Appreciate It*, ridden by the trainer's son, *Patrick Mullins*.

Ferny Hollow became the 5th horse by **Westerner** to achieve a Cheltenham Festival victory. All five winners have been successful at double figure odds: ***Western Warhorse*** (33/1) in the 2014 *Racing Post Arkle Challenge Trophy Chase;* **Cole Harden** (14/1) in the 2015 *Ladbrokes World Hurdle;* **Empire Of Dirt** (16/1) in the 2016 *Brown & Merriebelle Stable Plate*; ***Solar Impulse*** (28/1) in the 2016 *Johnny Henderson Grand Annual Chase Challenge Cup*; and the shortest priced **Westerner** sired winner, ***Ferny Hollow*** (11/1) in the 2020 *Weatherbys Champion Bumper*. In November 2020, ***Ferny Hollow*** won on his hurdling debut at *Gowran Park*, making him one of the leading contenders for the 2021 *Supreme Novices' Hurdle*, before he was ruled out for the season a month later when connections revealed that he had suffered a suspected stress fracture.

I have studied the festival performances of **Westerner**'s stock at length, and it is quite a challenge to come up with any trends or patterns. There is certainly a 'boom and bust' feel surrounding the 82 occasions in which **Westerner** has sired a festival runner, where 9 out of 10 runners do little more than make up the numbers and then every so often, up pops a winner at a big price. It has to be said that the majority of festival entries by **Westerner** are outsiders. Specifically, 47 horses by **Westerner** have lined up in festival races with a starting price of 25/1 or greater, which equates to 57% of this stallion's festival entries. Only two of these 47 competitors rewarded wagers, the aforementioned victories by ***Western Warhorse*** (33/1) and ***Solar Impulse*** (28/1). None of the other 45 runners could secure a top 4 finishing spot, the next best recorded results being a solitary 5th placing and three runners that finished 6th. Backing all 47 runners blind to a £10.00 each way stake would be rather boring and would have also resulted in a loss, although not that significant, just £54.00. Some of you may have spotted that both of these big-priced victories were secured in chases over the minimum distance, as was one of those horses that finished in 6th place. I shall refer to this topic later in the chapter.

At the other end of the scale, seven horses by **Westerner** have been fancied in the market, racing on ten occasions at single figure odds, but only once has a bet been rewarded, when ***Caid Du Berlais*** finished 3rd in the 2014 *Martin Pipe Conditional Jockeys' Handicap Hurdle* at a price of 9/1. It is striking to note that ***Caid Du Berlais*** is responsible for almost 10% of **Westerner**'s festival entries, and 50% of the recorded place positions, having appeared at the Cheltenham Festival on no less than eight occasions. The year preceding his 3rd placing in the *Martin Pipe*, he finished runner-up, at a price of 20/1, to *Flaxen Flare* in the 2013 *Fred Winter Juvenile Handicap Hurdle*. ***Caid Du Berlais*** was trained by *Paul Nicholls* for his first five runs at the festival, two of which occurred at the 2017 Cheltenham Festival, where having fallen at the 1st fence in Tuesday's *Ultima Handicap Chase*, he appeared two days later to finish in 8th place in the *Pertemps Network Final Handicap Hurdle*. That was to be the gelding's last appearance for *Paul Nicholls*, as ***Caid Du Berlais*** was transferred to *Mrs Rose Loxton* to embark on a career in Hunter Chases and Point to Points. Racing within this discipline, ***Caid Du Berlais*** has won seven of his ten starts for *Mrs Rose Loxton*, the horse's three defeats all happening in the past three renewals of the *St. James's Place Festival Challenge Cup Open Hunters' Chase*. ***Caid Du Berlais*** finished just outside the places in 5th place (12/1) in his first run in the *Festival Hunters' Chase* and that was his best result. Lining up for the 2019 and 2020 renewals priced up at single figure odds of 7/1 and 8/1 respectively, ***Caid Du Berlais*** was pulled up on both occasions. Now aged twelve, we will wait to see whether he makes the trip to Cheltenham for what will be his 9th Cheltenham Festival appearance.

Returning briefly to those horses by **Westerner** that were sent off at single figure odds, two of the sire's festival winners, ***Cole Harden*** and ***Empire of Dirt***, returned to Cheltenham after their festival victories but neither of them could quite match their previous year's successes. Following his 16/1 victory on his festival debut in the 2016 *Brown Advisory & Merriebelle Stable Plate*, ***Empire Of Dirt*** made the trip *to Prestbury Park* twelve months later for his second and final time at the festival when he lined up as the 11/4 second favourite in the Grade 1 *Ryanair Chase*. As it turned out, ***Empire Of Dirt*** never looked comfortable in the race, given an early reminder and niggled along mid-race, before trying but ultimately failing to make a late challenge. He finished just outside the places to finish 4th of the 8 runners.

Cole Harden's festival success came in the 2015 *Ladbrokes World Hurdle* and he attempted to do what *Baracouda*, *Inglis Drever* and *Big Buck's* had achieved this century, by winning this 3m Grade 1 *Stayers' Hurdle* more than once, but he too couldn't match his feats of 12 months earlier. In the 2016 renewal, like ***Empire Of Dirt***, he was sent off as the 2nd favourite, at odds of 15/2, but could only manage a 4th place finish, behind the convincing evens money favourite, *Thistlecrack*. Twelve months later, trainer *Warren Greatrex*, sent ***Cole Harden*** back to Cheltenham to compete in the *Stayers' Hurdle* for a third time. Lining up at the slightly bigger price of 9/1, ***Cole Harden*** matched the 4th place position achieved in 2016, this year's winner being *Nichols Canyon*.

The 57 horses by **Westerner**, therefore, that have been priced up at either single figure odds or 25/1 or bigger have achieved one 3rd place finish and two victories. All of which means that the remaining 25 outings by **Westerner**'s stock has delivered three wins and three places, which is a win or place for close to 1 in every 4 festival outings. Historically then, the 'sweet spot' for backing **Westerner**'s progeny at the festival would appear to be when they line up at odds from 10/1 and anything up to and including 20/1. Whether this sweet spot will remain is anyone's guess, but it is worth noting that a £10.00 each way wager on all 25 of **Westerner**'s offspring that have to date competed when sent off at prices of 10/1 or more up to and including 20/1, calculates into a £185.00 profit.

Earlier in this chapter, I highlighted that the two biggest priced festival winners that have been sired by **Westerner**, were successful in two-mile chases, ***Western Warhorse*** (33/1) winning the 2014 *Arkle* and ***Solar Impulse*** (28/1) winning the 2016 *Grand Annual*. **Westerner**'s offspring have lined up in the festival's 2m chase discipline just six times, twice in the *Arkle* and on four occasions in the *Grand Annual*. In the latter event, not only has **Westerner** sired the winner, but two of his other chasers, ***Three Stars*** (12/1 in 2018) and ***Theo*** (33/1 in 2019) both performed well, finishing just outside the places in 5th and 6th respectively. Performances by **Westerner**'s five *Weatherbys Champion Bumper* entries have stood up reasonably well too, where prior to ***Ferny Hollow***'s 2020 victory in the race, two other contenders recorded 5th place finishes in the 2016 and 2017 renewals. Although the offspring haven't performed as strongly in the hurdles discipline over two miles (a 2nd and 6th recorded in six outings), there is just the chance that **Westerner**'s stock perform best in the festivals' shortest races, where if we combine all disciplines of chases, hurdles and national hunt flat events over two miles, in a total of 17 appearances, the progeny have delivered three wins and one placing. Financially, a £10.00 each way bet on all 17 runners would have resulted in a substantial profit of £658.00.

The win strike rate for **Westerner**'s progeny when appearing in the festival's 2m contests is 18% with a win & place strike rate of 24%. This compares with a win & place strike rate of 8% and a win strike rate of just 3% in festival races that are over further distances. There is a significant difference when one compares the financial outcome of betting blind at level stakes. On the 65 occasions when **Westerner**'s offspring have competed in festival races of 2½ miles or further, betting £10.00 each-way on all runners would result in a loss of £794.50. The financial gap compared to supporting the progeny at the minimum distance is a massive £1,452.50.

The financial calculations above take into account all 82 outings by **Westerner**'s representatives ever since the very first of the stallion's runners appeared in a festival race. But I will take a moment to advise of the situation if we just take into account the dismal results from the past four festivals, where a £10.00 each way wager on all 52 runs would have resulted in a loss of £853.00. Within those 52 festival appearances, only 12 times have horses by **Westerner** registered a top six finish, but 5 of those 12 occasions happened when the offspring were competing in races at two miles, which consisted of four chases, three hurdle races and three bumpers. Five top six finishes from 10 outings over the minimum distance is a reasonable effort and there is the added bonus that the minimum distance includes the one victory of ***Ferny Hollow*** in last season's *Weatherbys Champion Bumper*. Financially, to the same staking plan of £10.00 each way blind, the losses in the past 4 years of backing **Westerner**'s progeny competing in races at two miles is just £48.00, a small fraction of the total losses of £853.00 if backing all 52 runners.

In conclusion, **Westerner**'s stock has provided supporters with a paltry one winner and one 4th place dividend from a total of 52 outings at the past four Cheltenham Festivals. Supporting the progeny of stallions with such a record is foolhardy at best, but albeit from rather limited data, there is some evidence to suggest that **Westerner**'s festival representatives may provide supporters with hope of a profit in the festival's events that fall within the 2m distance categories.

Westerner (GB) – Progeny with Official Rating of 135+

Horses by this sire with an Official Rating of 135 or greater on 9th February 2021. Horses registered with the Irish Horseracing Regulatory Board (I.H.R.B) are shown in *italics*.

					Official Ratings as of 9th February 2021	
Sire	***Horse***	***Age***	***Sex***	***Hurdles***	***Chase***	***Trainer***
Westerner	*Anything Will Do*	*6*	*g*	*133*	*136*	*Joseph Patrick O'Brien*
Westerner	Ballyhome	10	g	137	140	Fergal O'Brien
Westerner	*Captain Cj*	*10*	*g*		*143*	*Dermot Anthony McLoughlin*
Westerner	*Castlebawn West*	*8*	*g*		*161*	*W.P. Mullins*
Westerner	Keeper Hill	10	g	142	145	Warren Greatrex
Westerner	*Kupatana*	*8*	*f*		*140*	*Henry de Bromhead*
Westerner	Lough Derg Spirit	9	g		135	Paul Nicholls
Westerner	*Moyhenna*	*9*	*f*	*128*	*145*	*Denis Gerard Hogan*
Westerner	Port Of Mars	7	g		140	Olly Murphy
Westerner	Ribble Valley	8	g	146		Nicky Richards
Westerner	Rocky's Treasure	10	g		143	Kim Bailey
Westerner	Theo	11	g		141	Dr Richard Newland
Westerner	Truckers Lodge	9	g		153	Paul Nicholls
Westerner	West Approach	11	g	147	147	Colin Tizzard
Westerner	Western Miller	10	g		137	Charlie Longsdon
Westerner	*Western Victory*	*8*	*f*	*135*	*137*	*Declan Queally*
Westerner	*Westerner Point*	*12*	*g*	*127*	*143*	*Eoghan O'Grady*

Yeats (IRE)

Quote from the 2020 Cheltenham Festival Stallion Guide - "I anticipate **Yeats** being represented by around 7-8 of his offspring at this year's Cheltenham Festival, but unlike in previous years, it is the **Yeats**' geldings that look stronger. That isn't to say that the progeny is going to have a fantastic set of results at this year's festival. Far from it. Although we are working with a small sample of data of just nineteen festival results, one win and one placing squeezed in with seventeen largely forgettable performances indicate a watching brief would be the most prudent strategy."

Yeats (20-y-o)								
Race Format	*Miles*	*Won*	*Placed*	*Unplaced*	*Total*	*Win %*	*Place %*
Hurdles	About 2m	0	2	4	6	0%	33%
	About 2m 4f	0	1	9	10	0%	10%
	About 3m	0	0	3	3	0%	0%
Chases	About 2m	0	0	0	0	-	-
	About 2m 4f	1	0	2	3	33%	33%
	About 3m	0	0	5	5	0%	0%
	About 4m	0	0	1	1	0%	0%
Bumper	About 2m	0	0	4	4	0%	0%
Total	**2011-2020**	**1**	**3**	**28**	**32**	**3%**	**13%**

There were more entries by **Yeats** at last year's festival than I had expected. Thirteen in total. I advised readers last year that more information was needed from the sire's runners before determining specific betting strategies and that a watching brief at the 2020 Cheltenham Festival was the best approach. I didn't back any of **Yeats**' progeny at last year's meeting and based on the results recorded by the 13 horses by **Yeats** that participated last season, that was no bad thing.

As far as this stallion goes, we definitely have more data today to help us decide how to tackle the 2021 Cheltenham Festival, as we have results from 32 outings now as opposed to twelve months ago, when my analysis was based upon just 19 festival appearances. Nevertheless, the data is still somewhat inconclusive. I feel a little like a contestant on "Who wants to be a Millionaire", where from four possible options, I know that the answer is A or B, so I take the 50:50 lifeline, hoping that either A or B is removed, but the computer takes away C and D, leaving me none the wiser!

Let's start with the two positive results that were achieved by **Yeats**' progeny at last year's Cheltenham Festival and kick off with the traditional festival opener, the *Sky Bet Supreme Novices' Hurdle*, where the **Yeats** sired ***Chantry House*** (15/2), although well beaten, claimed a 3rd place dividend. ***Chantry House*** is owned by *John P McManus* who purchased the horse for £295,000 following a Point-To-Point victory in December 2018, so he is clearly highly regarded, even though he still has some way to go and a few big races to win, if he is going to repay the amount that was paid for him. Going into last year's *Sky Bet Supreme Hurdle*, although he had won his two first starts over hurdles, both events were Class 3 affairs, and in this Grade 1 event, ***Chantry House*** would be racing against hurdlers that had already shown form in graded class. In short, a couple of his rivals were simply better on the day and *Shishkin* (1st) and *Abacadabras* (2nd) were separated by a head at the line with ***Chantry House*** a clear 3rd albeit eleven lengths behind the front pair. Some 20 lengths further back from ***Chantry House*** finishing in 7th was another entry by **Yeats**, the only mare in the race, ***Heaven Help Us*** (100/1).

A place dividend from **Yeats**' representatives, therefore, was recorded by ***Chantry House*** in the very first event of the 2020 Cheltenham Festival and 26 races passed before the next one arrived, in the very last race of the meeting, the *Martin Pipe Conditional Jockeys' Handicap Hurdle*. The six-year-old, ***Pileon*** (9/1), trained by *Philip Hobbs*, was so close to delivering a festival victory for **Yeats**' supporters, but just missed out on the line, beaten a short head by the *Paul Webber* trained mare, *Indefatigable*.

And that was that. Thirteen appearances from horses by **Yeats** at last year's festival, with two placings recorded. Five of the thirteen entries were placed between 5th and 8th in their respective races, but with the exception of ***Ilikedwayurthinkin*** who finished 8th and just over 5 lengths behind ***Pileon*** in the *Martin Pipe*, in truth, the finishing positions are flattering and don't reflect the **Yeats**' runners being close up or just missing out on places. ***Heaven Help Us*** (7th in the *Supreme*), ***Longhouse Poet*** (8th in the *Ballymore*) and ***Aye Right*** (5th in the *RSA Novices' Chase*) all finished more than 30 lengths off the winner in their Grade 1 events. And, ***Shattered Love***, (who is the only one of **Yeats**' offspring to record a festival victory), was placed 6th of 7 finishers and 23½ lengths behind winner, *Min*, in the *Ryanair*.

Adding last year's thirteen runs to the nineteen festival outings that had preceded them, **Yeats**' festival statistics table now shows three place positions alongside ***Shattered Love***'s solitary festival victory. The win and win & place strike rates are poor at 3% and 13% respectively. There aren't any surprises financially had one backed blind to level stakes all of **Yeats**' festival runners. To a £10.00 each-way stake, the losses would amount to £424.50.

Although there is a possibility that one or two horses by **Yeats** may win or place at the 2021 Cheltenham Festival, the statistics to date certainly aren't motivating me to focus considerable energy deliberating which one or two of the offspring it will be. A watching brief again? I think so.

Yeats (IRE) – Progeny with Official Rating of 135+

					Official Ratings as of 9th February 2021	
Sire	***Horse***	***Age***	***Sex***	***Hurdles***	***Chase***	***Trainer***
Yeats	Aye Right	8	g		154	Harriet Graham
Yeats	Brave Eagle	9	g		153	Nicky Henderson
Yeats	Chantry House	7	g	147	147	Nicky Henderson
Yeats	*Conflated*	*7*	*g*		*144*	*Gordon Elliott*
Yeats	De Rasher Counter	9	g	143	155	Emma Lavelle
Yeats	*Flooring Porter*	*6*	*g*	*159*		*Gavin Cromwell*
Yeats	Fugitives Drift	6	g	135		Nicky Henderson
Yeats	*Kilfenora*	*9*	*g*	*145*		*Edward P.Harty*
Yeats	Little Bruce	9	g	122	135	Philip Kirby
Yeats	*Longhouse Poet*	*7*	*g*		*141*	*Martin Brassil*
Yeats	Master Debonair	7	g	142		Harry Fry
Yeats	Pileon	7	g		138	Philip Hobbs
Yeats	Precious Cargo	8	g		144	Nicky Henderson
Yeats	*Shattered Love*	*10*	*f*	*136*	*152*	*Gordon Elliott*
Yeats	Soldier Of Love	8	g		144	Paul Nicholls
Yeats	*Some Neck*	*10*	*g*	*130*	*142*	*John C. McConnell*
Yeats	Storm Arising	7	g	141		Paul Nicholls
Yeats	*The West's Awake*	*10*	*g*	*127*	*142*	*E. J. O'Grady*
Yeats	*Tudor City*	*9*	*g*	*144*		*A.J.Martin*
Yeats	Younevercall	10	g	156		Kim Bailey